CAMPUS AFLAME

by J. Edwin Orr

Dynamic of Student Religious Revolution

Evangelical Awakenings in Collegiate Communities

A Division of G/L Publications   Glendale, California, U.S.A.

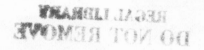

Published by
Regal Books Division, G/L Publications
Glendale, California 91209, U.S.A.

Library of Congress Catalog Card No. 71-185801
Hardcover 0-8307-0157-5
Softcover 0-8307-0156-7

Microfilmed 1971 as
Evangelical Awakenings in Collegiate Communities

TABLE OF CONTENTS

Preface

PREFACE

In standard church histories and in standard histories of higher education, reference is often made to the phenomenon of revivals of religion or evangelical awakenings in collegiate communities, particularly during the late eighteenth and the early nineteenth centuries. Frederick Rudolph in a standard text on American colleges and universities has devoted ten pages to a study of the phenomenon up until the year 1858. Other historians with an obviously profound knowledge of the history of colleges and universities seem to have found the phenomenon of evangelical awakenings in the colleges intriguing, to say the least. More often, the educationalist of the twentieth century is apt to regard such revivals of religion on campus as a form of hysteria happily past.

It seems strange that no qualified scholar thus far, to our best knowledge, has produced an authenticated account of evangelical awakenings in collegiate communities. Nor has anyone traced the impact that these awakenings in both college and community have had upon social progress at home and abroad, including the initiation of educational systems, primary and secondary and advanced, as part of a worldwide accomplishment.

And it is even more amazing to discover that the usually well-informed educational or ecclesiastical historian seems blissfully unaware that evangelical awakenings in collegiate communities—far from fading out a hundred years ago— are still occurring in the same form in the same kind of Christian colleges, and in different form through voluntary societies in the secularized universities of our own time, with a greater impact than ever upon missionary enterprise.

All this serves to show that the writing of an account of the course of evangelical awakenings in collegiate communities has been long overdue, and makes a contribution to history of practical value in education, rather than pedantic interest. With the facts available, judgments may be made.

i

In certain cases, judgments need to be reversed. It is inevitable that people of the latter third of the twentieth century be inclined to interpret happenings of the past in the light of their own reading or prejudices. For example, one has found that the achievements of the New England missionaries in the Hawaiian kingdom a century and a half ago are belittled and disparaged or outrightly denied because of the writings of a popular novelist or the equally fictional screenplay of a film producer; and all the protests of capable Hawaiian historians have gone almost unheard. Christianity filled the void of a broken society in Hawaii, rather than invading a Hawaiian paradise where everyone was having fun, in the fictional account. The missionaries made Hawaiian island populations literate in less than twenty-five years, rather than capturing power by teaching only chiefs and their children. As history, the novel and film were frauds.

However, there is so much material here presented in published form for the first time that it would be presumptuous to pronounce judgment in every case. This is somewhat of a pioneer study—if not regarding the early nineteenth century, certainly concerning later periods—and a fuller analysis of untreated aspects of the college revivals must properly await the study of interested historians now able to view the facts in perspective for the first time.

Studies could be made of the question of academic freedom in evangelical colleges where faculty members subscribe to a statement of faith; of the bases of support of these colleges which, in large measure, depend upon the gifts and bequests of ordinary Christian people and the benefactions of ordinary congregations as well as the support of loyal graduates, rather than massive grants from wealthy foundations and corporations or underwriting by denominational funds; and of the political alignment of evangelical colleges, a few of which have been buttressed by support from the political right, but the great majority of which are free of political alliances of any kind, minding their own business in the educating of the young with a concern for the gospel of redemption, individual and social. And the writer has refrained from writing at length on the future of the evangelical college in competition with state education.

There is no such a thing as Presbyterian physics or as Baptist chemistry—though some insist that Baptists are more interested in H_2O than other denominations. There is an evangelical attitude to philosophy, of course, and a desire to combat atheism in all its related fields. In 1965 as in 1905, evangelical educators have recommended the moving of Christian colleges to state university campuses and concentration on the subjects of Christian concern.

For the past quarter of a century, the writer has been engaged in a teaching ministry on the campuses of secular colleges and universities and of Christian colleges—while this dissertation was being written, for example, delivering twenty-eight lectures in four days as the guest of the state University of Arizona and conducting series of meetings in colleges from New York State to Washington State.

Residing near the campus of the University of California at Los Angeles, the writer had enrolled in an occasional course at Moore Hall, the School of Education—curriculum for computers, economics, and the like. It was suggested that a study of college awakenings had become necessary. In order best to engage in such research, the scholar needed experience in writing history, understanding of educational developments, acquaintance with psychology and anthropology, objective observation of the phenomenon of current evangelical awakenings on campus, and theological training.

The writer owes an academic debt to Prof. Ernest E. Smith (long ago) and Prof. E. Alfred Jenkins (more recently) for instruction and direction in the field of education at the Northern Baptist Theological Seminary in Illinois, where his master's work in education was completed. Added to these obligations is gratitude to a number of professors at U. C. L. A. teaching comparative education——Herbert W. Hendricks, Wendell P. Jones and James R. Liesch in Latin American, African and Asian education respectively. One also owed much to professors directing study in British, American, Latin American, African, Indian and East Asian history—Profs. Clinton N. Howard, Richard Weiss, Robert N. Burr, Leonard M. Thompson, Stanley Wolpert, Philip C. Huang, not forgetting D. C. Moore and Alexander P. Saxton (in history) and J. J. Espey and L. W. Erickson.

The writer gladly acknowledges a debt to Prof. Sol Cohen for stimulating instruction and direction in four courses in the history of Western education and American education, as much by friendship and counsel as by lecture and paper. Above all, the wise direction and careful criticism of Prof. C. Robert Pace, of the Higher Education department, has shaped this dissertation, in half a dozen courses and in the final dissertation research. It was a pleasure and privilege to tap the resources of such a man in scholarship and grace. A posthumous influence was the encouragement given by the dean of church historians, Prof. Kenneth Scott Latourette of Yale University.

Every scholarly treatise must have its limits in time and place. Nowhere in the world have Christian colleges multiplied as in the United States. Nowhere in the world have evangelical awakenings occurred so frequently on the campuses. Hence the major interest of this study had to be focussed upon happenings in American universities and colleges. However, the same effects on educational enterprises were achieved in movements occurring at the same time elsewhere in the Western world, due to evangelical awakenings manifested (in the absence of such positively Christian colleges) carrying over to missionary education. Again, experiments on the mission field had their effects on education in the homelands. So the minor interests of this study were switched to other parts of the world, chosen as typical examples of a worldwide influence, but limited in number for reasons of concentration. It has been clearly demonstrated that it is impossible to study evangelical movements on American campuses without reference to British precedents, or consequent effects overseas.

The locating of source materials had been a formidable task, tedious at times, but always rewarding and challenging. For the past hundred years, the main sources of information have been found in periodicals rather than published books, in biographies rather than in standard texts of history. But for the hundred years before that, much material is found in published histories of colleges, biographies and the like. Missionary records have been useful for tracing the impact of such movements overseas.

Fortunately for this study, there is a wealth of information available regarding the lives of certain great educationalists thrust out by the evangelical awakenings under study. So, far as educational methods and techniques are concerned, it would be futile to try and attribute these to evangelical influence. But it is much more appropriate to attribute the dedication and sacrifice of evangelical educational pioneers to their personal experience in evangelical revivals.

Out-of-print books have been made available by British friends of the writer's, experienced in student evangelism: for instance, the Most Rev. F. D. Coggan, the Archbishop of York, and Dr. Oliver Barclay, director of the Inter-Varsity Fellowship of Christian Unions of Great Britain. Thanks are due to two clergymen in Australia, Dr. the Rev. Howard W. Guinness, for access to his diaries and letters written in the decade before World War II, and the Very Rev. Dr. A. W. Morton, the Dean of St. Andrew's Cathedral in Sydney, for access to his thesis on education—both of them associates of the writer at Oxford University.

Thanks are also due to scores of presidents or other members of faculty of Christian liberal arts colleges in the United States for providing useful information to the writer: answers to a questionnaire, copies of articles, statistics of interest regarding students and graduates, reports of past and present-day awakenings on campus, comments and the like. It would be impossible to name them all in a paragraph, but it would be ungrateful not to mention Hudson Armerding and Wilbert Norton, the President and Dean of the Graduate School of Wheaton College, as well as Donald Demaray of Asbury Theological Seminary, for very great favors.

Material has also been provided through the good offices of Dr. John W. Alexander, the President of the Inter-Varsity Christian Fellowship—formerly a professor at U.C.L.A., and William R. Bright, director of Campus Crusade for Christ, Lorne Sanny, director of the Navigators movement, Hal Guffey, director of International Students, and Paul E. Little, of Trinity Theological Seminary. C. Stacey Woods, retiring general secretary of the International Fellowship of Evangelical Students also forwarded multilingual material. The kindness of Billy Graham and his staff is acknowledged.

CHAPTER I

THE EVANGELICAL HERITAGE

When a broad perspective is used to view the spread of education throughout the world, the part played by Evangelical Christianity is very clearly seen as one of the great factors.

By Evangelical Christianity is meant that way of life or mode of thinking which considers the New Testament as its source of authority, superior to tradition or rationalism—though not at all disregarding tradition and reason.[1]

In this treatise, more attention is paid to the contributions of Evangelical Christianity than to those of other Christian and secular philosophies, not with the idea of denigrating the contributions of either Roman Catholic orders or Russian Communist cadres—themselves poles apart—but because, so far as one is aware, there has been no thorough treatment of the Evangelical contribution to the spread of education, seemingly forgotten by many modern educators.

Some today consider the Christian college with students numbered in the hundreds as a back number. It is wise to recall that in the United States, as in other countries, there was a time when all higher education, not to mention elementary education, consisted of such Christian colleges with student bodies in the hundreds. The Christian college has no need to apologize for its existence. It was the pioneer.

Nor does the Christian college need to excuse itself for its motivation. Neither Confucianism, nor Buddhism, nor Hinduism nor any philosphic religion ever produced a system of education to compare with that of the Western world with its roots in Athens and Jerusalem. Islam, like Christianity a revealed religion, possessed its schools for the élite, such as Al Azhar in Cairo, but Muslim scholarship arose from the influence of subject Christian scholars upon their Arab masters; while Judaism developed rabbinical institutions but never gained a chance to educate the masses.[2]

It is difficult to find a specific warrant for education in the New Testament. True, the prophets of the Old Testament enjoined upon the Hebrew people the necessity of instruction for the children and for youth.[3] The fear of the Lord was recognized as the beginning of wisdom.[4] All this was taken for granted in the days of the Disciples. The Lord Jesus Himself was a master teacher, as any reading of the sacred record reveals.[5] And He adopted the words of Isaiah in espousing the ministry of 'good news to the poor, release for the prisoners, and sight for the blind' but not a word about educating the masses.[6] In commissioning His disciples, He explicitly commanded them to evangelize by preaching and teaching, but the latter was not interpreted as elementary education.[7] The good works of clothing the naked, feeding the hungry, caring for the sick, and visiting the prisoners, seemed to be expected rather than commanded, and that expectation undergirded the resolution of Christians in their good works of social benevolence.[8] Nothing was said about starting schools.

How then can we account for the fact that Christian folk, more especially in times when their religious zeal was great, unfailingly engaged in promoting the education of the masses? Medieval mendicants or reformed evangelists, without ado, embarked upon schemes of education for others than themselves. The only explanation which impresses the writer is that their Master had predicted that they would perform greater works than His, and that He would endue them with the Divine Spirit. It was the Divine Spirit,[9] rather than the explicit commandment which directed the campaign for the abolition of slavery, and which impelled ordinary people to establish schools for the education of the underprivileged.

Modern educationalists readily concede the debt which Education owes to both the Greek and the Judeo-Christian traditions.[10] And historians are agreed in crediting earlier movements of teaching, whether they were monastic schools or universities, to the energy of the more evangelical orders of the medieval Christian Church. The scope of education was severely limited. There seemed to be little concern for the education of the masses outside the ranks of nobility and clergy, only to provide leadership in State and Church.

In Europe, in the Middle Ages, monasteries and episcopal schools gave training not only to the clergy but to the sons of nobility. By the thirteenth century, a movement for education began, with religious and secular motivation, partly provoked by contacts with Muslim scholarship. And so universities began to appear in Europe.[11]

Jews[12] as well as Christians shared in teaching at the Medical School of Salerno in its early days. The University of Bologna grew out of the student guilds in operation there in the twelfth century.[13] As the century progressed, other Italian universities were founded. The University of Paris also began in the twelfth century, as did the University of Oxford, followed by that of Cambridge.[14]

It is important to remember that the early universities of Europe were Christian colleges in every way, and that their bodies of students were numbered in the hundreds. The religious interest was not only conservative but liberal, for John Wycliffe, John Hus, Martin Luther and John Calvin initiated the Reformation from transalpine universities.[15]

The effect of the Reformation controversy on education was disastrous.[16] As universities took sides, a wholesale abstention from studies followed. Those who remained in cloistered halls engaged in wrangling. Erasmus complained that where Lutheranism flourished, learning decayed.

Despite Luther's quarrel with Erasmus and the scholars, he took steps to forward the cause of education, writing to burgomasters in all German towns to urge the establishment of Christian schools.[17] In a notable discourse on the duty of sending children to school, he dwelt upon the obligation of the State to provide schools and compel attendance. Luther held that even if there were neither heaven nor hell, there would still be the need of good schools for boys and girls. If magistrates compelled their citizens to carry arms, there was more reason for them compelling school attendance. Slowly, these ideas provoked action.[18]

Philip Melanchton, Luther's theological adjutant, gave much time to creating educational institutions. Not only did he reorganize some of the older universities and establish newer ones, but he helped organize a secondary school system. Melanchton combined Humanism and Reformation.[19]

At first, the post-Reformation university courses gave promise of reverent and rational study of the Scriptures together with an enlightened but critical appreciation of the Classics. But in some quarters, university studies degenerated until endless dogmatic bickering absorbed them.[20]

Zwingli in Switzerland proposed educational reform, but died in battle before anything could be effected.[21] John Calvin recognized the fundamental importance of education.[22] His educational innovations spread throughout Huguenot France, Reformed Holland, Puritan England, and Presbyterian Scotland. Even in France, a large number of elementary schools and no less than thirty-two colleges and eight universities sprang up under the auspices of the Huguenot minority.[23] In Scotland, where the Calvinist system was more completely accepted than in any other country, the Genevan ideals in education came to full flower in the proposals of John Knox, and profoundly influenced Scottish education in due course.[24]

During the seventeenth century, the most developed parts of Europe were blighted by the Huguenot War in France, the Thirty Years' War in Germany, and the Civil War in England. Before the beginning of that century, John Amos Comenius was born in Moravia, becoming a schoolmaster and a minister of the evangelical Moravian Brethren.[25] Though driven from his native land, he continued his educational innovations among the exiles of the faith. Bishop Comenius had little patience with the pedantic pedagogy of his day. He added to his courses a teaching of economy, politics, history, geography, science, arts, handicrafts and singing. He organized a school system for Sweden, attempted one for England.

Most clearly, Comenius recognized the right of every person to education, not the privilege of the elite only: [26]

> Not the children of the rich and powerful only, but of all alike,
> boys and girls, noble and ignoble, rich and poor, in all cities
> and towns, villages and hamlets, should be sent to school.

The writings of Comenius were translated into a dozen European languages, and into Arabic, Persian and Turkish. His was the great educational genius of the seventeenth century, standing as an important prophet for centuries still to come. His antecedents were wholly evangelical.

4

Comenius owed much to the thinking of Roger Bacon, and between them Bacon and Comenius influenced the thinking of the English Puritans of the Commonwealth. Puritanism found its expression in a number of new schools, and in the writings of John Locke.[27]

By the time of the seventeenth century, a new religious movement revitalized the University of Cambridge, that of Puritanism.[28] Sir Isaac Newton served as a professor there between 1669 and 1702, and this was the period of impact on the higher educational foundations of the American Colonies. It was in the American Colonies, the refuge of persecuted Puritans, that the educational enterprise of the Puritans can best be studied.

It was a Puritan Londoner, the Reverend John Harvard, who bequeathed £779:17:2 toward the pious work of building a college, established in 1636 and named for its patron. John Harvard was born in England, educated at Emmanuel College, Cambridge, where he received his M.A. in 1635; he became the pastor of the Congregational Church in Charlestown, Massachusetts, dying in 1638.[29]

In Williamsburg, Virginia, was established a college with the avowed purpose of furnishing a seminary for ministers of the Gospel and for training youth in good manners. Concerning this 'project for souls', the British Attorney-General Seymour exclaimed to Commissary James Blair:[30]

'Souls? Damn your souls. Make tobacco.'

Blair enjoyed more encouragement from King William and Queen Mary, who warmly supported his project and gave £2000 directly. Blair raised an equal sum from private donors, and finally secured a charter from Virginia. Jefferson and Madison and Monroe proceeded from William and Mary College to the United States Presidency.

Another Christian college begun at that time, Yale College, was founded in 1701 through the munificence of Elihu Yale, who, although born in New Haven, Connecticut in 1648, spent his life from ten years onward in England and India, and did not return to America, becoming a Governor of the East India Company. He died in 1721.[31]

Thus the stage was set for the eighteenth century, one in which the Evangelical Revival implemented inherited ideals.

CHAPTER II

THE EVANGELICAL REVIVAL

Not much progress in education had been made during the seventeenth century. Except for parts of Germany and in Scotland, common people in Europe were receiving no education at all. In England, there were grammar schools for the privileged, but their standards had sadly deteriorated. Higher education had also suffered, universities at Oxford and Paris[1] having sunk to depths unknown in their history. Edward Gibbon, a contemporary of Wesley, recalled his days at Oxford as 'the most idle and unprofitable of my whole life.'[2]

Towards the end of the seventeenth century, a new movement began in Germany—Pietism, which (like its contemporary Quakerism) sought a more personal knowledge of God.

In 1675 Philip Jacob Spener published a volume which expressed the desire of many for a reform of the Evangelical Church.[3] As a result, believers who were dissatisfied with the dead formality of church life began to meeting in homes as voluntary societies; and the movement spread widely.

One of Spener's more ardent disciples, August Herman Francke, founded an orphanage at Halle in 1695.[4] Teaming up with an anti-scholastic and a rationalist, Francke helped found the University of Halle just before the beginning of the eighteenth century. With Thomasius and Wolff, Francke there introduced the principle of academic freedom.

In turn, a disciple of Francke, Johann Julius Hecker, set up a school in Berlin with practical subjects as the main interest. This Pietist venture became the forerunner of the whole German system of Realschulen.[5]

A Society for Promoting Christian Knowledge was begun in England, due in part to Pietist influence. August Francke hailed the venture with enthusiasm.[6] Within forty years, the Society had opened two thousand schools with forty thousand scholars enrolled—ten times as many as those of Dissenters.

Before the Evangelical Revival of the eighteenth century, there were five main types of schools operating in England, (1) the dame school, (2) the privately endowed school, (3) the grammar school, (4) the dissenting academy, and (5) the charity school.[7]

The dame school, to which the poet Wordsworth made an affectionate reference, taught reading, writing and a little arithmetic.[8] To this, the privately endowed school added Latin, philosophy and religion, part of its educational conviction including the idea that the poor should accept their situation in society.

The grammar school, aimed at the need of the middle class, had sadly deteriorated by the turn of the eighteenth century.[9] It taught reading, writing, arithmetic, philosophy, religion and Latin. The dissenting academy, closest to the evangelical ideal, taught the same subjects together with practical courses, such as history, geography, mathematics, astronomy and navigation. The academy operated by Dr. Philip Doddridge at Northampton was considered 'the best educational centre in the country,' at a time when historic universities were sadly disappointing.[10]

The charity school catered to a tiny fraction of the poor. In London, an 'infant army' of ten thousand blackguard boys roamed the streets and alleys. It seemed impossible to do anything to help them.[11] Yet the work persisted. It was too thinly distributed and its quality was far too uneven. But by 1799, there were 179 schools with 7108 children enrolled as pupils.[12] In the provinces, there were similar enterprises, touching only a very few of the children of the poor.[13]

In the American Colonies, there were schools in operation which displayed the features of their English models, but with American modifications.[14] The Colonies possessed a different type of poor, a more widely placed middle class, and a nearly non-hereditary aristocracy. There were Latin schools, which tended to classics and religion, and private schools which added the practical subjects. In some colonies, the 'dissenters' were established! In none of them were the poor caught in a treadmill of competitive hardwork, as was the case in industrialized England. And the colleges were more like higher educational academies.

The Evangelical Revival of the eighteenth century made its appearance first in Wales, a generation before Whitefield and the Wesleys began to preach their message with power. It was associated with the name of Griffith Jones, described as 'the greatest Welshman of the century,' and 'one of the greatest benefactors of the Welsh people.'[15]

Griffith Jones was proficient in Latin and Greek, but his inclinations were not only scholarly, for once in 1716 he was established in Llanddowror parish, he preached at large.

Not only was his evangelism fruitful, but he followed it up by attempting to educate the masses of ignorant young and adults.[16] Adopting the idea of itinerancy, he conducted school sessions in the various parishes, and recruited not a few schoolmasters to travel through the counties of Wales.

Griffith Jones not only taught reading, so sorely needed then, but laid 'a solid foundation of virtue, justice, temperance, industry, truth, wisdom and honesty.' The class idea he refused to consider, saying [17]

> It is by no means the desire to make them gentlemen, but Christians and heirs of eternal life.

By 1737, before Wesley began his mission, Griffith Jones had thirty-seven schools in operation, with 2400 pupils. Five years later, he had a hundred and twenty-eight schools with more than 12,000 enrolled. A quarter of a century later, in 1761, the Welsh schools conducted 3495 school sessions and 158,237 attended,[18] chiefly day pupils and mostly children, although night schools were conducted for interested adults. By 1777, three-fifths the total population of half a million had been taught in these schools.[19]

The Welsh schools were very limited in curriculum. The emphasis was on reading only, without writing or ciphering. The school sessions usually lasted three or four months, a whole year in places.[20] In derision, they were nicknamed 'dutch academies,' perhaps because of the influence of the work of Herman Francke of Halle, the evangelical leader. Griffith Jones died in 1761.[21] Madam Bevan of Laugharne continued to direct the enterprise, but died in 1789, leaving £10,000 for the schools. The will was contested, and the project died away, until revived in the nineteenth century.

The widest reading of history and the most particular scrutiny suggest that wherever concerned Christians find themselves in a collegiate community, they form voluntary societies either as seekers or finders of the Christian life.

The Puritan colleges of the New World appeared to be more congenial to the search for evangelical experience than those of the more cynical and sophisticated homeland. It is in the writings of the Rev. Cotton Mather, the New England divine,[22] that reference is first made to American student Christian societies.[23]

Before the beginning of the second quarter of the eighteenth century, there was organized at Harvard 'a Private Meeting' for worship, fellowship and service.[24] During the Great Awakening of 1740 onwards, a similar society existed at Yale, of which David Brainerd was a member, associating with his colleagues for mutual conversation and assistance in spiritual things.[25]

Both the Harvard and Yale societies maintained secrecy, a reflection on the degree of tolerance in New England society.[26] It was otherwise in England. Although the degree of open persecution was greater, the Holy Club formed at the University of Oxford operated openly.

On 9th December, 1732, a local journal featured a letter criticizing a group of young Anglicans who in derision were styled 'Methodists.' A copy was sent to the saintly William Law, who took the trouble of investigating the matter. In Oxford, he found no one who would say a good word about these Oxford men.[27] They were described as 'gloomy' and 'melancholy,' 'miserable enthusiasts and zealots'; but as no one questioned their honesty and sincerity, Law sought them out himself, and published (anonymously) a pamphlet that in defending the Holy Club recorded its operations for history. True, they took the Communion once a week in the Cathedral, but they found that 'religion is a cheerful thing.' They were observing churchly fasts and prayers, but they also visited the sick and the poor and the prisoners.[28]

As at Oxford, there was a laxity of morals at Cambridge, an emptiness of religious life. Chapel attendance was compulsory, but devotion was lacking. If there was a Holy Club of sorts at Cambridge, the fact is not recorded.

The Holy Club at Oxford University, in the days of Wesley and Whitefield, did not spend all leisure hours in reciting prayers at matins and evensong. These Methodists, as they were nicknamed, operated a charity school for the poor.[29]

Whitefield, during his Holy Club days at Oxford, had the oversight of two or three charity schools maintained by the band of Methodists.[30] He developed a passion for education, and once he gained the ear of the populace, he made use of his opportunities not to aggrandize himself but to raise money for educational projects. He enemies called him 'a spiritual pickpocket,'[31] partly because they had no sympathy for his evangelism, and partly because they had no sympathy for the ignorant poor, whom Whitefield (like his Master) loved. It is no mean tribute to Whitefield's influence to read that in 1741 Richard Hooker alleged that Whitefield was disturbing the national economy.[32]

It was the same in the American Colonies. As soon as Whitefield had become a national figure, he attracted huge crowds in Boston and Philadelphia and other towns. He had such a remarkable voice that crowds gathered on the Camden side of the Delaware to hear Whitefield preach across the river in Philadelphia. He immediately harnessed the warm financial response to his ministry to educational and other philanthropic enterprises.

Benjamin Franklin, admirer and friend of the evangelist, though not a disciple, advised Whitefield to found his school and orphanage in Philadelphia, the foremost town in the Colonies, and was much offended when Whitefield persisted in planning them in Savannah, on the perimeter of American settlement. Wrote Franklin in his recollections:[33]

> I happened soon afterwards to attend one of his sermons, in the course of which I perceived he intended to finish with a collection, so I silently resolved that he should get nothing from me. I had in my pocket a handful of copper money, three or four silver dollars, and five in gold. As he proceeded, I began to soften and concluded to give the copper; another stroke of his oratory made me ashamed and determined me to give the silver. He finished so admirably that I emptied my pocket into the collection dish, gold and all.

11

Whitefield adopted a schedule of classes much the same as Wesley's, the children rising at 5 a.m., engaging from 8 to 10 a.m. in useful industry, classes from 10 to 12 and from 2 to 4. He modified curriculum to suit the American way of life, and it was practical rather than classical.[34]

In 1764, Whitefield's memorial to establish a college was turned down by the colonial authorities. He did not give up easily. He was much impressed by the Log College operated by his friends in the Great Awakening, William Tennent and his sons.[35] William Tennent, an Ulsterman, was a graduate of the University of Edinburgh. In 1716, with four sons and a daughter, he came to Pennsylvania and became minister of the Presbyterian Church at Neshaminy in 1726. For about twenty years, he taught talented groups of young men in a log school, men destined to change colonial life. Observed Whitefield, a meticulous journal-writer:[36]

> The place wherein the young men study now is in contempt called The College. It is a log house, about twenty feet long and near as many broad; and to me it seemed to resemble the school of the old prophets, for their habitations were mean; and that they sought not great things for themselves is plain from those passages of Scripture wherein we are told that each of them took a beam to build them a house... All we can say of most of our universities is, they are glorious without. From this despised place, seven or eight worthy ministers of Jesus have lately been sent forth; more are almost ready to be sent, and the foundation is now laying for the instruction of many others.

Many of the Log College 'graduates' established other log colleges, out of which came a host of educational leaders, including the first president of the College of New Jersey, founded to succeed Tennent's school upon his death. In 1755, the college was moved to the town of Princeton, where soon it developed into the great university of that name.[37] Its first few presidents were evangelists-cum-educationalists of the Great Awakening, the great turning to God of the American people around about 1740. The movement profoundly stirred Presbyterians, who never lost their lead in the educational field, founding college after college westwards.

Out of George Whitefield's visits to Philadelphia came the foundation of the University of Pennsylvania. The building in which Whitefield customarily preached was used for an academy, largely through the efforts of Benjamin Franklin, and in 1753, it was chartered as a college and academy.[38] In 1791, this Philadelphia institution became the University of Pennsylvania, which in 1914 unveiled a statue to the famous Revivalist, calling him the 'inspirer and original trustee' of the University. Engraved upon the panel of the statue were the words of Benjamin Franklin: [39]

> I knew him intimately upwards of thirty years. His integrity, disinterestedness and indefatigable zeal in work I have never seen equalled and shall never see excelled.

Philadelphia's example was followed by the burghers of New York.[40] Trinity Church conveyed to the new college a valuable parcel of land, with the proviso that the president of the new college be a member of the Church of England. However, the college operated from the start on interdenominational principles and practices. King's College in due course became Columbia University.

Likewise, the Dutch Reformed friends of the Awakening desired to build a college, and in 1770 founded the Queen's College in New Brunswick, New Jersey, which continued as Rutgers University. In New Hampshire, Congregationalists founded Dartmouth College, an outgrowth of the Awakening. The Baptists opened Brown University, first known as Rhode Island College.[41] There were several other colleges arising from the educational passion of the Great Awakening.

Whitefield expressed criticism of Harvard, and was then dubbed 'an uncharitable, censorious and slanderous man' by the administration. After a disastrous fire, Whitefield solicited books for Harvard's library, and was thanked for this generous service to the college.[42]

Whitefield therefore made his mark as an educationalist, but it must be conceded that education was his avocation where evangelism was his vocation. Like Wesley, he was engaged in preaching all his adult life, an evangelist without apology. Far from being anti-intellectual, evangelism provoked educational enterprise.

Samuel Johnson, famous man of letters whose span of life was almost identical with Wesley's, opposed education for the masses. Said he: [43]

Learning cannot possibly be of any use. For instance, this boy rows as well without learning as if he could sing the song of Orpheus to the Argonauts . . .

Whereas Wesley said of his Kingswood School,[44] built near the spot where he began to preach in the open air at Bristol, 'I have spent more money, time and care on this than on almost any design I ever had.' And it was obvious that John Wesley, like Whitefield, was concerned with the need of society as a whole for education, this at a time when it was regarded as the privilege of the wealthy.[45]

It was not surprising that John Wesley, after sharing in the Holy Club school for the poor in Oxford, should operate a school for thirty or forty of the settlers' children in the infant colony of Georgia.[46] Alas, Wesley's venture overseas was a qualified failure; but upon his return, he experienced in heart what he had preached from his mind, the grace of God. One of his first side trips from his preaching to the multitudes in England was a journey to Herrnhut to observe the Moravians, the most evangelistic denomination of the day.

Wesley had been brought up in a home that owed much to forebears who had suffered the heavy hand of persecution of the Establishment upon Puritans and non-Jurors. He was already interested in the education of the poor. His new experience of conversion had given him a ready sympathy with the Moravians. He combined these varying elements in his own mind, and embarked upon an educational project almost from the start of his great ministry. His philosophy was a hundred years ahead of his time:[47] 'All alike, gentle and simple, rich and poor, are to be drawn into schools.'

Wesley followed Whitefield who had stated at Bristol: [48]

Were I to continue here, I would endeavour to settle schools all over the Wood, and also in other places, as Mr. Griffith Jones has done in Wales.

The need of the community was obvious; but what gave the evangelist the motivation? It was his spiritual conviction.

Wesley gathered his converts into societies and on 12th May 1739 he built his first meeting-house in Bristol. Within a month, he began to build a school at Kingswood, a day school for children, evening school for adults.[49] The same year, he opened his first meeting-house in London, the Foundry site on City Road; and there also he began a school, instruction arranged between 6 a.m. and noon, 1 p.m. and five.

The evangelist took time to study educational systems. After studying the schools of Jena and Herrnhut, the works of Comenius, Locke and Milton, he delivered a critique of English schools as he found them, objecting to [50]

1. the distraction of schools in great towns.
2. the indiscriminate admission of pupils.
3. the absence of arithmetic, geography or chronology in some schools, the poor teaching of Latin and Greek in others; and the poor quality of textbooks.
4. the teaching of obscene and profane passages by masters who delighted in shocking the innocent.

Wesley insisted that there was to be no learning by rote. 'Let the children not read or say one line without understanding and minding what they say.'[51] The children rose at 4 a.m., which hour Wesley deemed to have therapeutic value, making 'the children less nervous.'

Perhaps because of his dislike of callous sports at the school at Charterhouse, in which bullying was prevalent, Wesley set his face against play, adopting the adage 'He that plays when he is a child, will play when he is a man.' Rather Wesley provided 'healthy exercise for the dear children,' chopping the wood, digging the garden, drawing the water.

The curriculum at Kingswood included reading, writing, arithmetic, Latin, Greek, French, Hebrew, history (which included the American Colonies and Mexico), chronology, rhetoric, logic, ethics, geometry, algebra, physics, drawing and singing. The Oxford tutorial system showed itself in the ratio set of one master to five boys. [52]

Wesley's notes (and he was a prolific recorder of events, his diary enjoying the attention that a wife would receive in a happier marriage) show that he possessed no mere passing fancy for education. It was a lifelong passion.

Meanwhile, the prophets of a revolution were arising in Europe, among them 'that strange genius,' Jean-Jacques Rousseau, destined to have a profound influence upon the development of education.[53] Wesley had drawn from Locke and Comenius, but was repelled by Rousseau's irreligion. On the other hand, Wesley's disciple, Dr. Thomas Coke, who engaged in educational ministry, cited both Locke and Rousseau, acknowledging the latter's extensive genius while agreeing that he was mistaken in his religious ideas.[54]

Another staunch Evangelical Christian who was deeply influenced by Jean-Jacques Rousseau was Johann Heinrich Pestalozzi, born in Zurich in 1746, who put into practice Rousseau's theory of sympathy with the child. Pupils and teachers flocked to his boarding school-training college, and before he died in 1827 he had influenced generations to come.[55] Again, revolutionary secular ideas were being combined with Evangelical Christian ideals.

The flowering of the educational bloom on the tree of evangelism began in the eighteenth century, but it was not until the period of the Napoleonic wars and the dawning of the nineteenth century that the ripened fruit was seen appearing. The Evangelicals promoted educational schemes in Britain, in the United States, on the continent of Europe, in the infant colonies in Australia, New Zealand and South Africa as well as in Canada, in the territories of the East India Company and wherever possible.

Another Evangelical Awakening provided the dynamic for the engineers of the post-revolutionary period.

CHAPTER III

DESPAIR AND RECOVERY

During the latter part of the eighteenth century, there occurred a general decline in morals and religion in the United States of America. The unsettled state of society following a long-fought war and a revolution, the self-assertive feelings which accompanied independence, the changing social conditions, the lure of the western frontier, the rugged individualism of the frontiersman, the break-up of family and church relationships due to migration—all these were factors in the decline, but they were matched by the influence of the militant French infidelity which had swept the country.

In the wake of the American Revolution came a disastrous setback for Evangelical Christianity. The alliance between the American republic and the revolutionary republic of France, moved by a more violent form of insurrection, brought a flood of infidelity to the United States which the moderates were unable to stem.[1] Christian chroniclers complained that, for the first time in the history of the country, there was a surfeit of lawlessness, a profusion of gamblers, of gangs of robbers and slave-stealers. Drunkenness was common and profanity prevalent, they said. Immorality had increased as standards of honesty and veracity declined.[2]

The bitter writings of Thomas Paine and the gentler utterances of Thomas Jefferson had lent much aid to the rapid spread of a kind of deism and unbelief in the newly independent United States. Inevitably, the republicanism in the new nation showed hospitality to the work of noted sceptics and political radicals,[3] the French revolutionists capturing the place of the evangelical moderates.

The moral decline was reflected in the life of the students in colleges.[4] Collegians were intoxicated with the idea of independence, the responsibilities of which made little appeal while the laxities produced a surge of debauchery.

College students of revolutionary times were aptly described by one of the sharpest observers of the day, Timothy Dwight, whose words (if translated into modern vernacular) sound like a report on the fatuous Age of Aquarius: [5]

Youths particularly who had been liberally educated, and who with strong passions and feeble principles, were the votaries of sensuality and ambition, delighted in the prospect of unrestrained gratification, and, panting to be enrolled with men of passion and splendor, became enamored with the new doctrines. The tenor of opinion, and even of conversation, was to a considerable extent changed at once. Striplings scarcely fledged suddenly found that the world had been enveloped in general darkness through a long succession of preceding ages, and that the light of human wisdom had just begun to dawn upon the human race. All the science, all the information that had been acquired before the last thirty or forty years stood in their view for nothing. Experience they boldly proclaimed a plotting instructress who taught in manners, morals and government nothing but abecedarian lessons fitted for children only. Religion they discovered, on the one hand, to be the vision of dotards and nursemaids, and, on the other, a system of fraud and trick imposed by priestcraft for base purposes upon the ignorant multitude. Revelation was found to be without authority or evidence, and moral obligation a cobweb which might indeed entangle flies, but by which creatures of stronger wing nobly disdained to be confined. The world they resolutely concluded to have been probably eternal, and matter the only existence. Man, they determined, sprang like a mushroom out of the earth like a chemical process; and the power of thinking, choice and motive were merely a result of elective affinities. If, however, there was a God and man was a creative being, he was created only to be happy. As therefore, animal pleasure is the only happiness, so they resolved that the enjoyment of that pleasure is the only end of his creation.

George Washington received a letter from an intimate friend in 1796, predicting that national affairs were leading to some crisis, some revolution; and Washington agreed, saying that he was unable to foretell what might happen. [6]

Lyman Beecher, described a typical campus in 1795:[7]

> College was in a most ungodly state. The college church
> was almost extinct. Most of the students were skeptical and
> rowdies were plenty. Wine and liquors were kept in many
> rooms; intemperance, profanity, gambling and licentious-
> ness were common . . . most of the class before me were
> infidels and called each other Voltaire, Rousseau, . . . etc.

What was true at Yale in New Haven was true at Princeton
in New Jersey, there being in one year no more than two
students who professed religion, only five or six who scrupled
the use of profane language in common conversation—and in
this 'filthy speech' movement the profanity sometimes was
of a very shocking kind.[8]

So far as religion was concerned, the colleges were the
seed-beds of infidelity.[9] The University of Pennsylvania,
Transylvania College, Columbia College in South Carolina,
and others had influential 'free-thinkers' on their faculties.
An anti-Church play was featured at Dartmouth. At Yale and
Princeton, as at William and Mary, the student bodies were
overwhelmingly sceptical, if not infidel. At Bowdoin, as at
Yale, the number of believers was counted on one hand.

During the last decade of the eighteenth century, the
typical Harvard student was atheist.[10] Students at Williams
College[11] conducted a mock celebration of Holy Communion.
When the Dean at Princeton opened the chapel Bible to read,
a pack of playing cards fell out, some radical having cut a
rectangle out of each page to fit the pack.[12] Christians were
so unpopular that they met in secret and kept their minutes
in code.[13] The radical leader of deist students led a mob in
burning the Bible[14] of a Raritan valley Presbyterian church.
Students disrupted worship services with both profanity and
sputum. They burned down buildings; and they forced the
resignation of college presidents.[15]

Many historians have agreed that conditions on campus
and in society were deplorable. The last two decades of the
eighteenth century were the darkest period, spiritually and
morally, in the history of American Christianity, the low-
water mark of its lowest ebb-tide,[16] when infidelity rode
roughshod over the feelings of the disoriented majority.

In the United States, the two largest denominations, the Methodists and Baptists, were losing more members than they were gaining.[16] The Episcopal Bishop of New York quit functioning for lack of duties.[17] Chief Justice Marshall wrote to Bishop Madison of Virginia declaring that the Church was too far gone ever to be redeemed.[18]

It was the same in the countries of the European continent. The British historian, G. M. Trevelyan, marked the date 1776 as the low-point of the decline in religious fidelity in Great Britain,[19] marking off the jubilee years of Evangelical Revival in the eighteenth century from the recovery of faith manifested toward the end of that century into the beginning of the next. Fear of Napoleon and the excesses of the French Revolution caused a turning back to God earlier in Britain than in the United States. There was revival in England, Wales, Scotland and Ireland, among Anglicans, Presbyterians and Methodists and other denominations.[20]

In Scandinavia, an awakening began under Hans Nielsen Hauge before the end of the century, followed by awakenings in Denmark, Sweden and Finland.[21] These movements helped to shape the course of events in each of the Scandinavian countries.

The critical years on the Continent of Europe came a little later because of the outbreak of the French Revolution, the Napoleonic period of revolutionary domination delaying a recovery of faith in Switzerland, France, the Netherlands and Germany until after the battle of Waterloo.

In despair or hope or both, a score of New England men posted a call for a nationwide 'Concert of Prayer,' entreating the Almighty to intervene in American affairs. Ministers of every denomination joined in.[22] Soon reports of revivals were received from various parts of New England, and even the Maritime Provinces of Canada, throughout the Middle Atlantic States and the South, and across the mountains in the trans-Allegheny West, where phenomena beyond description were witnessed.[23] The Second Great Awakening of American history had come. The spread of infidelity was effectively halted, and a vast new movement of benevolence began, affecting religion, philanthropy and education—just as in the Mother Country.

Already in Britain, signs of spiritual awakening were manifest during the distressing times of Napoleon's Wars. The spirit of revival abroad in Britain in the early nineteenth century affected the Dissenting denominations, and produced some great men of God. It affected the Established Churches also.

News of the camp-meetings among Methodists on the American frontier sparked a new movement among British Methodists: Primitive Methodism. The Primitive Methodists not only renewed the aggressive evangelism of Wesley's day but developed a strong social conscience, contributing spiritual strength to the trade unions in the struggle to better the lot of the working man.[24]

Anglican Evangelical leaders began to devote all of their energies to the indoctrination of a body of clergy who would carry evangelical ideas into their parish pulpits and parsonages.[25] Their leader was Charles Simeon of Cambridge, who combined the fervency of evangelism with the regular discipline of the Church. In this he made a profound impression upon the younger clergy in training at Cambridge, and soon the Simeonite clergy became a dominant force in English life.

There were similar awakenings in Wales and Northern Ireland, and a great reviving in many parts of Scotland, two ex-naval officers, James and Robert Haldane, preaching in crowded churches or in the open air to vast throngs.[26]

The power of the Scottish Revival of the early nineteenth century was carried to the continent recently freed from the tyranny of Napoleon but still dominated by sceptical thinkers. In 1816, in Geneva, Robert Haldane began his lecturing to any students willing to listen to him. He hired a room and used an interpreter as well. In sceptical Geneva the students flocked to hear the able Scot who 'knew his Bible like Calvin.' The awakening spread to the nearby parts of old Huguenot France, and from there, to the Reformed Churches of the Low Countries. This movement, known as Le Réveil, had the profoundest effects at home and abroad.[27]

Following the defeat of Napoleon at Waterloo, there was much rejoicing in Germany over the providential deliverance from the foreign yoke. Spiritual awakenings occurred in all the German states.[28] Zeal produced philanthropy.

The Awakening in Germany lasted for a whole generation. The leaders raised up in the revival extended its work throughout their homeland and exported it through dedicated missionaries to the far corners of the earth.

Norway, scarcely moved by the Reformation and lightly touched by Pietism, enjoyed a vital revival toward the end of the eighteenth century. In spite of his persecution by the state Church, Hans Nielsen Hauge urged his followers to stay in its fellowship, which they largely did.[29] Out of the fertile soil of Haugeanism grew socieities for home and foreign missions. Hans Nielsen Hauge was a man of genius. The nationwide revival that stemmed from his conversion to God was unique. He helped unite the common folk in a national and spiritual consciousness which prepared them for national responsibility soon to come as Norway emerged from its centuries-long eclipse.

Denmark, close to Germany, was affected less by Anglo-Saxon Evangelicalism and more by the German 'Aufklärung.' Nevertheless, a series of evangelical awakenings began and gave rise to missionary enterprise at home and overseas. The awakenings coincided with a golden age of Danish culture. From the 1820s onward, a dynamic and brilliant Lutheran clergyman, N. F. S. Grundtvig, directed a national church movement which stressed the sacramental rather than the evangelistic way of life. Both movements helped the Church of Denmark struggling against German rationalism.[30] There were similar awakenings in Sweden—'frontier-style' in their phenomena—and in Finland, under Paavo Ruotsalainen.[31]

There were also evangelical communities outside North America and Europe, in the Cape of Good Hope and the South of India. Evangelical Awakenings occurred among the Dutch and English at the Cape during the Napoleonic Wars, giving rise to an immediate evangelistic and social outreach to the Hottentots and other races nearby; and among the Tamils of South India, making the diocese of Tinnevelly at the tip of India the home of half of India's Evangelical Christians for half a century to come.[32]

Thus the Evangelical Awakenings of 1800 and thereabouts were effective all over the world, wherever communities of evangelical believers were found.

The contributions of Evangelicals to education overseas, whether primary, secondary or advanced, is a part of the story of missionary enterprise. It properly began with the Awakenings of Napoleonic times.

At the conclusion of the eighteenth century, Evangelical Christianity influenced a tiny part of the population of the world. It was dominant in Great Britain and in Scandinavia, and had major influence in the Netherlands and Switzerland. It shared the German States with Roman Catholicism,[33]was a minor force in Hungary and France, and was almost non-existent in Italy, Spain and Portugal and the rest of Europe.

In the Americas, there were vigorous bodies of Evangelical Christians in the coastal states between the Alleghenies and the Atlantic, a few settlers in the Ohio Valley and none at all in the West, while Mexico, Central and South America had only a handful of foreign Evangelicals.[34]

Africa, away from the Mediterranean littoral, was an unexplored continent with a scattering of nominal Evangelicals at the Cape of Good Hope, scarcely regarded as a beachhead for civilization and Christianity on a hostile continent.

The Muslim countries scarcely knew what an Evangelical Christian was. There were only a few thousand converts in all of India, while in China and East Asia only a handful of believers existed. The Pacific islands were the haunts of cannibals, and Australia was almost empty.

At the time of the early nineteenth century Revivals, very little of the world was open to the Protestant missionary. An intransigent Roman Catholic hierarchy jealously held the door closed to the Latin American countries. The Islamic ecclesiastical authorities barred the door of the Muslim countries. The whole continent of Africa was terra incognita, except the northern littoral and tiny enclaves in West and South Africa. The vast empire of China was also closed, and it was by no means easy to gain a foothold in India. Japan and Korea were sealed off completely.

Yet, in the nineteenth century, Evangelical missionaries impelled by the great awakenings, not only planted churches in Africa, Asia and Latin America, but profoundly influenced the course of education throughout the world, in some places being a major factor in the founding of educational systems.

CHAPTER IV

COLLEGIATE AWAKENINGS, 1800—

So far as can be ascertained, the first of the series of college awakenings occurred as early as 1787. At Hampden Sydney College in Virginia, a few students, none of them an active Christian but all of them concerned about the moral state of the college, met for prayer. They locked themselves in a room, for fear of the other students. One of them said: 'We tried to pray, but such prayer I never heard the like of.' He added: 'We tried to sing, but it was in the most suppressed manner, for we feared the other students.'[1]

The ungodly students created a disturbance, and their President came to investigate. He rebuked the rowdies and invited the intercessors to his study for continued prayer. This continued in power, until an awakening was felt at last. Within a short space of time, more than half the number of students professed conversion in a movement which stirred the local churches also.[2]

In college after college, the students took the initiative in beginning Christian fellowships. It would be impossible to divorce the student movement from the awakenings that were beginning in the nearby communities. At Harvard, Bowdoin, Brown, Dartmouth, Middlebury, Williams and Andover, new societies were formed.[3] To resist the ungodly influences that prevailed, they committed themselves to mutual watchfulness, ardent prayers, frequent fellowship, mutual counsel and friendly reproof.[4] In most cases, they were tiny societies. For example, three students at Brown University formed a 'college praying society,' which met weekly in a private room, 'for fear of disturbance from the unpenitent.'[5] About the same time—11th December 1802— three juniors and four sophomores formed themselves into the Harvard Saturday Evening Religious Society.[6] It also was a secret society in its early years.

When the brilliant Timothy Dwight, grandson of Jonathan Edwards, came to the presidency of Yale College in 1795, he invited his students to attack freely the truth of the Scriptures, and he answered them in a series of pungent sermons in chapel. Among his topics were 'The Nature and Danger of Infidel Philosophy,' and 'Is the Bible the Word of God?' Then he proceeded to grapple with the problems of materialism and deism in his direct exposition of theology.[7]

One of Dwight's main contentions was that the philosophy which opposed Christianity in every succeeding generation has uniformly worn the same character, rested on the same foundations, proceeded from the same disposition, aimed at the same ends, and produced the same means. He claimed that Hume's concessions to adultery and suicide were pale reflections of Greek philosophers who taught the same. He met the prevailing ridicule with quiet argument. He pointed out that infidel philosophy possessed no means of restraining vice or promoting virtue.[8] He lectured brilliantly.

After Timothy Dwight's notable baccalaureate sermon of 1796, in which he exhorted his beloved students to 'embrace Christianity,' the tide began to turn at Yale, and came in full flood in 1802. One third of the student body made profession of faith that year.[9]

Thus began a movement in American schools of higher learning. There followed revivals of religion in Andover, Princeton, Washington and Amherst and other university colleges, inaugurating half a century of student awakenings. In not one of these eastern college awakenings was there any extravagance reported. Revivals began quietly and continued without fanaticism of any kind. There was undoubtedly an appeal to the hearts of the students, but first their minds and consciences were moved.[10]

Anti-Evangelical sociologists seem to delight in stressing the emotional extravagances of the Awakenings on the far frontiers of Kentucky and Tennessee, ignoring the fact that the frontiersmen were generally illiterate and that at the same time in the college towns there were occurring deep and thorough religious revivals without any extravagance whatsoever.[11] To this day, the emotional response of people is affected by temperament and education.

At Hampden-Sydney College, President Smith determined to use all means to prevent physical manifestations of feeling from expressing themselves among the students. There was a marked lack of extreme emotion in every subsequent movement on campus.[12] Freedom from abnormal excitement became a marked characteristic of the collegiate awakenings.

Full half a century later, Bishop Charles P. McIlvaine of Ohio, an Anglican, in commending the sane and serious 1858 Awakening throughout the United States, compared it with the collegiate revivals of his youth, when, at his alma mater, he witnessed a revival of religion which was 'quiet, unexcited, and entirely free from all devices or means' peculiar to what he considered 'promoted revivals.' [13]

The college awakenings had a significant effect upon the corporate life of the colleges. The colleges appointed as president and professors the most dynamic Christian men available; campus prayer days were held regularly in term; and the college sermon became a regular feature of worship and religious education. By 1815, for example, the day of prayer had become a regular feature at Yale and Williams, Brown and Middlebury.[14]

The evangelistic impact of the days of prayer on campus was noteworthy. Amherst, Dartmouth, Princeton, Williams and Yale, to name a few, reported the conversion to God of a third to a half of their total student bodies, which in those days usually numbered between a hundred and two hundred and fifty. In 1802, Yale reported 75 converts; in 1815, 80. The figure for the 'unpopular war' year of 1812 was only 20. Between 1820 and 1830, half of those who entered Amherst 'without piety' professed conversion. In 1803, Dartmouth added 25 names to its roster of believers; in 1815, 60. At Princeton, more than 50 professed conversion in 1815. Of these converts, about fifty percent became ministers of the Gospel to serve the revived churches of the seaboard and frontier states.[15]

A student Christian society was formed at Yale, and other colleges were quick to follow suit. The Student Moral Society at Yale discouraged profanity, immorality and intemperance. Soon it comprised between a third and a half of the student population.[16]

Following the Awakening at Williams College, several new converts formed a confidential society.[17] At Harvard College, the Saturday Evening Religious Society—formed to combat French infidelity—united in 1821 with a Wednesday Evening Society to become the Society of Christian Brethren. Dartmouth's theological society in 1813 dismissed a member for being intoxicated with liquor. It is noteworthy that these collegiate societies carried on a voluminous correspondence between campuses. As a result, voluntary student Christian societies were formed in rapid succession, more than ninety being established between 1810 and 1850.[18]

It may be asked, if the revivals of religion on campus were so thorough, why was it necessary to seek a further awakening? At Yale in 1802, half the students entered the ministry, and after their departure the number of active Christians dwindled to a dozen or so.[19] Then followed the awakening of 1808, which transformed the student body again. At Bowdoin, in 1811, there was not one who professed religious faith, with quite a few men reckless in conduct and openly immoral in character.[20] There followed another revival of religion.

There were other factors at work in influencing students. At Yale in 1802, of 63 converts received into church, 55 were children of pious parents; in 1831, of 70 converts, 60 were the offspring of church members.[21]

The collegiate awakenings continued through enrollment after enrollment of college classes, generation after generation of students.[22] Between 1820 and 1835, there were 1500 professed conversions in thirty-six colleges.[23] In the year 1853, eleven New England colleges with a total enrollment of 2163 students reported 745 active Christians, of whom 343 were candidates for the Christian ministry. It was noted that two-thirds of those professing an experience entered the ministry, of whom a quarter had been converted in course.

The collegiate awakenings of the early nineteenth century continued effective for half a century. They perpetuated themselves in a long period of vigorous activity of profound social and religious significance. They were a major force in the founding of colleges, in the work of philanthropy, and in the extension of the Church at home and abroad. College awakenings moved the best and produced the best.

In Great Britain, there was no situation comparable to the one prevailing in the United States. The universities of Oxford and Cambridge were preserves of the Church of England. Chapel services were compulsory, but they were far from evangelical in most cases. The universities of Scotland were predominantly Presbyterian, following the establishment of religion in the northern kingdom. Such Dissenters as Baptists and Congregationalists received an education in Nonconformist Academies, which lacked the rank of universities but seemed to give their students quite as useful a training.

The Awakening of Napoleonic days had its effect upon Cambridge,[24] in which arose developments comparable to those observed in Oxford in the eighteenth century. Charles Simeon, an Anglican Evangelical, moved to Cambridge and became Fellow of King's College and Vicar of Holy Trinity. He not only preached an evangelistic message, but devoted his life to combining evangelistic zeal with ecclesiastical discipline, in order to retain the dynamic of the Awakening within the national Church. In this he made a profound impression upon the undergraduates at Cambridge.[25] Within a lifetime, the Simeonite clergy had become a dominant force in English life,[26] as rightly recognized by G. M. Trevelyan. From Cambridge went forth such outstanding men as Henry Martyn to India.[27] Others remained at home, and became leaders in social reform.

William Carey, the pioneer of modern missions in India, was a product of Nonconformist non-university education in England.[28] That it was not inferior to Henry Martyn's studies at Cambridge may be seen in the fact that Carey became a master of Latin, Greek, Hebrew, Sanskrit and other tongues in less than seven years. Had Carey been born forty years later, he would no doubt have qualified for a degree through the newly chartered University of London,[29] organized by scholars dissatisfied with religious tests in universities.

The Awakening of Napoleonic days was just as strong in Britain as in the United States; but it produced no series of college revivals, for the simple reason that there were no such dozens of colleges in the Mother Country. It produced student societies besides transforming individuals.

The universities on the Continent of Europe had fallen under the influence of Napoleon and the French Revolution. It was not until the final defeat of the Corsican that any revival of evangelical zeal appeared therein. Rationalism reigned supreme for a whole generation.

The post-Napoleonic Awakening in Germany revived the dying causes in the universities of the German states. The extraordinary social reformer, Theodore Fliedner, studied at Giessen and Göttingen but was moved by the evangelical revival at Halle.[30] Throughout Germany, many graduates of the German universities experienced evangelical renewal, and sparked a movement of evangelical zeal and philanthropy among the privileged classes, affecting the nation.[31]

Robert Haldane, a nephew of Admiral Lord Duncan who had succeeded Nelson in the affection of the British people, left his successful work of revival in Scotland and moved to Geneva in 1816, directly after the year of Waterloo. He hired a room and an interpreter, and invited the students of the Swiss university to come and listen.[32] His method was simple: if a student asked a question, simple or complex, he replied: 'What does the Scripture say?' This was so very different to the obtuse methods of the professors in rationalist Geneva that students flocked to hear the Scot who 'knew his Bible like Calvin.' Before long, the wrath of the faculty and clergy was incurred, but a thorough revival of evangelical Christianity ensued, spreading throughout French Switzerland and France and into the Low Countries, everywhere known as 'le Reveil.' Several of the revived students became internationally known—Merle D'Aubigne, Louis Gaussen, Cesar Malan, Henri Pyt and Charlies Rieu, scholars all as well as evangelists.[33]

It is necessary to know the facts of the Awakening in countries outside North America to appreciate the point that the college awakenings in the United States in the days of Napoleon were only part of a worldwide movement. That the American movements on campus were much more intense could be attributed to the concentration of evangelical principle and practice in the American institutions of higher learning. Simply stated, there were many more evangelical collegiate communities in the United States than elsewhere.

CHAPTER V

THE IMPACT ON EDUCATION

Apart from the collegiate awakenings and the foundation of colleges which followed in the United States, it is difficult to separate the movements and trends in the United Kingdom from those occurring in the younger English-speaking nation. Chiefly because of the earlier industrialization, social reform was first achieved more often in the mother country.

France was the chief enemy of the British nation in those times of revolution. Fear of Napoleon had a salutary impact upon his threatened victims across the English Channel. A turning to God occurred in Britain before the United States.

In the concluding quarter of the eighteenth century, the traditional grammar schools of the Church of England had sunk to a sorry state,[1] Lord Chief Justice Kenyon in 1795 describing them as 'empty walls without scholars, and everything neglected but the receipt of salaries and endowments.' The new vitality that arose from the Evangelical Revival of Napoleon's day was sadly needed.

In 1780, a social reformer named Robert Raikes stood among the unruly children of Gloucester's depressed workers and asked himself: 'Can anything be done?' A Voice answered: 'Try.' And he tried. He gathered the illiterate children on Sundays and taught them to read, using the Bible as the inevitable textbook. Raikes too was a product of Revival.[2]

The Sunday School movement was founded, not as familiar junior churches of modern times, but as schools of rudimentary education which used the Holy Scriptures as a main text. The Sunday School movement thus became a vehicle of Evangelical Revival.[3] By 1820, it had half a million scholars in England and Wales, representing four per cent of the population; by 1830, it had a million and a half, representing ten per cent; and by 1850 nearly two and a half million were thus enrolled—approximating fifteen per cent of the population.

In the opinion of some,[4] this was 'the root from which sprang our system of day schools.' It had a considerable effect upon secular education, as well as creating a worldwide system of religious instruction.

Within the Established Church, a godly woman, Hannah More, became concerned about the illiteracy of rural folk in the Mendip Hills. While sharing a contemporary Anglican notion of full education for only the governing elite, Hannah More set out to provide elementary education for the children of the rural countryside. Her concern also arose from her Evangelical convictions.[5]

Dr. Edmund J. King, University of London scholar, told the present writer that, in comparative studies, it was interesting to observe that not only did experiments in the homelands affect the various countries overseas to which missionaries were being sent, but that experiments made by the missionaries overseas contributed to the progress of education in the sending countries.

Such was the case with Andrew Bell.[6] Sent to India as a missionary, he found himself baffled by the problem of teaching and keeping order in an overcrowded school of Tamil boys. He hit upon a device of delegating authority to his pupils, and thus succeeded in directing and teaching while maintaining reasonable order.

Andrew Bell, born 27th March 1753, graduated by St. Andrew's University in Scotland, went out to Virginia in 1774,[7] and returned from there in 1779—as an Anglican feeling but little sympathy with the revolting colonists. Five years later, he was ordained to the Anglican priesthood, soon afterwards proceeding to Madras as a missionary chaplain, where he served 1787-1796.[8]

In 1796, Andrew Bell returned to England and published the year following an account of his experiment in education. It was widely read by educational pioneers.[9] Bell's treatise was read by Joseph Lancaster, who, as a youth of twenty, had already opened a school for poor children in London, with a hundred in attendance. He too developed his passion for education from the Revival. Lancaster promoted, with vast enthusiasm, this idea of using monitors. With the help of a host of friends, he extended it over the world.

When a child was admitted, a monitor assigned him to his class; while he remained, a monitor taught him (with nine other pupils); when he was absent, a monitor ascertained the fact, and another found out the reason; a monitor examined him periodically and when he made progress a monitor promoted him; a monitor ruled the writing paper; a monitor made or mended the pens; a monitor had charge of the slates and books; and a monitor general looked after all the other monitors.[10]

Of course, the monitoring system was not new even in England. Raikes's teachers taught twenty children in four classes under four monitors and the delegated responsibility lightened the load.[11] Centuries before, at Eton, it was noted that the pupils shared the task of instructing:[12]

Ye Vth forme learn ye versyfycall rulys of Sulpicius gevyn in ye morning of some of ye VIth forme, and this Vth forme gevyth rulys to ye fowrth.

The very essence of the Lancasterian system was the monitor. As suited to the needs of the time, it was a huge success. Lancaster joined the Society of Friends, but was never an ardent Quaker. Nevertheless, Elizabeth Fry solicited gifts for his work from among the wealthy Quakers[13] and many other Dissenters rallied to his support. Lancaster was known[14] as a 'skilful, persistent and unblushing beggar.' In 1805, he enlisted the support of George III, who had demanded to know how a single teacher could keep in order several hundred pupils.[15] 'By the same principle,' replied Lancaster, 'that thy Majesty's Army is kept in order!'

Lancaster's school on Borough Road grew by leaps and bounds.[16] Foreign princes, ambassadors, peers and ladies of distinction and commoners, bishops and archbishops and Jews and Muslims, all visited the Lancaster schools with wondering eyes.[17] In 1810, the Royal Lancasterian Society was formally constituted, becoming in 1814 the British and Foreign School Society,[18] sharing most of its title with the British and Foreign Bible Society, founded in the same period. Alas, Lancaster encountered double major difficulties, one due to his own folly and the other to sincere conviction.

The very success of his project brought him ready funds, which he spent with a 'recklessness, extravagance and ostentation' which soon led to his arrest[19] He formed a society which attempted to liquidate his personal debts of £5000, but he soon had a quarrel with his committee. The British and Foreign School Society attracted substantial supporters who agreed to promote Lancasterianism without Lancaster, and thus rejected he left in 1818 for America[20]

Joseph Lancaster founded Lancasterian schools in New York, Philadelphia, Baltimore and Washington; and was well received by the United States House of Representatives. He remarried (his first wife had died insane) and journeyed with his second wife to Venezuela upon an invitation of the Liberator Simon Bolivar, but he soon parted from Bolivar. Lancaster died in New York in 1838.

Lancaster had exchanged friendly notes with Andrew Bell, but an Anglo-Catholic Englishwoman (Mrs. Trimmer, who distrusted Lancaster's notions of non-sectarian education) sowed the seed of sad disagreement between them.[21] In 1811, Andrew Bell and his friends founded the National Society for promoting the Education of the Poor in the Principles of the Established Church throughout England and Wales.[22] By 1830, it was serving a third of a million children.

One of Lancaster's supporters had sought to introduce non-sectarian schools into England, but the opposition of the Archbishop of Canterbury had brought Samuel Whitbread's Parochial Schools Bill to naught.[23] From then on, the issue of Anglican-controlled or non-sectarian schools bedevilled education in England until the twentieth century. In Free Churches, there was support for non-sectarian schools; but in the Church of England there was opposition.

Robert Owen, a radical young thinker in Scotland, adopted these methods of Lancaster and Bell in his school for his factory employees' children at New Lanark[24] Owen's experiments had effect upon the thinking of Samuel Wilderspin in England and David Stow in Scotland, both of them products of the Evangelical Revival.[25] The former founded the London Infant School Society in 1824, and the latter the Glasgow Infant School Society in 1826. Scottish education owed much to David Stow's Glasgow Normal Seminary, founded in 1836.

Boyd's opinion that the system followed by Lancaster and Bell was very poor, but better than no system at all, is substantiated by students of this movement.[26] The monitorial system permitted no asking of questions and no development of personality: it was, in fact, a kind of educational mass production. In view of the appalling need of the times, mass production was in order. The system worked, up to a point; the pupils learned something; quiet order was maintained among the rowdy offspring of the rough lower classes; and the system was economically cheap, extraordinarily so.[27]

Bell and Lancaster may be regarded as the creators of the English elementary schools, their work a forerunner of the Elementary Education Act of 1870,[28] which recognized that the task of educating a nation's children was too great for the Church or for non-sectarian voluntary societies. The same conclusion was reached earlier in the United States.

* * *

In the meantime, a public school system was developing in the United States, superseding the private schools of the church-related pedagogues. While Roman Catholic educators still felt the need of maintaining schools and high schools, the majority of Protestants felt no threat, inasmuch as the same sort of teachers were teaching children in the same way. The few academies that remained survived by providing a select education for children of the families able to pay for more expensive tuition—Groton School, founded by a pious churchman, Endicott Peabody, for example.[29]

Interest was transferred to public schools by other men. They were often deeply religious. While not attached to the established denomination, Horace Mann, Charles Brooks and Henry Barnard shared the Puritan convictions of the local community regarding education.[30] De Witt Clinton, who gave a striking lead in public education in New York State,[31] was a godly Presbyterian, as was Robert Breckenridge of Virginia.

It does not require a religious experience to work out some better scheme of education, any more than it requires such a commitment to discover a cure for leprosy. But religious commitment more often shows itself in willingness to risk both health and life in some backward tribal society, and in this way the Evangelical Awakenings aided education.

In the United States, therefore, the public conscience had been stirred by the private example of committed Christians, so that there was no longer the urgent need of originating schools for the masses. There was a great need of training an elite for leadership, of providing higher education for all aspirants to service in the professions.

The impact of the college awakenings was felt in the founding of colleges and academies throughout the West. The principal dynamic behind the college founding movement was undoubtedly evangelical religion. The realization by the once fearful churches that the sceptical and rowdy revolutionary students were being converted by the hundreds on campus after campus certainly fired enthusiasm for establishing college after college out west.

The high proportion of collegiate converts going into the Christian ministry created a need of theological seminaries of graduate level.[32] Seventeen theological schools came into existence between 1807 and 1827, among them Princeton Theological Seminary, 1812; Yale Divinity School, 1822; and Union Theological Seminary in New York, 1824. The revived graduates of the old and newer theological schools provided the ministry for the burgeoning churches of the western as well as of the seaboard States. They also provided personnel and plans for the home missions on the frontier.

Samuel J. Mills,[33] the student Christian leader, 'plunged into the depths of the western wilderness, and between 1812 and 1815, traversed the Great Valley as far as New Orleans, deeply impressed everywhere with the famine of the Word, and striving to provide for the universal want by the sale or gift of Bibles.'[34] After a second trip, Mills proposed the organization of the American Bible Society, accomplished in 1816. This is a typical example of student pioneering.

Following the Awakenings of the early nineteenth century, the Baptists and the Methodists had extended their stakes rapidly with the help of farmer-preachers and circuit-riders. They had little use for higher education, but they soon fell in with the college-founding movement and multiplied their own schools of higher learning. The Presbyterians, on the other hand, committed as they were to an educated ministry, never lost the lead they developed in the founding of colleges.[35]

Most of these colleges were financed by the sacrificial giving of church members. There were no wealthy corporations to endow foundations. The people who gave generously were open-hearted in offering education to all and sundry, making no tests of doctrine for students;[36] but they did expect the students to attend the chapel services, and this was not an unreasonable request under the circumstances. There was nothing to hinder unbelievers from starting colleges with their own donations; but seldom did any of them try. Most unbelievers preferred to propagate their unbelief with public tax money, while opposing all voluntary religion on campus. This demanded little personal sacrifice.

Well did Frederick Rudolph observe that, if the colleges were not the work of missionaries, they were sometimes the work of people who might have been missionaries had they not decided to go west as permanent settlers.[37]

In 1811, the Reverend John W. Browne was drowned as he crossed the Little Miami River in Ohio.[38] He was on a preaching mission, but he had brought a wagonload of books and $700 for the newly founded Miami University. In 1832, five young Presbyterian ministers kneeled in the snow in the woods of Indiana and asked the blessing of God upon their projected institution of higher learning, Wabash College.[39] A volume could be written on the subject of such sacrifice.

In the booming state of Ohio, which had early passed all but four of the original thirteen states in population, the Baptists founded Denison; the Congregationalists, Oberlin and Western Reserve; the Disciples, Antioch and Hiram; the Episcopalians, Kenyon; the Lutherans, Wittenberg; the Methodists, Ohio Wesleyan, Baldwin and Mount Union; the Presbyterians, Franklin and Muskingum; the Reformed, Heidelberg; and the United Brethren, Otterbein.[40]

Of 180 denominational colleges in the West in 1860, 144 or so were founded and maintained by the more evangelistic denominations.[41] Led by teachers with strong convictions, it is not surprising that religious awakenings recurred.

There was no comparable movement in Great Britain. A proposal to provide for Dissenters and others disqualified from attendance at the historic universities resulted in the foundation of the University of London,[42] an academic leader.

CHAPTER VI

EDUCATIONAL PIONEERING OVERSEAS

Williams College in Massachusetts had been the scene of discouraging anti-Christian demonstrations, and there the new converts formed a secret society. One summer afternoon in 1806, five students met in a maple grove for private prayer, but a sudden thundershower drove them to shelter under a haystack. There they prayed about a plan to reach the unevangelized world with the message of Christ.[1]

The thundershower was of short duration, and as the sun broke through the clouds, one of their number, Samuel J. Mills, gave the decisive word, 'We can do it, if we will.' As a result, their burden increased with their numbers. Four years later, at Andover Theological Seminary, they proposed to ministers of their denomination that several of them be sent overseas in missionary enterprise. After much debate, it was decided to form the American Board of Commissioners for Foreign Missions, the first American mission society, soon to be followed by denomination after denomination.[2]

Polynesia became a target of missionary enterprise. All of the primary records have disclosed the hazards of existence in the Islands of the Pacific. Romantic ideas of 'ports of paradise' were contradicted by the facts of life as lived in the South Seas before the coming of Christianity. Though the Islanders often were comely and brave, life was cheap and wars were bloody. Infanticide, widow murder and cannibalism were common.[3]

The European impact in Polynesia had been far from generally beneficial. The beachcombers were often men of low morals who exploited the natives and introduced depravity of a vicious sort in a community already debased by lack of the moral sanctions of civilized society. Whalers and sealers cruised between the islands, adding fuel to fire by selling weapons of war to tribal warriors. Shamelessly at times, traders exploited people innocent of crude commercialism. Men off ships abused native women and often kidnapped the able-bodied of either sex to work in indentured service not far from slavery. They introduced epidemic diseases and venereal disorders which spread like plague in olden days.

The student awakening in New England had an indirect impact upon Hawaii, then a Polynesian kingdom in the North Pacific. A Hawaiian youth Opukahaia (or Henry Obookiah) found his way to Yale, attracting the attention of Samuel J. Mills, the student evangelist and missionary zealot. In 1818, Opukahaia died,[4] but a year later a party of missionaries, challenged by his untimely death, sailed for Hawaii.

The missionaries fully expected to find much drunkenness and prostitution among the natives, aided and abetted by the lawless European and American whalers who frequented those parts, not to mention gross idolatry and taboos. They arrived in 1820 to learn that native movements had succeeded in destroying much idolatry and in discouraging pagan taboos, movements due to news received from Tahiti and Tonga.[5]

Tahiti was reached in 1796 by a party of missionaries of the London Missionary Society who tried to educate, then to evangelize the inhabitants. They failed. Tonga was reached by British Methodists, who first evangelized and succeeded. Then the Tahitian mission returned and overcame the local paganism, thanks to the support of a chastened king.[6] Other islands were won, and the news reached Hawaii.

King Kamehameha I had united the islands by force of arms. His successor granted permission to the missionaries to land and to carry on their work. They made remarkable progress in their first decade, winning converts in the royal family and among the chiefs, instituting public services of worship, influencing local legislation to build up morality, educating thousands of children in schools, and defying the opposition of the foreigners who preferred a lack of moral control—a very different picture to that painted by novelists. By 1836, they had seventeen churches and a sixth of the islands' population was enrolled in their mission schools.[7]

In 1837, a Hawaiian 'Great Awakening' began in Hilo and, within five years, more than twenty-seven thousand converts —a fifth of the population—were added to the churches.[8]

Another area open to missionary education was the far south of the African continent, inhabited by a non-Negro race of yellow-skinned peoples, the Hottentots and the Bushmen.

At the time of the 1800 Awakening, there was a colony of 25,000 Dutchmen at the Cape of Good Hope. There were enclaves of traders at spots widely separated on the Atlantic coast of Africa. The rest of Africa, to the south of the Sahara, was scarcely known to the civilized world.

The evangelical awakening also affected the churches of Capetown, and so revitalized the congregations that some of the burghers gave up the comforts of Capetown to become pioneer Dutch Reformed missionaries to the Hottentots.[9]

At the same time, the Moravians reopened their mission at Genadendal, and the London Missionary Society sent Jan Theodor van de Kemp as a pioneer, succeeded by the Scots, John Philip, Robert Moffatt and David Livingstone.[10] Thus the great northward march of missions was begun.

Once a visiting judge and an investigating officer, asking a humble worker at the Bethelsdorp Mission what missionaries had done for Hottentots, were told by interpreter:[11]

When the missionaries came among us, we had no clothing but old sheepskins; now we are dressed in British cloth. We were unable to read; now we can read our Bibles or hear them read. We were without real religion; now we worship God in our families. We were without Christian morals; now every man has his own wife. We gave way to license and drunkenness; now we are hard-working and sober. We owned no property; and now the Hottentots at Bethelsdorp have fifty wagons and cattle as well. We were liable to be shot like wild beasts; and the missionaries stood between us and the bullets of our enemies.

The Hottentot way of life was doomed, but out of Hottentot interaction with South Africans of European blood came, with an admixture of slave stock of Malay and Malagasy origin, the Cape Coloured folk and the Griquas, both of them interesting and attractive peoples with as high standards of education and civilization as any in Africa next to the advanced communities of Europeans living in peculiar privilege, and closest to them culturally as well as linguistically.

University education in Latin America started a century before its North American counterpart. Peru, Mexico and the Dominican Republic claim the oldest universities. But such university education in Hispanic America was patterned after the older European system to provide a classical education for the elite, little help to the middle and lower class. It was rare for the humble and poor to aspire to education, above the most rudimentary.

In the first quarter of the nineteenth century, a Scottish agent of the British and Foreign Bible Society succeeded in gaining an entrance to the southern republics![12] He was also an agent of the British and Foreign School Society, which promoted schools on the Lancasterian model.

James Thomson sailed from Liverpool to Buenos Aires, reaching that port on 6th October 1818, after a voyage of three months. He was well received by the Government of Argentina, to whom he proposed the establishment of schools on the Lancasterian plan. Even the clergy gave him support, for just then the native-born clergy were open to new ideas, and within three years he had set up schools in Argentina and Uruguay with a total of five thousand pupils.[13] He was made an honorary citizen of Argentina.

Thomson arrived in Chile in mid-1821 and established schools on the same monitorial plan.[14] Some of the monastic orders were dispossessed of their convents to provide room for his schools. It seemed that his work had been established, for he was made an honorary citizen of Chile also.

No less a personage than the Liberator, San Martin, installed Thomson as first director of public instruction in Peru.[15] Navarrette, a local priest, was one of his most ardent supporters in all his educational and colportage plans. Also in Colombia, Thomson initiated a school system. In Mexico, ten primary schools became a thousand within a generation.

In Argentina, Chile, Peru and Colombia, Thomson's good start was lost both to education and evangelism. His well-organized school system and plans for extension and continuance languished for want of trained teachers. He lacked the organized support of British and American Churches. A major factor was the unrelenting opposition of the Catholic hierarchy. His work was destroyed by clerical reaction.

At the beginning of the nineteenth century, all of East Asia was closed to missionary forces, and the missions could do little more than hope for footholds on the perimeter. Consequently, the educational impact there was nil.

A more hopeful opportunity was afforded in India, where an extension of British commercial and imperial power opened a vast sub-continent to the influence of Europeans. Among those who early heard the call of India were Henry Martyn, a brilliant linguist and dedicated Churchman moved by the Evangelical Awakening at Cambridge University, and William Carey, disqualified from attending the universities, but a master of Latin, Greek and Hebrew in his 'teens.[16]

In 1793, William Carey arrived in India. In spite of vast difficulties, the debts of a colleague and the insanity of his wife, the demands of his employment and the opposition of the authorities, Carey persisted, transferring his residence at the end of the century to Serampore, under the Danish flag.[17] There he and Marshman and Ward set up a printing press, opened a school for children of Indians and Britons.

The energy of the Serampore missionaries was astounding. Not only did they translate the Scriptures into various Indian languages but they found time to experiment in the growing of sugar, coffee, cotton, cereals, and fruit trees.

An Indian civil servant, Charles Grant, used his influence with Wilberforce and the 'Clapham Sect' to open up India. The changes made in the Charter of the East India Company in 1813 opened India to the British missionary societies only, and those that followed in 1833 made it possible for societies from other parts of Europe and from the United States to begin their work in the sub-continent.[18]

One of their first objectives was education. There existed in India a traditional love of learning, but the chaotic conditions prevailing in the country at the time of the break-up of Moghul power had brought the indigenous system to a sorry condition. Appalling ignorance and superstition prevailed.[19]

It was recognized by both missionaries and their critics that their educational projects were a by-product.[20] Their main objective was the conversion of Indians to the Christian faith, and their minor purpose to meet the educational need. Yet this 'by-product' became a major force in India.

The long battle of the missionaries against suttee, that distressing custom of burning a widow on her husband's pyre, convinced their leaders that education was needed to impel Indian people themselves to welcome reform.

By 1813, evangelical associations in Britain had persuaded Parliament to provide a hundred thousand rupees from India Company revenue to promote education.[21] Important as were the school projects which received financial support from the Government, they were far surpassed by the projects of the missionaries themselves. In 1819, the Baptists reported 7000 children in their own schools, the Anglicans and London Missionary Society 4000 each, perhaps 50,000 in all schools of the various Societies in 1824. No government projects could remotely match the achievement. Baptists at Serampore reported printing 71,000 school-books in various languages by 1828, and other Societies had similar outputs.[22]

A controversy—bitter, deep and pivotal in all Indian education—developed between Anglicists and Orientalists regarding the medium of school instruction. Both agreed that vernaculars were useful for elementary instruction, for advanced studies quite inadequate. Anglicists advocated the teaching of advanced subjects in English, Orientalists in an Oriental classical language. Missionaries compromised, but Anglicists among them gained in influence. The Serampore missionaries taught Sanskrit also, but only for better understanding of its daughter languages, not for spiritual content. So, by 1824, the Directors of the Company were being persuaded that English was needed for the kind of education designed to help Indian people.[23] Most missionaries agreed heartily.

The Evangelical Awakening in Scotland had begun to shape the educational system of that forward-looking nation. It was the Church of Scotland which sent out several men who were to influence educational policy in India.[24] Alexander Duff introduced far-reaching new methods in the missionary approach, developing Christian institutes of higher learning using English with an expectation of attracting young men of the higher castes desirous of a European education. And the occasional converts of these colleges provided educated leadership for emerging churches.

44

Duff, in his educational projects was often opposed, very strongly, by the missionaries, with one illustrious exception, William Carey.[25] But his objective won its way. It is significant that Duff was supported by the enlightened Hindu Ram Mohan Roy when he opened his first school in Calcutta, attracting a couple of hundred boys to study in English and Bengali. Duff's college became justly renowned.

Duff's success had a powerful effect upon the educational policies of the Government. Such Anglicists as Trevelyan and Macauley were beginning to win support, and in 1835 Lord Bentinck threw his backing to the use of English as the medium of instruction. Within twenty years, the main lines of education for India were laid down.

John Wilson, like Alexander Duff, a product of the Revival in Scotland, arrived in Bombay in 1830. In 1832, he started a school which soon became a high school, out of which Wilson College grew. John Anderson similarly founded a work in Madras which became the Madras Christian College. Yet another convert of the same Scottish Revival, Stephen Hislop, founded a college in the city of Nagpur. Schools and colleges began to spring up all over the country as missionaries promoted their educational projects, for secular and spiritual betterment. The converts from the higher castes became Anglican clergymen and Presbyterian ministers, national pastors and teachers, to provide leadership for a growing number of Indian churches.[26]

Dr. Kenneth Ingram has observed that the 'promotion of Christianity called for the extension of education to assist in the attack upon the superstition and mental slavery fostered by ignorance.'[27]

William Carey and his colleagues adopted enterprising schedules, preparing or printing portions of Scripture in Sanskrit and Assamese, Bengali, Gujerati, Hindi, Kashmiri, Marathi, Oriya, Telugu and other tongues, with Chinese included. Within thirty years, they had the whole Bible ready in five languages and the New Testament in fifteen more.

The British and Foreign Bible Society lent valuable aid. But secular and classical literature was not neglected, for the Serampore Press published school histories and geographies, and other varied texts in the vernaculars.

One of the greatest of all educationalists in India, Sir Philip Hartog, paid his tribute as a Jew to the work of the Christian missionaries: [28]

. . . imbued from the first with a zeal not only for religion but for spreading secular knowledge in the vernaculars as well as in English . . . a great and inspiring influence in Indian education in all its stages. As one who belongs to another faith, I desire to bear my testimony to the noble and unselfish work of Christian educators in India . . .

Forty years after 1813, the total number of educational institutions managed, inspected or aided by the Company was no more than 1474, in which 67,569 pupils were instructed. In the same period, the Protestant missionary societies alone raised their total of schools to 1628 (exclusive of 1867 Sunday Schools) with 64,043 pupils (exclusive of Sunday Schools).[29]

Realizing the paucity of missionary finance, the well-informed surveyor, M. A. Sherring, stated: 'One is amazed and almost overwhelmed at the stupendousness of this undertaking.' [30]

The missionaries maintained grade schools for the lower classes, hence developed a strong emphasis upon vernacular education. They also opened schools for orphan children, and began projects of education for women in the teeth of strenuous opposition—not only day schools for girls, but zenana work among women in their own homes.[31]

Between 1813 and 1833, the missionaries concentrated their educational enterprise on elementary schools, relying upon the vernacular. Between 1833 and 1853, the emphasis began to shift to secondary schools and colleges using the English medium. This followed American patterns.[32]

The American Board of Commissioners for Foreign Missions teachers opened schools in the Tamil-speaking area in the 1830s, then spread into the Marathi districts. American Baptists opened a work in Andhra and another in Assam. American Presbyterians entered the North West Provinces and the Punjab.[33] Personnel came from the revived colleges.

At the mid-nineteenth century, the missionary enterprise in education (including the Roman) still exceeded that of the agencies subsidized by the State.[34]

CHAPTER VII

THE MID-CENTURY DECLINE

By the middle of the nineteenth century, it was evident that the series of awakenings on college campuses in the United States had run its course. As in the days of the Restoration of Charles II, following the Commonwealth of Oliver Cromwell, it seemed obvious that 'righteousness' tried and tired the generation that followed the dedicated puritans. This was true not only in ordinary society, but among the college students.

Reaction to evangelical religion found expression in the rise of the Greek-letter fraternities.[1] Founding chapters were established as early as the second quarter of the century. They spread rapidly through the colleges of New England and the Middle Atlantic States. They were most often sponsored by students themselves, and rarely had the backing of college administrators. Their function was social and emotional, rather than academic or religious. It was too much to expect the oncoming, unregenerate classes of students to appreciate the religious enthusiasms of their predecessors, who had experienced spiritual realities in the times of awakening. As a collegiate historian observed:[2]

Fraternities offered an escape from the monotony, dreariness and unpleasantness of the collegiate regimen which began with prayers before dawn and ended with prayers after dark.

The same historian pointed out that fraternities really institutionalized the various escapes from the boredom of regimented life—escapes that, as in military life, were all too natural but also all too unspiritual, considered (in fact) sinful by the practising Christian: drinking, smoking, card playing, singing and seducing. The fraternity provided new ways of enjoying a cigar, a drink, a song or the company of a coquette. It was a freemasonry of gaiety.

47

In one other way, the fraternity was at variance with the Christian society. Confession of sin had a disciplinary and purgative effect upon the spiritual company;[3] the fraternity adopted a loyalty of concealment, students standing by each other in matters both innocent and mischievous.[4] Plainly, concealing and revealing did not go together, so the Greek letter men tended to resist the influence of evangelical awakenings. Not that the fraternities became anti-religious; rather they were devoted to the values of the present age, not those of eternity; and they succeeded in emphasizing such things as friendship, comeliness, fashion, and family connections, not to mention affluence. Students were less likely to be 'convicted' of these accomplishments than of outright drunkenness, gambling, fornication, and the like.

It cannot be overemphasized that the student world did not live to itself. It was affected by the currents of thought in outside society; and the decline in religious zeal in the world at large at the mid-century had an immediate effect upon the colleges in the 1850s.

There was turmoil and revolution in Europe at the mid-century.[5] In Great Britain, there were Chartist demonstrations; in Ireland, republican agitation. Insurrections broke out in Berlin, Paris and Vienna. Reaction followed, giving a new lease of life to absolute rule.

In England, the Anglo-Catholic Revival countered the expanded power of Anglican Evangelicals; in Scotland, a great Disruption rent the Presbyterian establishment; and in the German States, a new rationalism blighted Lutheranism. In Switzerland and the Netherlands, there was dissension.

Between 1845 and 1855, religious life in the United States of America was in decline.[6] There were many reasons for decline, political and social as well as religious. The question of slavery was of paramount importance, and men's passions and energies were being diverted into contention. The issue also polarized student opinion.

At first, the student community seemed to support the idea of re-colonizing Africa with liberated slaves. Samuel J. Mills, the Christian student leader, embarked for Africa on a trip to survey suitable territories for resettlement of the slaves, and died overseas.[7] Later, many students began

48

to question the wisdom of African resettlement. They tended to divide themselves between Colonization and outright anti-Slavery societies, and often were prohibited by authorities from agitation on these issues.[8]

At Amherst, the Anti-Slavery Society enlisted more than a third of the student body, all but six of their members active Christians. They refused to disband, saying that they could not 'conscientiously disband and relinquish the right of inquiring into, discussing, and praying over the suffering and woes of more than two million of our population.'[9] In Ohio, Theodore Dwight Weld, a convert of the brilliant C. G. Finney, arranged a debate upon Slavery at Lane Theological Seminary, as a result of which four-fifths of the students left the Cincinnati institution and moved to Oberlin, where Finney's anti-slavery sentiments prevailed.[10]

Many people at the time lost faith in spiritual things because of the extremes of apocalyptists who followed William Miller and others in predicting Christ's return and reign in 1843 and in 1844.[11] Public confidence became shaken as the excitement died down, some disappointed victims becoming bitter infidels while others embraced a cynical materialism. So widespread was the delusion that the churches became the subjects of ridicule, and faith in religion was impaired, so that between 1845 and 1855, there were several years in which church accessions scarcely kept pace with the severe losses due to a relenting discipline and a relentless death rate.

The Millerite movement also had its effect upon college life.[12] Miller had predicted the Second Coming in 1843, then 1844. These years, and those immediately following, were years of discouragement on typical campuses. The cynical reaction to the misplaced enthusiasm was having its effect upon the free-thinking offspring of the generation that was disappointed in its expectations.

The 1850s were very disappointing years for evangelical activity in American colleges.[13] At Williams College, for example, there were no results worth recording in the years 1854-1857. Of course, conditions were better than before the rise of the student societies in the early 1800s. In the mid-fifties (for example) eleven New England colleges taught a total of 2163 students, of whom 745 professed faith:[14]

49

Bowdoin College	152	37
Waterville College	86	46
University of Vermont	123	30
Middlebury College	60	35
Amherst College	187	113
Williams College	207	106
Brown University	243	80
Harvard College	319	30
Yale College	446	130
Wesleyan University	103	78
Dartmouth College	237	60 [15]

It is significant that the fifty years following the Unitarian capture of Harvard College had produced the lowest percentage of students professing Christian faith among these New England colleges.[16] Harvard reported less than one in ten; Yale, the only comparable institution, reported nearly one in three. Harvard's friends were glad to announce that the pious John Harvard's foundation was "a college where hot-gospelling was poor form, hell was not mentioned, and venerable preachers treated the students not as limbs of Satan, but as younger brothers of their Lord and Saviour." This gentle handling failed to persuade more than ten per cent of them to declare their faith.

The mid-century brought to the fore a problem which faced those educators who were dedicated to evangelism as well as to education. The colleges in which occurred an epidemic, phenomenal revival—a spiritual movement that affected the total community with New Testament phenomena —were evangelical communities. They had been chartered not only to teach the arts and sciences but also the Christian life; their administrations and faculties were generally not only capable teachers but ardent or acquiescent evangelists; their students were either willing or reluctant auditors of a message which neither they nor their parents challenged. The colleges were underwritten by the gifts of dedicated Christians in foundation and maintenance. They were clearly evangelical communities in which evangelical revivals were expected or desired—as in evangelical colleges in the late twentieth century or in the earliest years of settlement.

The mid-nineteenth century, however, was producing two other types of colleges, the state university and the secularized private college. In the state university, there was no specifically Christian charter; and in the secularized private college, it was allowed to lapse. In the state university, an excellence in teaching was demanded and evangelism was officially undesirable; and this became more and more the practice in the secularized private college. And secular funds became available to both state university and private college. Neither was reckoned an evangelical community.

Not only was the expectation of evangelical awakenings lessened; their realization was made difficult or impossible. The focus of the evangelical community was communal worship, and chapel attendance was required. By the mid-century, the student revolt against compulsory prayers was widespread. Even in the 1850s, students at Williams College indulged in 'deliberate absenteeism, indifference, disrespect.' They wrote obscene verses in their hymnals and spat in the aisle during the sermon![7] In the deep South, it was no better, for in 1857 a student at the University of Georgia danced in the aisle of the college chapel during prayers![8] In the West, the younger brother of the president of Illinois College was suspended[19] for 'repeated disorders tending to disturb the worship of God in chapel.' In the 1850s, the abandonment of evening prayers began, and within a generation or so they were obsolete in most institutions. Ways were sought to make voluntary services more attractive to the unregenerate.

With the passing of compulsory chapel attendance, the likelihood of reaching the whole community in evangelistic ministry passed also. The epidemic, phenomenal revival continued on only in those Christian colleges which chose to maintain communal prayers. Henceforth, revivals in their strictest sense occurred in voluntary societies; awakenings in the wider academic community came about by evangelism undertaken by committed students stirred by revivals.

This does not mean that those concerned convened their representatives and planned a change of strategy. The next 'outpouring of the Spirit' seemed to initiate the changes, without prior human planning. This is a factor that cannot be ignored. The great changes were unprogrammed.

In American society at large, from Atlantic to Missouri, there were secular factors operating as well. The financial and commerical prosperity had had an adverse effect upon the American people at the mid-century.[20] The zeal of the people was devoted to the accumulation of wealth, and other things (including religion) took a lesser place. Cheap and fertile land attracted multitudes of settlers as the frontier was pushed farther and farther west. Cities and states were founded in rapid succession and the population in them increased at an astounding rate. Harvests were plenteous. Boom times caught the public fancy.

Secular and religious conditions combined to bring about a crash.[21] The third great panic in American history swept the giddy structure of speculative investment away. Thousands of merchants were forced to the wall as banks failed, and railroads went into bankruptcy. Factories were shut down and vast numbers thrown out of employment, New York City alone having 30,000 idle men.[22] In October 1857, the hearts of people were thoroughly weaned from speculation and uncertain gain, while hunger and despair stared them in the face.

There had been a commerical revulsion, quite as widespread and unexpected, in the year 1837. It was tenfold more disastrous, yet it produced then no unusual turning to religion, no revolution of the popular mind, no upheaving of foundations.[23] The people as a whole were far more intent upon examining the political and economic causes of their pecuniary pressure than searching for a spiritual explanation. Now, in the United States, distress preceded an awakening.

Within a matter of months, the churches of the nation of every denomination were overcrowded nightly, and at noon even the theatres were packed with praying people.[24]

CHAPTER VIII

THE 1858-59 AWAKENING

Three outstanding scholars have produced a massive, two volume, historical interpretation of American Christianity with representative documents, and have written of the 'wide sweep and immense popularity of the great revival of 1857-58. . . . In city after city, hugely attended prayer meetings, often held at noon, became a feature. The press devoted many columns to the exciting news. Lay leadership was conspicuous in the work.'[1]

Historians have often dismissed the Awakening of 1858 as 'the bank-panic revival,' ignoring the fact that both the intercessory and evangelistic phases of the movement had begun before or independent of the bank panic of 1857.[2] The great movement has been traced to prayer meetings begun in Manhattan in September of 1857, which became newsworthy in March of 1858. Bank-panics do not automatically produce religious awakenings, as noted in the 1929 crash.

Just before the bank panic, the movement began in lower Manhattan. Prayer meetings grew during autumn and winter. Church after church in Manhattan was opened and filled at the noon hour.[3] Then the crowds filled the theatres also. In these meetings, apart from the opening exercises, there was no formality. Anyone was free to pray publicly.

At first, the newspapers reported that 6,110 people were attending noon prayer meetings in New York (Manhattan only in those days).[4] Then the numbers increased beyond easy calculation. And before very long, 10,000 New Yorkers had been converted to God and committed to the care of local churches.[5] In May, a good authority gave the total for the city as 96,000 converts.[6] American papers from coast to coast carried the news of the awakening in the metropolis to their readers. Already, less publicized awakenings were occurring elsewhere.

Soon similar manifestations were seen in New England, the Ohio Valley, Pennsylvania, and the South, even to the farthest West. The phenomenon of the packed-out churches together with startling conversions occurred everywhere. The influence of the wonderful Awakening was felt throughout the nation. It first captured the great cities, but it also spread through every town and village and country hamlet. It swamped schools and colleges. It affected all classes regardless of condition. There was a remarkable unanimity of approval by religious and secular observers alike.

The population of the United States at that time was about thirty million.[7] Some indication of the scope of the movement may be gathered from the numbers of converts added to the churches, not counting the numerous church members who were also converted. Within a year, more than a million joined the various denominations.[8]

Bishop Charles P. McIlvaine, addressing the Convention of the Diocese of Ohio on the Revival of Religion, observed that the 1858 Awakening was (1) simple in means——prayer, reading, brief exposition, and singing; (2) quiet, marked by calmness and freedom from unwholesome excitement; (3) harmonious, exhibiting brotherly love; (4) restrained, having a conservative influence; (5) far-reaching, of the very widest extent; and (6) reputable, commanding the respect of the world in unprecedented ways——all well substantiated.[9]

Critics were unable to lay the charge of fanaticism or hysteria, or any of the usual accusations against revivals. So they contented themselves with declaring that a revival which filled other churches, but not their own, could not be of Divine origin.[10] Their criticism provoked very little attention or controversy in either secular or religious press. It was difficult to find anyone with unkind words to say.

It was a laymen's movement,[11] in which the laymen of all denominations gladly undertook both normal and extraordinary responsibilities in the service of God and humanity. The social influence of the Awakening was first felt in wartime services, but much impetus was held in suspense until the cessation of hostilities, after which the social conscience asserted itself, reinforced by the social achievements of the same Awakening following 1859 across the Atlantic.

It was as strong in the frontier towns as in Philadelphia. Even more surprising was the full interdenominationalism: every denomination was affected, whether informal as were the Baptists and Methodists, or formal like the Lutherans and Episcopalians. The Young Men's Christian Association took a leading part in the movement, for it was primarily a lay effort, although the clergy rejoiced in it.[12]

Historians have neglected the Awakening in the colleges. In 1914, Clarence P. Shedd completed his history of the development of the College Young Men's Christian Associations, as part of the research required for his Master of Arts degree. Twenty years later, to fulfill the requirements for a Yale Ph.D., this able and widely read scholar added a thorough study of the college awakenings prior to 1858, when the College Y.M.C.A. movement made its appearance. The whole story was published to describe 'two centuries of Student Christian movements.' It is a gold mine of information and a treasury of insight, and it is rightly considered the standard text on the subject.[13]

Shedd's great work is marred by an astounding oversight. His fifth chapter is devoted to 'Student Religious Societies, 1810-1858,' with sub-sections such as 'Extent of Student Societies——1810-1858,' and 'Student Religious Societies prior to 1858.' His sixth chapter is entitled 'The Widespreading League of Christian Youth,' and contains a score of references to the year 1858 as a turning point in college social developments. His seventh chapter describes 'The Spread of the Young Men's Christian Association in the Colleges (1858-1877),' in which he states that more than fifty colleges organized Y.M.C.A.s between 1858 and 1877, which statement he italicizes for emphasis. And yet, in the three chapters—and in the whole of his work of research—there is not a mention of the Awakening of 1858 throughout the nation, nor in any single college.[14]

In a detailed bibliography supplied by Frederick Rudolph in his treatise upon American colleges and universities, the question is asked: 'Who has written the book that tells the story of religion in the American college in the eighteenth and nineteenth centuries? What would a study of the revival of 1858 reveal?'[15]

As early as November, 1857, an awakening was reported from that citadel of evangelism, Oberlin College in Ohio, in which the student body numbered 845, a considerable number in those days.[16] The Oberlin Church received forty additions to membership, half of them students 'hopefully converted.' Oberlin owed much to Charles G. Finney, the evangelist.

It was not long before an Oberlin paper, operated in the Finneyan tradition, declared that the most precious feature of the 1858 Awakening was the revival in the colleges.[17] The news of revival came from the east and west and south, as awakenings occurred in almost all of the colleges.

So far as denominational colleges were concerned, there were, during that decade,[18] thirty-four Methodist colleges, twenty-five Baptist, forty-nine Presbyterian, fourteen Roman Catholic, twenty-one Congregationalist, eleven Episcopalian, six Lutheran, five Disciples, five Reformed, two Quaker, and eight others. Nearly all were immediately affected.

State universities had begun in the Old South, but were emerging more rapidly in the great Midwest where frontier philosophy supported the idea on purely pragmatic grounds. But, in the late 1850s, the state universities were practically indistinguishable from their denominational counterparts, and their students also experienced the Awakening.

It was impossible for collegiate communities to remain uninfluenced by the nationwide religious upheaval. Stirring awakenings occurred in most of the colleges. They began as meetings for prayer and continued as manifestations of repentance, confession and restitution. No single evangelist was responsible, nor did visiting clergy initiate the campus movements. The biggest single factor was the services of intercession going on all around.

The historian of the American college and university, Frederick Rudolph, has cited briefly the awakenings north, south, and west in the colleges in 1858.[19] Although he rightly assessed the scope of the movement, he was wrong in calling 1858 'the last great revival year': 'Evangelical religion— with its emphasis upon a great outpouring of spirit, of individual professions of experience, with its goal of total victory waiting to be achieved—would never have as good a year again as it had in 1858.'

New England, home of so many first-rate colleges, was mightily moved in the 1858 Awakening—cities and schools. By March 1858, the awakening in Boston[20] (like its counterpart in New York City) had become news to the whole nation. The movement in New England generally was even stronger than in the metropolis. The most numerous denomination reported in the revival period 11,744 added on profession; and another claimed 8,479 in a few months.[21] Two hundred and sixty smaller communities announced in two months' reporting more than ten thousand conversions.[22]

In Northern New England, great crowds attended prayer meetings in Portland and other towns of Maine. In Vermont and New Hampshire, a hundred towns reported hundreds of conversions resulting from crowded prayer meetings. This was not without effect on Dartmouth College, where a 'deep and pervading interest, accompanied by quiet good order and serious deportment' was reported.[23] In the spring, the work was still progressing through the 'fervent prayers' and the 'active efforts' of students and faculty.[24] The town and the college of Middlebury both experienced an awakening even before the winter had ended—'such a refreshing,' they said. More than half of all the Middlebury students became inquirers during the movement, a third of the undergraduates professing conversion. It was observed that there was an uncommon freedom in expressing feeling and a great frankness in confessing sin.[25]

At Williams College, where student rebellion had broken out not long before, an awakening had scarce begun before thirty students—some of them the wildest on campus—had been hopefully converted.[26] An unprecedented awakening had swept the local churches and citizens of Williamstown, and soon the college campus was affected, conversions taking place every week from the beginning of January. Although some of the rowdiest students had become 'the subjects of renewing grace,' the Williams College awakening was said to be 'very quiet,' becoming very general.[27]

In Massachusetts,[28] a total of one hundred and fifty towns were moved by this revival of religion, with five thousand citizens professedly converted before the end of March, the month when the movement began. In the Connecticut Valley,

President William Augustus Stearns claimed that all of the collegiate community at Amherst had been moved, and the whole college penetrated.[29] In upper classes, only three or four seniors remained unconverted. A full year later, it was described as 'a wonderful revival of religion.' Nearly all the students had experienced a change of heart.[30] The movement went on for weeks, it being said (significantly) that there was 'no sudden rush into the kingdom, but each convicted sinner took up his cross as if alone with God.' The president insisted that there had been 'no extravagance' and 'no irregular zeal or enthusiasm,' the most noticeable result being the 'reformation of character.'[31]

One found no record of a startling movement at Harvard College,[32] where it was recognized that preaching the gospel in the halls of ivy was 'poor form,' though it must be said that Unitarians were not untouched by the Awakening,[33] and that Professor Frederic Dan Huntington began a weekly devotional service in Appleton Chapel, 'well attended,'[34] a sign of 'new vigor' at Harvard. Some more orthodox people wondered about the doctrinal content of this ministry, even though the spirit of revival was in evidence at Harvard. Shortly thereafter, the distinguished professor of Christian morals abandoned his Unitarian loyalty and entered the Episcopal ministry, doctrine thus following experience.[35]

In the State of Connecticut, the revival swept the communities in an unprecedented way.[36] One of the largest churches in New Haven was full to capacity for an 8 a.m. prayer meeting, repeating that proceeding daily at 5 p.m. Equally large prayer meetings were begun in Hartford and in New London. At Bethel, business was suspended for an hour every day between 4 and 5 p.m., and two hundred persons were reported converted in two months, three-quarters of whom joined the Congregational Church. In Connecticut also was reported a town where no unconverted adult could be found.[37] No fanaticism was reported anywhere.

The awakening in New Haven soon communicated its enthusiasm to the undergraduates and faculty at Yale College, where a tradition of college revivals had long persisted. In short time, the students were participating in union prayer meetings, where they encountered a conviction of sin.

The most powerful revival since 1821 was reported at
Yale, experiencing a movement in which it was 'impossible
to estimate the number of conversions,' though later it was
reported that 45 seniors, 62 juniors, 60 sophomores and 37
freshmen had responded, a large proportion of the total of
the student body.[38] In review, it was said that 'the work in
college scarcely finds a parallel in the whole history of the
institution.' And, more than a year later, Congregationalist
authorities reported a greater number of conversions than
in any previous revival. Yale's student body was composed
of 100 seniors, 107 juniors, 117 sophomores, and 123 freshmen, in 1858 a total of 447, of whom almost half professed
faith. By the end of May, Yale College Church had received
63 converted students as new members; another twenty became communicants; and between thirty and forty were
being considered for membership, making a total of more
than a hundred and twenty accessions, not counting student
converts adhering to the other denominations. Many 'bitter
scoffers' were among the converts. The movement of 1858
was unprecedented at Yale, insofar as the numbers were
concerned.[39]

Besides the awakening in New York City and its reper-
cussions at Columbia University and the College of the City
of New York, a wave of religious interest swept the State of
New York, up the Hudson and along the Mohawk. Town after
town reported hundreds of conversions. Albany, the capital
with 60,000 population, saw unusual happenings.[40] An early-
morning prayer meeting was begun by state legislators who
started with six men in the Court of Appeals rooms opposite
the Senate Chamber. Soon afterward, the rooms were overflowing. Civic noon prayer meetings attracted great crowds.
Nearby in Schenectady, church bells sounded every evening,
calling to meetings crowds that filled each church.[41] The ice
on the Mohawk was broken for believers' baptism, churches
being too small for warm hearted candidates for immersion.
A fervent spirit swept the students at Union College there,
converts being won on campus as in city.[42] As early as January
of 1858, a 'gracious revival of religion' began in Genesee
College in Lima, a small town in western New York State,
more than a hundred students being deeply moved.[43]

The students at Hamilton College, sharing in the movement among the townsfolk at Clinton in the Mohawk Valley, organized their own noonday prayer meeting, supporting two other regular meetings as well. Numbers were converted during the time of 'precious religious interest.'[44]

Unprecedented movements of religious enthusiasm were sweeping Newark and sixty New Jersey towns, with sixty thousand converts recorded within a few weeks.[45] Of the work in Newark, which won 2785 converts to a couple of dozen churches within a couple of months, it was said that the great revival was winning the most mature minds in the community. Hundreds joined the churches in New Brunswick, the home of Rutgers, heads of families in the town outnumbering students from the campus.[46] There were 272 students at Nassau Hall when the awakening reached Princeton, and 102 professed faith, 50 dedicating their lives to the ministry.[47] Princeton reported the reorganization of the Philadelphian Society, a move of great significance in future developments among college students all over the world.[48]

An example of the direct effect of the general awakening upon the colleges may be found in events in Philadelphia. A group of young men associated with the Y.M.C.A. moved a prayer meeting (begun 23rd November 1857) to the larger Jayne's Hall, where meetings commenced in the ante-room on 3rd February 1858.[49] Attendance grew from twenty, thirty, forty and fifty to sixty. In March, the revival erupted.

At first, only the small room was occupied, with a few in attendance. Then it became overflowing, and the meeting removed to the main saloon, meetings starting there on 10th March. Twenty-five hundred seats were provided, and were filled to overflowing.[50] The sponsors next removed a partition from the main floor space and platform; next the floor, platform and lower gallery, then floor, platform, and both galleries filled up; fully six thousand people gathered daily.

For months on end, each separate church was opened at least each evening, some of them as often as three and five times a day, and all were filled. Simple prayer, confession, exhortation and singing was all that happened, but it was 'so earnest, so solemn, the silence . . . so awful, the singing . . . so overpowering' that the meetings were unforgettable.[51]

In order to continue the work, which (as in New York) flooded churches with inquirers and converts, a big canvas tent was bought for $2000 and opened for religious services on 1st May 1858.[52] During the following four months, an aggregate of 150,000 people attended the ministry under the canvas, many conversions resulting. The churches in Philadelphia reported five thousand converts thus won.

It was inevitable that the enterprising young men of the Y.M.C.A. in Philadelphia should consider the needs of the students at the nearby University of Pennsylvania. Although owing its foundation to the Great Awakening, the University of Pennsylvania was the first in America to have no clergymen on its governing board, which possessed no denominational affiliation whatsoever. This did not mean an absence of religious interest, just a lack of a sponsor. So, between 1858 and 1860, the Y-men conducted prayer meetings on the campus, these being widely advertised and largely attended. It was not long before the students themselves became fully responsible for the continuing meetings.[53]

In the spring of 1858, an extraordinary awakening swept Jefferson College in Canonsburg, near Pittsburgh, in the western part of Pennsylvania,[54] prayer meetings and spontaneous conversions being supported by unabated interest. The rural colleges of Pennsylvania shared in the Revival— just as did those in New York and New England.

In plantation society, the sons of the wealthy were often in need of discipline. A professor at Davidson asked:[55]

Indulged, petted and uncontrolled at home, allowed to trample upon all laws, human and divine, at the preparatory school ... (the student) comes to college but too often with an undisciplined mind and an uncultivated heart, yet with exalted ideas of personal dignity and a scowling contempt for lawful authority and wholesome restraint. How is he to be controlled?

At Davidson, students had been suspended for drunkenness and for immorality in earlier years. In April of 1858, an awakening of 'great power and blessed results' began, in a short space of time registering forty inquirers. Students (besides attending chapel) conducted for themselves a weekly prayer meeting going on for eighteen months.[56]

At Oberlin College, a base of anti-slavery agitation from its foundation, an editor observed: 'If this great revival revives pure religion, it will purify the public conscience and . . . beget a deeper abhorrence of slavery.'[57]

This hope was fulfilled in many parts of the country, and (to quote Prof. Timothy L. Smith) the 'revivalists were convinced that the conquest of social and political evil was at hand.' The 'terrible logic of events,' cited by an evangelical journal which had enthusiastically chronicled the Revival, crystallized the anti-slavery feelings of Northern Christians into anti-slavery action when God 'loosed the fateful lightning of His terrible swift sword' as Truth went marching on.[58]

But the Northern abolitionists were unwilling to believe that the Lord could bless the South. Writing of the Revival of 1858, Charles G. Finney stated:[59]

> Slavery seemed to shut it out from the South. The people there were in such a state of irritation, of vexation, and of committal to their peculiar institution, which had come to be assailed on every side, that the Spirit of God seemed to be grieved away from them. There seemed to be no place found for Him in the hearts of Southern people at that time.

This was a very irresponsible statement for a lawyer— Finney's trained profession—to make. It was adopted by a number of historians, including Beardsley.[60] It was untrue. Bishop Candler, on the other hand, insisted that the results of the revival were 'in proportion to the population, greater in the South than in any other section,' and his good account of amazing revivals of religion in Confederate Armies in the War between the States seemed to contradict the contention that pro-slavery sentiment hindered revival in the South.[61]

Some allowance should be made for the fact that the South then possessed no great industrial cities like the Northern metropolitan areas, and that its population was scattered over an agricultural countryside; hence it was less spectacular down South, where newspapers could not immediately influence crowded cities as north of the Mason-Dixon Line. The press reported great revivals were sweeping the South, Richmond, Charleston, Nashville, Memphis, New Orleans, Mobile, Savannah, Augusta. Columbia, and Raleigh.[62]

At the time of the 1858 Awakening, there were fewer than five hundred college students in the State of Georgia. At Oxford, the Methodists had established Emory College, whose student body numbered about 120. The University of Georgia, a state foundation which was directed by one clergyman or another as president for half-a-century before and after, educated more than 110 at Athens. Oglethorpe College at Milledgeville had been founded by Presbyterians and cared for less than a hundred men. Mercer College was the smallest, with fourscore students in residence.[63]

Oglethorpe University (Presbyterian) had been founded in 1835 for 'the cultivation of piety and the diffusion of knowledge.' During the 1858 Awakening, not a solitary young man was without some degree of conviction of sin.[64] Emory and Mercer and the University of Georgia shared the revival.[65]

At the University of North Carolina, there were residing in 1857-58 a total of 453 students, 293 of them from North Carolina itself, the classes being 94 seniors, 119 juniors, 116 sophomores, and 94 freshmen, and some in detached courses.[66] The Awakening swept the communities, and Wake Forest and the University of North Carolina experienced student awakenings also.[67]

The college records in the Old South have chronicled the details of the 1858 Revival. It is safe to say that a majority of colleges and universities in the South enjoyed evangelical awakening in that year of grace. The student population was affected by the general movement among the citizenry.

In 1858, the University of Virginia tutored 633 students, 351 of them from the Old Dominion, 45 from Alabama, 41 from South Carolina, 40 from Mississippi, 38 from Louisiana, 18 from Georgia, 13 from Kentucky, and others from various parts of the Old South.[68] The University, founded by Thomas Jefferson—the statesman of high ethical standards and deistic convictions, possessed no denominational affiliations nor any reputation for infidelity or irreligion either.

One of the results of the Awakening of 1858 in Virginia was a revival of Christian zeal in a University of Virginia society which maintained numerous prayer meetings.[69] The students had maintained the usual prayer meetings, and had witnessed conviction of sin and conversion to God.

On 12th October 1858, the revived students organized a Young Men's Christian Association, the first of a widespread movement on American campuses.[70] University of Virginia students engaged in prayer meetings, Sunday School teaching and mission work among the Negro people and in the nearby mountains.[71] Without doubt, the first of the College Y.M.C.A. fellowships was evangelistic rather than social.

The College Y.M.C.A. thus arose to meet the need of the students on secular or secularized campuses. It was not a planned development, but it multiplied its opportunities on campus after campus, until the movement had become the main vehicle of Christian witness in American colleges.

There was a similar development in the University of Michigan. The State of Michigan had been swept by the 1858 Revival. Downtown churches in Detroit were crowded out by businessmen of all denominations.[72] A single Methodist church there enrolled one hundred and forty new converts. In the smaller towns, such as Kalamazoo, Baptist, Congregational, Episcopal, Methodist and Presbyterian people united in the services of intercession.[73]

All the evangelical churches of Ann Arbor shared in the Awakening in Michigan in 1858, and many were the converts added to church membership, not a few being students from the nearby University of Michigan. Observers on campus reported to the New York press:[74]

There has been at times a deep and solemn thoughtfulness among the students of the State University . . . and the able and convincing lectures of the President, Dr. (Henry P.) Tappan, which have been frequent, have done not a little under the super-added influence of the Holy Spirit towards banishing the last remains of skepticism and placing the claims of the Gospel before the young men, on their broad, rational and natural foundation.

The 1858 Awakening at the University of Michigan led to the foundation of an unexampled development in student life, a Student Christian Association being formed, affiliating with the Young Men's Christian Association in due course. As in Virginia, it was clearly and unequivocally evangelistic, as its earliest records reveal.[75]

Within two months of the outbreak of revival, four hundred and eighty towns in the Middle West were reporting fifteen thousand conversions.[76] The Awakening stirred Cleveland, Cincinnati, Louisville, Indianapolis, Detroit, Chicago, St. Louis, and Dubuque, as well as smaller cities, villages and country places in all the settled states and territories; and everywhere the colleges were awakened.

A score of colleges which experienced campus revivals between March and May of 1858 reported more than five hundred conversions, and it was supposed that at least five thousand students declared their faith in the general revival throughout the country.[77]

At Denison College, the series of awakenings continued until the coming of peace between North and South. In the autumn of 1865, so many students professed conversion that the Baptist facilities proved inadequate, and President Samson Talbot was seen bravely baptizing candidates in the cold waters of the creek, shivering with cold in his chilled body but glowing with warmth in his fervent spirit.[78]

Miami University, situated at Oxford in Ohio, graduated the largest class in its history in 1858, and among them a record number of candidates for the Christian ministry. It was the same in many another college in Indiana or Illinois, to the far frontiers.[79]

The newspapers of Chicago, a budding metropolis with a hundred thousand inhabitants, were reporting 'unusual and almost unprecedented' events in a movement which first of all filled the Metropolitan Hall with two thousand men at noon for prayer, then in turn filled every church in the city in the evenings.[80] In this movement, a young shoe salesman, Dwight L. Moody, not a college graduate and scarcely an ordinarily schooled young man, began his remarkable work as a Christian layman—one which made him the world's most effective evangelist, and afterwards a powerful force among the students of Britain and America.

Far to the west, in Wisconsin, the faculty, students, and friends in Beloit College engaged in a time of fasting and prayer for Divine blessing. At the end of the school year, it was found that more than half the number converted (70) had decided to enter Christian ministry at home or abroad.[81]

In the town of Liberty, in the troubled state of Missouri, there were ninety students attending William Jewell College when the 1858 Awakening swept the state. The students organized a Baptist Evangelical Society, and sustained their own meetings for prayer, evangelism and missionary zeal. The new president was Dr. William Thompson, whose term of office was marked by an overflow of 'new life.' The years immediately following provided the college with the 'most hopeful and substantial period in its history up to that point.' Alas, the whole school was closed down during the Civil War, for military operations and civil turmoil made its classes impossible.[82]

News of the Awakening reached California in hundreds of thousands of 'affectionate letters,'[83] provoking united prayer meetings in the lesser California towns and San Francisco. The College of California was founded across the bay by the Presbyterians, 'to augment the discourse of reason, intelligence and faith.' It was taken over by the State and became the University of California at Berkeley.[84] Chapman College was set up by revived Christians in the Los Angeles area.

Wilberforce University, maintained at Xenia in Ohio for students of African blood, catered for 70 students from 15 states. In the 1858 Awakening, 30 professed conversion. It is obvious that the Revival reached not only the Negro mass of population, but the tiny elite as well—many of those who were converted in 1858 being slaves released specifically for higher education.[85]

The Awakening also moved young women in the colleges. Elmira College, in upper New York State, was typical of the higher educational institutions maintained for girls. At Elmira, the students organized and sustained a daily prayer meeting, and quite a number professed conversion, 'a very delightful religious interest' prevailing.[86]

Not only did the Awakening of 1858 revive the student populations across the land, but it encouraged the Churches to plan additional colleges, just as its predecessor of the early 1800s had done. The endowment of a projected school, the University of Chicago, progressed encouragingly in the elation of the Awakening, but it was another thirty years before the Baptists built the massive institution.[87]

The outbreak of the War between the States, the ghastly slaughter of a generation of young men, the Reconstruction, all served to inhibit higher education and delay the rising of a new movement of college building.

In standard church histories, the Great Awakening of 1858 has received a couple of lines here and a couple of lines there. In the opinion of the writer, one of the reasons for neglect lies in the fact that the Awakening was entirely devoid of fanaticism of any kind, not an instance of screaming aloud or jerking or dancing for joy, as recorded in the frontier awakenings among illiterates in post-Revolution times.

In the same way, the student awakenings of 1858 were in every way solemn and serious, not one charge of fanaticism being found in any record. But this also was the case in the early 1800s in the colleges, survivors of which in 1858 were comparing the general awakening in the American population with the college awakenings of fifty years before—solemn, serious, sane and sober.[88]

Student diaries of the period give glimpses of the movements on campus in 1858. G. L. P. Wren, whose diary for the period 27th February until 27th May 1858 has been preserved, noted briefly:[89]

Monday April 19, 1858: 'Yesterday I went to hear preaching, but little did I think of hearing such as sermon as I did . . .'
Tuesday April 20: 'Being some rain in the fore part of the day, we could not meet in the woods for prayer and we met in the Phi Gamma hall, and in a very few minutes there were six or eight converted and we repaired to the church where there were several more converted before we left.'

How many thousands of students were converted during the 1858 Awakening? More than a million ordinary people experienced transforming power. How many students laid down their lives in the most deadly war of the nineteenth century, the War between the States? Who can tell? But a large number survived to carry on their commission, some at home and some abroad, making their native land a better place to live in, improving conditions in less fortunate countries, and influencing multitudes for righteousness.

News of the American Awakening amazed the Christians in the United Kingdom, but not long afterwards the same sort of movement manifested itself in the North of Ireland, three out of four of whose inhabitants had emigrated in earlier generations to provide the American Colonies with the cutting edge of western settlement—the Scotch-Irish pioneers.[90] In 1859, however, the Revival in Ulster resembled the frontier awakenings in producing such intense conviction of sin that physical prostration occurred in ten per cent of the converts. The social impact was as astounding as it was lasting.

The same awakening followed in Scotland, with similar results, and the Church of Scotland recorded its thanks to Almighty God for the unspeakable blessing on the people. At the same time as the Irish Revival, a movement began in Wales, with a wholesome transformation of society.[91]

In England, the awakening began in 1860 and spread to every county, reaching every class and condition.[92] Upper class people packed St. Paul's Cathedral and Westminster Abbey every Sunday evening for five years. The theatres, including Sadler's Wells, the Old Victoria, Covent Garden and the like, were packed by the poor in the greatest movement ever known in London, for the churches were incapable of caring for the multitudes.

One of the first effects of the 1859 Revival in Britain was the creation of a new and intense sympathy with the poor and suffering. 'God,' insisted Lord Shaftesbury, a leader in the Revival, 'has not ordained that in a Christian country there should be an overwhelming mass of foul, helpless poverty.' A revival school of practical philanthropists arose, going straight to the heart of the slums of industrial England with a sensible Samaritanism, yet always ready to cooperate in all wise legislative improvements.[93] As 'schemes, organizations, places of worship, were multiplied,' 'numberless philanthropic institutions—homes, asylums, refuges, brigades, schools—were founded in all parts of the country.' The Salvation Army and Dr. Barnardo's Homes may be taken as examples. All this was happening while the Armies of the Union were locked in deadly struggle with the Confederacy, explaining why the social effects of the '58 Awakening in the United States were delayed, or re-imported from overseas.

At the time of the 1859 Revival in Britain, Oxford and Cambridge were the two major residential universities in all of the United Kingdom, for the University of London, founded college by college after 1820, was largely non-residential, as were the Scottish universities.

The twin cultural capitals of England, the Universities of Oxford and Cambridge, were profoundly moved by the 1859 movement to prayer. In the autumn of that year, there was started a Universities' Prayer Union, and an appeal was made for prayer for revival at Oxford and Cambridge. Canon A. M. W. Christopher of St. Aldate's in Oxford sponsored a week of prayer on a city-wide, parish and inter-collegiate basis.[94] The response was immediate.

At that time, Oxford University was anything but an evangelical stronghold. Wadham College was regarded as the most evangelical college, and to it came Hay Aitken, fresh from a tour of evangelism with his titled relatives in the Highlands of Scotland.[95] He vowed to speak to every undergraduate about his spiritual welfare. Before long, 'a sort of evangelical revival amongst undergraduates had taken place.'

Weekly prayer meetings at Oxford coalesced, forming the Daily Prayer Meeting held each day in term for more than a hundred years to date. There was much the same sort of movement to prayer at Cambridge, with the undergraduates seeking 'wholehearted consecration' to God.[96] Two saintly Anglican bishops, Francis Chavasse and Handley Moule, traced their spiritual careers to these prayer meetings. The Cambridge Inter-Collegiate Christian Union and its Oxford counterpart formed the advance guard of the universities' Christian Unions, which in Great Britain were not sponsored by the Y.M.C.A.[97] In post World War I days, these Christian Unions were associated to form the Inter-Varsity Fellowship of Christian Unions, known throughout the United States as the Inter-Varsity Christian Fellowship.[98]

Converted undergraduates in London, Glasgow, Edinburgh and other university cities shared in the general awakening. A medical student in Edinburgh, accompanied by a woman missionary, invaded and transformed a house of prostitution. A Dubliner, Tom Barnardo, studying medicine in London, took time out to found an extensive orphanage system.[99]

69

The 1858-59 Awakening in the United States and United Kingdom was the turning point in the development of the Y.M.C.A. It boosted the work of the Bible Societies. And it loosed a multitude of lay workers, many of whom were the graduates of colleges on either side of the Atlantic.

The question is often asked: why is there an immediate impact of Evangelical Awakening upon personal ethics but something of a time delay in social responsibilities? The best way to explain the time lag, sometimes lasting a decade or even a generation, is to point out that an individual who comes under evangelical influence knows immediately that he is held responsible for his personal behavior; social repentance faces the opposition of social custom long ingrained, and the revived individual must persuade others of their joint responsibility. And even when the responsibility is recognized, there are often honest differences of opinion concerning how best to achieve the reform.

William Wilberforce did not wait to persuade the church convocations of Canterbury and York in order to accomplish the abolition of the slave trade. He entered Parliament, in which the power of reform resided, and persuaded men of all faiths and of none that the cause was just. Unfortunately, the question was not peacefully settled in the United States, and a civil war broke out before the country made up its mind to emancipate the slaves.

It is worth taking notice of the impact of the Awakening on the initiation and extension of educational systems overseas. Wider areas of the world were open to the evangelical missionary, and results were forthcoming in a number of countries hitherto untouched.

CHAPTER IX

POST-1860 OVERSEAS IMPACT

It is utterly impossible to divorce the story of student awakenings from the course of missions in countries overseas.[1] From the beginning, one of the most immediate and dramatic effects of college revivals has been the recruitment of personnel for the work of Christ abroad. Of course, the believing Christian has a simple explanation for this— that the Divine Spirit that worked collectively upon the conscience of the collegiate community likewise operated upon the will of the individual respondent to present him with a call to life-service, whether in ministry spiritual or service secular. The unbelieving must propose his own theory.

Just as in the college revivals of the first half of the century, so in the mid-century awakenings. In the records of the societies, the theme of missionary responsibility kept recurring. It is true that many of the students converted or revived entered the Christian ministry at home, some to go forth with the pioneers on the Oregon or Santa Fe trails, others to found schools and academies and colleges, out west. But it should not be forgotten that a medical student in London (as a result of the 1860 Revival) founded the China Inland Mission; an engineering student converted in Iowa went out to India, helped build the Buckingham Canal in the Telugu country, and baptized 2222 patiently waiting Indians in one day. An Englishman from Birmingham pioneered in Congo; an American from Atlanta pioneered in Brazil.[2]

The 1858-59 Awakenings in the United States and United Kingdom were followed by similar movements in South Africa, beginning among the Zulus, breaking out in phenomenal power among the Afrikaners, and continuing among the English-speaking settlers through the visit of William Taylor of California, who was moved in the Awakening of 1858, thence stirring up the churches of Australia and New Zealand.[3]

Not only did the Awakening move the Afrikaners to engage in missionary activities on their northern frontiers, schools being founded along with churches, but the Taylor Awakening profoundly moved the Xhosa and Zulu communities, leading to 'an era of education' among them, to quote a South African historian.[4] The mid-century Awakenings certainly prepared the South African Bantu nations for their leading place in educational achievement in all of Africa, in primary as well as higher education.[5]

Using Southern Africa as a base, missionary societies penetrated Central Africa. As late as the year 1875, there were in Malawi 'no schools, no teachers, no pupils, and nobody who could read.'[6] The Church of Scotland, influenced by its educational tradition and its recent renewal in the Awakening, initiated a successful educational system based at Blantyre, with 57 schools and 3643 scholars; and the United Free Church of Scotland, Livingstonia-based, maintained an even more remarkable system of schools, 15,765 pupils attending 207 institutions—all built up in thirty years of self-sacrifing enterprise.

What of East Africa, which was entered after 1860? The explorer Speke, in 1862, declared that the kingdoms of Uganda were by far the most inviting in all Africa for such missionary enterprise.[7] Stanley was of the same opinion and his challenge stirred the Church Missionary Society to enter Uganda as pioneers. French missionaries followed directly in ecclesiastical competition.

Conditions in the Ugandan kingdoms were far from ideal. The kings and chiefs had the power of life and death. Two missionaries were killed. Converts of the Christian missions refused to submit to a vice of the Kabaka taught him by the Arab slavers. So he roasted three martyrs slowly to death, and burned alive thirty-two young men in a funeral pyre, two hundred Roman Catholic and Protestant martyrs dying by fire.[8] But the king was overthrown, and the missionaries were free to educate as well as evangelize a nation.

Meanwhile, the Fourah Bay College founded by the C.M.S. in West Africa continued in its grand design, the higher education of Africans.[9] Affiliated with Durham University, it educated a majority of post-1860 West African leaders.

It was the same in other continents after 1860, as surely the social ferment caused by the leavening of Evangelical Awakenings spread far and wide. In India, it had resulted in the foundation of schools and colleges during the first half-century. After 1858-59, it produced yet another missionary initiative in the educational field.[10]

The curse of India in the nineteenth century was cholera. Epidemics swept huge areas, the fondness of Indian folk for pilgrimages and religious festivals multiplying the danger, wiping out tens of thousands.

Indian opposition to the practice of European medicine in India was varied. Long acquaintance with tropical disease had provided native doctors with proven remedies, but effectiveness was often nullified by mixed-in religious super-stition. The problem of training Indian doctors in the practice of modern medicine arose. Dead bodies were defiling to the touch of a Hindu who therefore could not study dis-section to learn anatomy. Alexander Duff's College students in Calcutta informed a government commission of inquiry that their studies in the English medium had removed their religious scruples in such matters. Hence, Indian practice of medicine moved into realms of the possible as a Medical College of Calcutta was founded to teach Western medicine to Indian students.[11]

Few of the missionaries sent out in the first quarter of the nineteenth century were medically trained, but all were 'well disposed' to medicine. The American Board of Missions first began to send out medical evangelists as such. Dr. John Scudder arrived in Madras in 1836,[12] and his son Henry Scudder began a medical work in Arcot in 1851 which in its second century is famed in all of Asia and the world as the Vellore hospital and medical college complex, developed by Dr. Ida S. Scudder and her colleagues.

It was after the 1858-59 Revivals in America and Europe that medical missionaries came alive in all India. The Scottish Presbyterians began a medical work in Rajasthan in 1860, employing medical evangelists who dispensed medi-cine and the Gospel.[13] Other Scots established hospitals at principal mission stations in the same period. Other missions adopted similar plans.

Before the 1858-59 Awakenings, there were no more than seven medical evangelists in the entire Indian sub-continent, but their numbers quadrupled by 1882 and increased to 140 in 1895, with 168 Indian doctors assisting them.[14]

In the decade of the Revival, Clara Swain as a fully qualified doctor began her work among Indian women at Bareilly, where she opened a women's hospital in 1874.[15] Other lady doctors followed, British sponsors founding Zenana Medical Missions to meet the needs of women, who were kept in purdah (seclusion) all the days of their married life, from puberty until death. This resulted in the education of women, first in purdah, afterwards outside the homes.

Christian Institutes for training doctors and nurses followed the foundation of hospitals. In 1881, a training hostel was begun at Agra, and in the years following, Dr. Edith Brown founded a School of Medicine for Christian women in Ludhiana, Dr. William Wanless one for men at Miraj, and Dr. Ida Scudder another for women at Vellore, serving north and central and south India, attracting capable students in whatever caste or class.[16]

Their standards were necessarily low, but, as a result of upgrading, the Medical Colleges at Vellore and Ludhiana and Miraj became fully-fledged Christian Medical Colleges for men and women from all parts of India. The writer was told by an Indian cabinet minister's lady that she chose outright to patronize a Christian hospital (at which he lectured in 1970) because of its 'tender loving care.'

The evangelical impact on nursing was felt in India too, and it is sufficient to say that 90% of all nurses throughout India (surveyed in World War II) were Anglo-Indian or Indian Christians, and that four-fifths of all Christian nurses were trained at mission hospitals.[17]

The missionaries tackled the 'white scourge.' The leading tuberculosis sanatorium in all India is that of the Union Mission in southern Andhra.[18] Sixty hospitals, homes and clinics for lepers are operated or subsidised by the Mission to Lepers which began in 1874 when three ladies in Dublin collected money for relief of leprosy. Cochrane and Brand, evangelical missionaries, are world famous specialists in Hansen's disease—as the writer has personally known them.

74

From the days of William Carey, evangelical missionaries sought to improve Indian agriculture. Carey had published valuable horticultural catalogues, and urged the missionary societies to send out men qualified to teach agriculture and to preach. The contribution of missionaries to agriculture in India is beyond computation. A case in point is Allahabad Agricultural Institute, founded by Sam Higginbotham, well-known agricultural missionary and evangelist.[19]

Mission schools, though by no means the last word in technology and education, introduced not only better animal husbandry and agricultural methods, but inculcated much-needed ideas of personal and social hygiene, prophylaxis against disease and improvement of diet, resulting in a vast enlargement of living standards which discouraged superstitions.

The 1858-59 Awakenings were felt in India in the 1860s. Not only did they bring out a contingent of dedicated missionaries, but they stirred the Indian Christian communities too. Kerala, at the southwest corner of India, shared in a like movement beginning in 1861 and climaxing in 1873.[20] People in Travancore were 33% nominally Christian; their Rajahs were enlightened rulers; and among non-Christians, women were held in higher respect than in other parts of India.

Jawaharlal Nehru, in denigrating British imperial benefits in India, cited Kerala as an example of native superiority. The Church Missionary Society's entrance to Kerala had effected startling changes in the ancient Syrian Christian community there. English schools were begun in 1834, and thirty years later a vernacular education committee using Malayalam was established by the State. Kerala early had the benefit of two Christian colleges, Kottayam begun by the C.M.S. and Alwaye, a wholly Indian Christian institution. A University was established at Trivandrum.[21]

Within thirty years of 1860, there were 2418 institutions of all classes and grades with 104,616 pupils. Ten years or so later, there were a hundred and fifty thousand, 25% in state schools. In another generation, there were 2700 in the Kerala colleges, more than fifty thousand in English schools and half-a-million or more in primary schools, and Kerala led the rest of India in literacy, with 23.9%.[22] The initiative had come from the missionaries and Indian Christians.

Missionary education in China developed the same way as in India, with obvious differences, the absence of a conscientious colonial power, the lack of a caste system, the use of a hallowed system of classical education.

The Protestant missions became involved in education, beginning with primary schools, then secondary schools and a few colleges. The moot question, whether English should be taught as a language or medium of instruction was debated. The missionaries' schools and high schools and colleges were not designed to prepare for the traditional civil service examinations leading to literary degrees for scholars and official posts for civil servants.[23] But they were the pioneers of the Western education which later replaced the ancient Chinese classical system.

During the 1859 Awakening in Wales, David Morgan conducted a meeting in a Carmarthen village, reporting pessimistically: 'It was a very hard service.' One of the converts, a lad named Timothy Richard, went to China and became the best-known and most influential Baptist worker, to whom the eminent historian Latourette ascribed 'an optimistic spirit, a daring and creative imagination, and a dauntless courage which led him to think and act in large terms.'[24] The 'large terms' included a national university system for China.

Richard engaged in famine relief in Shansi. In the capital, Taiyuan, he sought to interest the Chinese scholars in Western science. He later proposed to his London committee the founding of a college in each of the eighteen provincial capitals. He resigned from the society and set about influencing the literati of China in other ways. The great reformer, Kang Yu-Wei, said: 'I owe my conversion to reform chiefly to the writings of two missionaries, the Rev. Timothy Richard and the Rev. Dr. Young J. Allen.' Richard's proposals were later carried out by government decree.[25]

In Japan, there existed a national system of education, and to this advantage was added an avid desire for Western civilization. It was not necessary for missionaries to convince young Japanese of the benefits of Western education.

One of the first pioneer missionaries to Japan, J. C. Hepburn, a Presbyterian, arrived in 1859.[26] He prepared an English-Japanese dictionary as well as a major part of an early translation of the Scriptures. He and Mrs. Hepburn eagerly provided a Western education for all and sundry, beginning the first Western-type school for girls. Among their pupils were men who rose to high station in national affairs. Hepburn, a trained medical man, practised medicine and founded a medical school in Tokyo.

Samuel R. Brown, a Reformed Church missionary with experience of pioneering education in China, spent twenty years in Yokohama and round about, pioneering in Western education.[27] Another mission pioneer, also Dutch Reformed, was Herman F. Verbeck, who operated a school at Nagasaki, then an official school for interpreters and finally a school in the capital which became the Imperial University. [28]

Thus, one of the first activities undertaken by missionaries was to open schools for the training of Japanese youth. The motive of such young people in coming to missionary schools was not to learn Christianity, but ways of the West. The missionaries, on the other hand, while they offered instruction in the ways of the West, were primarily interested in winning the Japanese to the Christian faith. Of the missionary enterprise, secular writers commented: [29]

> For the most part, it may be said that the missionary schools in the early days were staffed by men of better education than were many of the foreign instructors who were then hired rather indiscriminately by local Japanese authorities. For this reason, many mission schools rapidly acquired a name for scholarship.

Neesima, a remarkable Japanese, journeyed at some risk to United States and studied at academy, college and seminary in Massachusetts, where he declared his faith. There also he conceived the idea of founding a Christian school to become a university in Japan. A wholly Japanese company took title to property in Kyoto, the old capital, and thus began Doshisha University,[30] where in 1883 an extraordinary revival started, expanding the Christian Church throughout Japan.

Within thirty years of the opening of Japan, Protestant missionaries had established 250 churches—more than a third self-supporting—with 25,000 members, and they operated a hundred schools with ten thousand pupils.[31]

The Awakening of the mid-nineteenth century effected many changes in the Island World. The Hawaiian Mission—itself the fruit of the New England college revivals of the 1800s—undertook the evangelization of other island groups. Mass movements began in the Indonesian archipelago. The pioneers were martyred in parts of Melanesia. Madagascar was delivered from one of the worst persecutions ever recorded. Awakenings swept Australia.[32]

The Awakening of 1858-1859 provided the enterprise and the volunteers for the second invasion of Latin America by missionaries from Britain and the United States. This time the educational projects were backed by the denominations, and staffed by revived and converted students graduating.

Father John J. Considine, in his popular writings in which the development of Evangelical Christianity in Latin America is described, has noted the stress laid upon the educational institutions therein: so also Padre Pedro Rivera, S.J.[33]

Immigration had opened the closed doors of the southern Latin American countries. Americans from the Army of the Confederacy founded a promising colony in Brazil, and found a missionary permanently settled there since 1859. Although evangelization was their main object, the pioneer missionaries in Brazil devoted much attention to education. Their schools were later recognized as the forerunners of the Brazilian system of education that evolved in due course.[34]

Fernando de Azevedo, in his outstanding work on Brazilian culture, attributed a large share of the inspiration for the educational reforms of Leoncio de Carvalho in the late 1870s and of Caetano de Campos and Cesario Mota in the early 1890s, to the work of Evangelical institutions. These early Presbyterian, Methodist and other schools, Azevedo said,[35]

> helped to change the didactic processes, influenced by the imported ideas of North American pedagogical technique, and for a long time they were to be among the few innovating forces in education—those living forces which keep the temperature of spiritual institutions from a kind of moral cooling off due to uniformity and routine.

In 1869, a Presbyterian missionary, Nash Morton, laid the foundation of Colegio Internacional in Campinas, near

São Paulo.[36] In 1870, Escola Americana was founded in São Paulo, becoming later the Mackenzie Institute, comprising educational projects from kindergarten to university.[37] In 1891, Mackenzie College was chartered by the Regents of the State of New York, graduating its first class in 1900.[38] It conferred degrees in Literature and Science. A Brazilian leader wrote to the president of Mackenzie University:[39]

A great change has come over us here in São Paulo. We firmly believed that scientific thought and religious thought were incompatible or equally hostile. We have, however, found that religious thought is perfectly compatible with efficient scientific thought. You people at Mackenzie do not parade your religion, but you have made it felt and stand for it on any suitable occasion, and you are doing the best scientific training that is being done in Brazil today.

The writer has lectured in many missionary-sponsored schools in Brazil, including Colegio Jose Manuel de Conceicao in São Paulo State, Colegio Agnes Erskine in Pernambuco, Colegio Isabella Hendrix in Minas Geraes, Colegio Americana in Rio Grande de Sul, Colegio Bennett in Rio de Janeiro—institutions accepted as part of civic life.[40]

Between 1858 and 1908, more than three million immigrants from Europe entered the Argentine.[41] The majority were Roman Catholics, a minority Protestants from Britain, Germany and Italy (Waldensians). Unlike Brazil, the Evangelical missionaries did not establish a school system in the Argentine. Evangelical influence was otherwise exercised.

One of Argentina's greatest presidents was Domingo F. Sarmiento, an educator, journalist, and author.[42] Argentine politics drove him to exile in Chile. Sarmiento became an ambassador to the United States in 1865, President of the Republic in 1868. He completely reorganized the Argentine educational system.

Sarmiento knew that Thomson's Lancasterian schools had perished through the lack of trained teachers and the hostility of conservative churchmen. He decided to set up a stronger system of normal schools, and he personally enlisted a number of dedicated teachers from the United States to begin operations.[43]

The imported teachers were not officially evangelical missionaries but, of the sixty-five outstanding pioneers, sixty were Evangelical by conviction and five were equally dedicated Roman Catholics. They came from a population which had enjoyed an evangelical revival within the decade. Sarmiento thus harnessed missionary idealism for a secular project. Among the teachers who came to head, reorganize or establish eighteen normal schools were a United States Army chaplain, Thomas Wentworth Higginson; Mary Elizabeth Gorman, daughter of a Baptist minister; and others of like background.[44]

The Bishop of Cordoba excommunicated the parents of those who patronized the new schools, the Bishop of Salta following suit. Sarmiento dismissed one, suspended the other.

In 1870, 20% of the Argentine population was literate; in 1895, 50%. Jose B. Zubiaur declared: 'This is the work of the normal schools, of which not one existed in 1869.'[45]

In 1885, a Chilean government chartered the Evangelical missionaries to 'promote primary and secondary instruction according to modern methods and practice.' From then on, their schools and colleges of a permanent nature influenced the life of Chile.[46] It was the same in some other republics.

In the 1860s, Evangelical work began in the Peruvian port of Callao, continued by a Bible Society agent, Penzotti, who suffered imprisonment for his faith.[47] In 1891, the American Methodists took over the work in Callao and opened a work in Lima, establishing Colegio Maria Alvarado in Lima and Colegio de Callao. In both, and in the Colegio San Andreas, run by Scottish Presbyterians, the writer has addressed the college assemblies.

Not until 1859 was the first Evangelical communion service celebrated in Mexico. In 1865, Melinda Rankin founded her school in Monterrey.[48] In 1867, a Liberal Government set up a free, obligatory and lay school system, but this seemed to be limited to urban communities. As missionaries multiplied, so did their schools in rural areas, the first ray of hope for the mestizos in many a neglected district. The missionaries were also schoolmasters.[49] Professor Moises Saenz, sub-Secretary of Education for a number of years, was a product of this rural movement.

CHAPTER X

THE MULTIPLYING FELLOWSHIPS

In 1860, there were approximately 180 denominationally related colleges operating in the United States, about 144 of them of Baptist, Congregational, Methodist or Presbyterian affiliation. Fifty years later, there were more than 400 such Protestant colleges, which does not suggest a decline, in spite of the emerging state universities and the secularized private institutions, for, in 1862, Congress passed the Land Grant College Act, and state after state began building state colleges and universities far removed in concept from the continuing Christian colleges.[1]

Civil wars, even more than foreign wars, inhibit higher education, military service draining off the best and the worst of the students. But the young men who enlisted in the armies of the Union and the Confederacy did not leave behind them the influence of the revival and evangelism. In spite of engrossing warfare, remarkable revivals and extraordinary evangelism extended the 1858 Awakening in church and college into front-line combat with major impact.[2]

The records of the war are full of instances of such awakenings and evangelism on the battlefields. In a New York regiment, an evangelistic campaign ran for thirty nights in succession in a tent furnished by the commanding general, and more than one hundred soldiers professed their faith in God.[3] Supplementing the work of chaplains was the United States Christian Commission, a part-ministerial, part-lay organization which served the troops by word of mouth and printed page, offering care and comfort.[4] One of their most successful workers was D. L. Moody, supported by Y.M.C.A. friends in Chicago.[5] Moody made frequent trips from Illinois to the theatres of war, preaching in the camps and ministering on the battlefield. Thirteen hundred ministers served as volunteer chaplains with this organization.

Religion in the armies of the Confederacy was even more conspicuous than among Union troops. Converts numbered 150,000, according to some.[6] In the main Army of Northern Virginia, a major evangelical awakening occurred, sustained by Baptist, Episcopalian, Methodist and Presbyterian clergy and ministers.

General Robert E. Lee, respected North and South for not only his military strategy but for 'whole-hearted, pure-minded, and devout' Christianity, accepted at the close of hostilities the presidency of Washington College, afterward Washington and Lee College. Lee 'dreaded the thought of any student going away from the college without becoming a sincere Christian,' yet he did not believe in compulsory chapel attendance.[7] It is not surprising that a College Y.M. C.A. was organized at the Lexington campus by interested students in 1867. President Lee contributed generously out of his scanty financial resources.

Already, up north, college students were converting their societies into College Y.M.C.A. During the academic year, 1864-65, students at the University of Rochester transformed the Judson Society of Missionary Inquiry, a dozen years old, into a Young Men's Christian Association.[8] Its records have shown that this Y.M.C.A. was as evangelistic as its predecessors at Michigan or Virginia. Rochester's Association exercised a wide influence on campus, there being an almost total absence of profanity and obscenity on the college grounds.[9]

College Y.M.C.A. were founded not on state university campuses alone, but also in the halls of ivy. In 1867, the students at Williams College organized fourteen prayer meetings weekly in different districts of Williamstown, and several conversions resulted. First a town and then a 'gown' Association were formed.[10]

Ten years after the 1858 Awakening, the Y.M.C.A. as a movement first appointed a national secretary, and within another ten years the multiplication of college Associations necessitated the formation of the Intercollegiate Young Men's Christian Association.[11] At the time, 1877, fifty or so of the two hundred student Christian societies scattered across the country were affiliated with the Y.M.C.A.

Meanwhile, in Britain, the 1859 Revival had given rise to daily prayer meetings among the students at Oxford and Cambridge in the 1860s. The biographer of the Bishop of Liverpool, Francis J. Chavasse,[12] observed that, in 1865, 'a sort of evangelical Revival amongst undergraduates had taken place, especially at Wadham, where W. Hay M. H. Aitken, afterwards the famous missioner, had been in residence.' Chavasse described the activities of the student group as 'incessant.' The daily prayer meetings, regularly held each day in term since 1867, continued into their second century. (In post-World War II years, they were held in the Northgate Hall in Oxford, of which the present writer was honorary warden while engaging in doctoral research.)

Prayer meetings began in Cambridge also, beginning in 1862 and continuing each day in term into their second century. The prayer meeting, wrote the Cambridge men in the spring of 1863, 'has met with the disapproval of many of the most esteemed men in our University.'[13] But many famous men were there transformed, including Handley C. G. Moule, Cambridge principal and saintly Bishop of Durham later.[14]

In 1877, a conference was held in the Guildhall's minor hall in Cambridge, attended by about 250 men, including a contingent from Oxford.[15] Its purpose was to unite the various Christian unions, as the British called them, in the various colleges of the universities. They chose the title: Cambridge Inter-Collegiate Christian Union. Oxford's Inter-Collegiate Christian Union was formed in 1879. (In the 1970s, this new movement was intercontinental, attracting ten thousand or more to student rallies in the United States.)

The student awakening at Oxford and Cambridge was but a small part of a general awakening brought about in Great Britain by the evangelistic ministry of D. L. Moody, himself an unlettered man. Moody, and his singer Ira D. Sankey, had arrived in Liverpool in 1873, without a single firm invitation. After modest beginnings at York, they moved north, and in Edinburgh and Glasgow they made a far-reaching impact on the life of Scotland.[16] They moved Belfast and Dublin, then tackled the cities of England and Wales.[17] Their meetings in London, lasting twenty weeks, attracted a total of 2,500,000.[18]

*   *   *   *

Samuel J. Mills and his colleagues in the early nineteenth century collegiate awakenings had initiated an intercollegiate correspondence between the scattered student societies. It fell to a student more than sixty years later to bring about the realization of the idea of cooperative union.

Luther D. Wishard was born in a log-cabin in Indiana in 1854.[19] In 1870, he entered Indiana University, but was forced to drop out for reasons financial. In 1872, he entered a smaller college, Hanover College, where he remained until 1875, when he transferred to Princeton University. He was impressed by President James McCosh, who had been active in the extraordinary 1859 Awakening in Northern Ireland.[20]

Wishard immediately connected himself with the campus Philadelphian Society, which had been revived following the 1858 Awakening.[21] Its re-written constitution of 1874 stated as its objects: 'to promote the piety of its members, the cause of missions, and the interests of religion in College.' In 1875, its membership included 110 active members, about one-half the number of professing Christians on campus. As in other student societies, its members engaged in local evangelistic enterprises.

In the autumn of 1875, D. L. Moody was conducting great evangelistic meetings in nearby Philadelphia.[22] Wishard and his colleagues were eager to cooperate with the evangelist, and engaged in sustained prayer meetings for that objective until William Taylor and D. L. Moody came to Princeton. The prayers of the students and the preaching of the visitors resulted in an awakening described by Prof. John T. Duffield as 'the most remarkable that ever occurred in the history of the institution.' [23] Nearly a third of the student population professed conversion, and the revival moved the churches of the town, adding a hundred and fifty to membership.

One of the results of this student awakening was the union of the Philadelphian Society with the Y.M.C.A. Wishard's keen collaborator included a 'modest, serious-looking fellow from Virginia' named Tommy Wilson, who served with the society, became President of the University and President of the United States — T. Woodrow Wilson.[24] Wishard's part in the movement brought forward his undoubted gifts of leadership, destined for exercise around the world.

Wishard sounded out his colleagues about the feasibility of an intercollegiate union of student Christian associations. He found strong opinion against the development of such a union within a wider organization, such as the Y.M.C.A.[25] It was urged that an exclusively student movement would much better suit the need, an Intercollegiate Christian Union.

This was the way in which the British movement developed in the years to come, and within three generations the inter-university fellowship of Christian unions in Britain began to take the place of the American organization as the vehicle of student evangelism in the United States.

But Wishard felt strongly that an organization of students and faculty would lose much for lack of association with the wider work.[26] At the time this factor impressed him, the larger body (the Y.M.C.A.) was the more evangelistic. It doubtless never crossed his mind that the Y.M.C.A. would switch its emphasis from evangelistic-social to social-and-evangelistic to social only. But this is the way with specific organizations subordinated to other organizations with less specific or more general objectives.

In the middle 1930s, C. P. Shedd of Yale was still able to write of the contributions made in fifty years by the student Y.M.C.A. to the larger body of the Young Men's Christian Association.[27] In one more generation to come, the student organization faced dissolution, having lost its sense of the purpose for which it was called into being, that of reaching the world with the Evangel, and the continuing British organization in its Canadian and American development had taken its place, sharing the field with an entirely new work devoted to the same objectives.

In June 1877, at the Louisville Y.M.C.A. Convention, the Intercollegiate Young Men's Christian Association was set up.[28] Without a doubt, its objects were mainly evangelistic and its dynamic was the continued outpouring of the Spirit recently witnessed in the Awakening of 1858. In the light of the developments of the latter half of the twentieth century, one could say that the Inter-Varsity Christian Fellowship and the Campus Crusade for Christ inherited the mantle of the Intercollegiate Young Men's Christian Association. The movement of student evangelism was never lost.

Just before the historic Louisville Convention, Robert Weidensall of the Y.M.C.A. declared that no field of service was so inviting as that of student evangelism:[29]

One student may do more in leading other students to Jesus during his college course than he could ever do in a like time afterward; for he duplicates himself every time a student is converted through his instrumentality.

Wishard laid out his proposals for intercollegiate work, its objectives being stated as follows:[30]

1. The importance of seeking the salvation of students for their own sake and their influence as educated men.
2. The importance of securing their salvation while in college. 3. The value of united work and prayer.

The methods deemed essential for success were stated under four headings:

1. Diligent study of the Word of God.
2. Prayer. 3. Personal Work.
4. Efficient organization.

The student conference proposed also that exchange of ideas be encouraged by inter-association correspondence; that inter-association visitation be provided, especially in times of revival; and that a full-time secretary to supervise and organize the work be appointed. The logical choice was Luther Wishard.[31]

So the work of lining up the student societies was begun. Many of the older ones used titles that repelled the average student: 'The Society of Christian Brethren'; 'The Sodality'; 'The Praying Circle'; 'The Christian Fraternity'; and the like.[32] Wishard surveyed the college situation, and decided that there were about 350 institutions of higher learning; that more than sixty thousand students studied therein; that eight thousand of them participated in voluntary Christian organizations on campus.[33] By 1880, nearly a hundred colleges entertained collegiate Associations, five thousand students enjoying membership. Within a decade, there were more than 250 student Associations with 12,000 members.[34] The rapid growth was due to evangelism and revival.

Across the Atlantic, D. L. Moody had made an impression upon a brilliant young Scot, Henry Drummond. Drummond had shown real ability in at least two fields, science and theology, and commanded the respect of faculty and students in the University of Edinburgh.[35] Drummond lined himself up with Moody, and engaged in evangelistic personal work in university circles during Moody's campaigns and afterwards.[36] Drummond and student helpers participated with great effect in Moody's meetings elsewhere. Often Moody would summon Drummond by telegram to share in the conclusion of a campaign and continue the work. This cordial association between the unlettered Moody and the literate Drummond was to have effect upon the student world not only in Britain and America, but around the world.

In the Christian unions at the universities, the leaders were studying D. L. Moody carefully, wondering whether he would be able to reach the cultured and sophisticated undergraduates of Cambridge and Oxford. Edinburgh and Glasgow were not residential universities, their students residing in lodgings nearby in their respective cities. Nor were the Scots inclined to snobbery. Would Moody be able to touch Oxford and Cambridge? Little did they know that he would be able to reach universities around the world thereby.

CHAPTER XI

THE STUDENT VOLUNTEERS

One of the many upper-class Englishmen moved by D. L. Moody was Edward Studd, a wealthy, retired tea-planter, who had made his fortune in India. Studd had three sons at Cambridge: Kynaston, George and Charles. Kynaston was a member of the university cricket team; George was captain of cricket; and Charles, better known as C. T., was an all-England cricketer of national fame.[1]

Three hundred Cambridge men had petitioned Moody to come to Cambridge during his earlier British tour, but now Kynaston Studd had rounded up support among his colleagues to invite the American to conduct a mission at the University. Handley Moule signed the invitation reluctantly, and so did other Cambridge men. The Cambridge Prayer Union through its committee invited its friends to join in asking Almighty God 'that it would please Him to grant to our university a measure of the religious revival which has lately been vouchafed to other parts of His church.'[2]

Moody was already famed in Britain when, in 1882, he consented to conduct a preaching mission in Cambridge for university students.[3] The aristocratic undergraduates were utterly outraged that 'an illiterate American' presumed to lecture to them. They determined to show their objections and rebuff the trespassing evangelist. Word soon spread of the pranks that were to be played. Even Moody's friends were concerned, Handley Moule (the future Bishop) penning in his diary: 'Lord, be Thou really with me in this coming anxious, responsible time.'[4]

'There never was a place,' said Moody, 'that I approached with greater anxiety than Cambridge. Never having had the privilege of a university education, I was nervous about meeting university men.' He was not concerned without good reason, as events quickly proved.[5]

It was arranged that Moody and Sankey should speak and sing in meetings for the townspeople first, and these went off without an incident. The Corn Exchange, ill-suited to purposes evangelistic, was well-filled each time.

Seventeen hundred university men, attired in cap and gown, noisily crowded into the hall for the university meeting. Seventy undergraduates, displaying rare courage, joined in singing hymns, but the majority responded with vulgar songs. The Rev. John Barton, vicar of Holy Trinity parish, opened with prayer, to which some 'ill-mannered youths' responded with 'Hear, hear!' Sankey's first solo produced derisive shouts of 'Encore!' Cambridge proctors ejected several of the more rowdy disrupters.[6]

The proceedings went on in an uproar. Moody decided to preach upon 'Daniel in the Den of Lions,' a very appropriate topic. The Hebrew name Daniel has three syllables, and in English it may be pronounced with two, but Moody managed in one, which brought the house down in cheering and jeering, clapping and stamping. It was a trying time for Moody, but he kept his temper and his poise.[7]

Next day a ringleader, Gerald Lander of Trinity College, called at Moody's lodgings to apologize, saying that he had supposed that Mr. Moody was unfit to speak to gentlemen, but concluded that he, unlike his critics, was a gentleman.

Although seventeen hundred students had been counted in the first meeting in the Corn Exchange, only a hundred attended the second in a seated gymnasium, but they included Gerald Lander. On Wednesday, before a larger crowd, Moody gave an evangelistic appeal and after repeating it saw more than fifty men make their way to the inquiry room. One was Gerald Lander—afterwards Bishop of Hong Kong.[8]

Next night, a hundred or more waited behind for counsel. All through the week, clear-cut conversions were professed by intellectuals and athletes, many of them proving to be both deep and lasting. The final meeting in the Corn Exchange brought eighteen hundred hearers, and concluded a mission which proved to be the beginning of a worldwide, interdenominational student movement. Moule, kneeling beside Moody on the platform, heard him say: 'My God, this is enough to live for.'[9]

The next day, without the benefit of a Sunday start, Moody opened his mission in the Corn Exchange in Oxford, which was filled to overflowing. Bolder, he quenched attempts at rowdyism several nights running and gained a hearing for his messages. Audiences moved from Clarendon Assembly Rooms to the Town Hall, where Moody gathered inquirers in an aftermeeting, and a number made personal decisions.[10]

Moody's Oxford and Cambridge campaigns, like his earlier visits to Edinburgh and Princeton, had continuing effects in the lives of key personalities.

C. T. Studd had played for England against Australia, but was away in Australia playing against Australia's cricket elevens during Moody's Cambridge campaign. His brothers communicated the Moody challenge to him, so he responded. Together with Stanley Smith, another outstanding athlete, he visited Edinburgh and stirred another generation of students, encouraging numbers waiting behind for counsel.[11] Kynaston Studd and his brother Charles assisted Moody in his great London meetings. It is recorded that, on one occasion, D. L. Moody called upon a clergyman to offer prayer in the huge gathering, but the man of the cloth was so overwhelmed by the privilege of addressing Deity on behalf of so many thousands of people that he prayed on and on and on—until Mr. Moody cheerfully invited the assembly to join in singing a hymn while 'our brother is finishing his prayer.' This utter frankness intrigued a young atheist, a medical student, who had wandered into the meeting. He returned and heard the Studd brothers speak, and thereupon committed his life, the story being well known in the lifework of Sir Wilfrid Grenfell of Labrador.[12]

Sir Montague Beauchamp, William Cassels, D. E. Hoste, Arthur and Cecil Polhill-Turner, Stanley Smith and C. T. Studd, all Moody's helpers and some his converts, offered themselves to work in China under the China Inland Mission, founded by Hudson Taylor in the wake of the 1859 Revival. They first became a remarkable witness team, named the Cambridge Seven, touring the British universities with their message, stirring up the students. No doubt, part of their extraordinary influence was due to their family circumstances as well as their reputations as athletes.[13]

Beauchamp was a nephew of Lord Radstock; Cassels was the son of an importer from Portugal; D. E. Hoste was the son of a brigadier-general; the Polhill-Turners were sons of a Member of Parliament; Stanley Smith was the son of a London West End surgeon; and C. T. Studd was the son of a wealthy man, a Master of the Hounds, a turf enthusiast. They were not all as famous as C. T. Studd as athletes; but they had each a reputation in sport.

The Cambridge Seven as a team or in pairs set about visiting Edinburgh and Glasgow, Liverpool and Manchester, Leicester and other English towns, delivering the message. All this had an exciting effect upon the universities of Great Britain![14] Their visit had brought to white heat (to quote John Pollock, historian of the Cambridge movement) the religious revival among the students at Edinburgh kindled by Moody. There the theological colleges were overcrowded with Scots preparing for the ministry and missionfield.[15] At Cambridge, five years of religious enthusiasm followed, with a marked increase in attendance at the Daily Prayer Meeting.

D. E. Hoste, not a Cambridge graduate, was a dashing young officer of the British Army, whose brother William had been impressed by Moody at Cambridge. Hoste was converted through his brother's witness and Moody's ministry at Brighton, in 1882.[16] He succeeded Hudson Taylor as the general director of the China Inland Mission, which, until the 'liberation' of China by the Communist armies, was considered the largest Protestant missionary society in the world. Cassels became the first Anglican Bishop in West China.[17] Each of the others served in China with distinction. (Later, Studd was to found a mission in the heart of Africa—this in turn became the Worldwide Evangelization Crusade, an international organization.)[18]

Moody invited Kynaston Studd—in the present writer's youth, Sir Kynaston Studd, Lord Mayor of London and father of his good friend, Commander Ronald G. Studd—to spend an academic term on American campuses.[19] Another wave of awakening swept twenty colleges in those thirteen weeks. At Cornell, a law student named John R. Mott made a full commitment of his life, and emerged as the best-known student leader for half a century.[20]

Evangelical awakenings generally develop in four phases, reviving, evangelizing, missionary and social. The student movement of 1858 was primarily one of reviving the work of God among students, then evangelistic; Moody's ministry at Princeton and Cambridge, for example, was evangelistic with overtones of revival; now the rolling movement seemed about to develop into a missionary enterprise, one of the most remarkable in the history of the Christian faith.

A friend of Luther Wishard, Robert Mateer of Princeton, became leader of an Inter-Seminary Missionary Alliance which held its first convention in 1880 with two hundred and fifty students from thirty or more seminaries present.[21] These missionary-minded students, like their Y.M.C.A. friends, were strongly evangelical and evangelistic.

Luther Wishard, as organizer and evangelist of the Inter-Collegiate Y.M.C.A., had tried hard to interest Moody in collegiate ministry, but had been rebuffed by the modest Moody, conscious of his academic deficiencies.[22] In 1884, after Moody's powerful impact on Cambridge became known, Wishard pleaded again with Moody, who consented to preach at a few colleges in 1885, including Dartmouth, Princeton and Yale. His college-slanted sermons, he knew, were few. He looked for help from his many faculty friends.

An outcome of Moody's growing interest in the student world was the convening of a college conference at Mount Hermon in Massachusetts in the summer of 1886, when some two hundred and fifty students from one hundred colleges attended, and Moody was as popular as any eminent lecturer. This first conference was entirely unprogrammed, and the students followed a course of lectures and activities which came about 'as the Spirit directed.'[23]

One of the college delegates was Robert P. Wilder, son of a retired missionary to India, who had already formed a student foreign missionary association at Princeton.[24] The Wilder family, whose head had been one of the Williams College group of missionaries in the early 1800s, had been praying that a thousand students from American universities might be enlisted for foreign missionary enterprise. To every student who would listen, Robert Wilder presented the call of missions.

Wilder succeeded in persuading Moody to set aside time for missionary talks, and this combination of prayer and presentation had its effect. One hundred delegates signed a declaration signifying their willingness to serve overseas.[25]

Consciously following the example of the Cambridge Seven, a team of committed students was formed to carry the call of missions to the college campuses: R. P. Wilder of Princeton; John R. Mott of Cornell; W. P. Taylor of Yale; and L. M. Riley of DePauw. Only Wilder was able to go, but he enlisted the help of a Princeton classmate.[26]

Robert Wilder and John Forman toured the universities and succeeded in enlisting about two thousand volunteers for missionary service.[27] McCosh of Princeton asked: 'Has any such offering of living men and women been presented in our age?'[28] Seelye of Amherst replied that the movement was of larger proportions than anything of the kind in modern times. At first, Moody was cautious about the overflowing enthusiasm of the youngsters,[29] but he continued to help them. The volunteers increased their own numbers to about three thousand in the academic year, 1887-88.

Before Robert Wilder commenced his second missionary journey, it was decided to create a new organization, to be called the Student Volunteer Movement for Foreign Missions. Mott was made chairman of the new movement, a position that he held until 1920.[30] John Forman crossed the Atlantic to communicate the enthusiasm for service to student hearers in the universities of Aberdeen, Edinburgh, London, Oxford, Cambridge and Belfast.[31] Prof. Henry Drummond crossed the Atlantic and addressed the students.[32] He received a welter of invitations to address scientific societies, but refused almost all of them.[33] He returned to minister in American universities,[34] Williams College being stirred, Dartmouth suspending all classes, Princeton pre-empting his time from morning till night, Yale giving him one of the busiest weeks of his life. Even Harvard heard him graciously. Drummond was attacked by conservatives for his attempt to bring both religion and science into harmony, and, although Moody had lined up with the conservatives, he stood by Drummond as a zealous evangelist and a great scholar. Drummond thus extended his student ministry around the world.

Luther Wishard returned the British visitors' calls by touring the universities of Cambridge, Oxford, Edinburgh and Glasgow in the spring of 1888. The summer he spent in Germany, France, Switzerland and Sweden.[35] Wishard extended his journey around the world, reporting conversions and calls to service everywhere.[36]

James B. Reynolds, another student volunteer, crossed the Atlantic to Oslo University.[37] He also visited Stockholm, Lund and Copenhagen in 1889. In 1891, Robert Wilder visited universities in Britain, enlisting three hundred volunteers for missionary service.[38]

In 1890, Henry Drummond sailed for Australia and spent a profitable time challenging students in the universities of the southern continent. His days were numbered, however, for he fell ill in 1894 and died in 1897.[39] John R. Mott had organized the Student Volunteers in the universities of New Zealand and Australia before Drummond died.[40]

In 1893, a conference was called at Keswick, attended by a hundred delegates from twenty universities, and from it was created the Inter-University Christian Union.[41] Donald Fraser, later a successful missionary in Central Africa, became the first secretary of this British organization.

These various developments resulted in the formation of the World's Student Christian Federation. The chief engineer was none other than John R. Mott.[42] The federation was fully consummated at the castle of Vadstena in Sweden, Dr. Karl Fries becoming chairman and John R. Mott secretary. (Both Mott and Fries—the writer met them in the 1930s—were ardent evangelists all their days.)

The Student Volunteers sought to enlist every Christian in the objective of evangelizing the world. Their watchword was 'the evangelization of the world in this generation.' In their main objective, they were hugely successful, for in half a century, more than twenty thousand students reached the foreign mission fields of the Church, an astounding and heartening achievement. The greatest of church historians, Kenneth Scott Latourette declared his measured opinion that it was through the Student Volunteers in the various countries that a large proportion of the outstanding leaders in the spread of Protestant Christianity were recruited.[43]

CHAPTER XII

SPORADIC REVIVALS OVERSEAS

It is tempting to think that the outpourings of the Spirit in collegiate communities, these 'college revivals,' may have been a peculiarity of American Protestantism, or, in view of known facts, a Western Protestant phenomenon.[1]

There is enough evidence from colleges racially distinct from those just designated to show that the occurrence of evangelical awakenings in collegiate communities were in fact worldwide, regardless of culture and race.

An example may be found in the greatest educational institution established in Africa in the nineteenth century, the Lovedale complex of schools for Bantu-speaking people in South Africa.[2] Lovedale, a Presbyterian foundation, was much indebted to a visit from Alexander Duff, the Scottish educator who so profoundly influenced the educational system in India.[3] A government inspector commented:[4]

> A visit to Lovedale would convert the greatest sceptic regarding the value of native education . . . The staff is large and able and the civilizing effect of the whole institution is remarkably felt. It may have its defects, but the scheme at present is the most complete, the largest and most successful in the country, and the institution as a whole is probably the greatest educational establishment in South Africa.

James Stewart had been the companion of Livingstone on his central African journeys, and he pioneered in Malawi before becoming principal of the Lovedale Institution.[5] In 1872, following the practice during the worldwide awakening, noonday prayer meetings were begun, preparing the faculty and students for an extraordinary revival which commenced in 1874,[6] described by Dr. Stewart as 'the most remarkable in the whole history of Lovedale.' The movement continued for years, provoking Bantu students to offer freely for lifetime service among dangerous tribes—as, for example, William Koyi who helped pacify the bloodthirsty Ngoni.[7]

In the following generation, Luther Wishard and Donald Fraser, representing the American and European Student Volunteer organizations, visited Lovedale in 1896.[8] Another awakening occurred, no less than forty black students becoming missionary volunteers.[9]

In Central Africa, Industrial Missions were maintained by several societies so specializing.[10] At the turn of the twentieth century, the Zambesi Industrial Mission cultivated thousands of acres, largely in coffee and cotton, and useful trades were taught in forty schools based on ten stations. This mission not only won hundreds of Bantu to Christian faith, but provided them with a means of livelihood—most useful at a time when there were thousands of refugees from the terror of the Ngoni and other raiders.[11]

Meanwhile, thousands of Student Volunteers were streaming to the missionfields of the world, among them ardent evangelists and eager educationalists. George Pilkington, Senior Classic at Cambridge, a brilliant intellectual converted and called to the ministry, volunteered for Uganda. Through his personal renewal on the field, an awakening began, in which the number of lay teachers increased from 75 to 2032, communicants from 230 to 18,041, baptized from 1140 to 62,716, and catechumens from 230 to 2563, all in fifteen years.[12]

By the end of the nineteenth century, the Church Missionary Society alone was maintaining in East Africa a total of 262 schools, with 26,847 pupils.[13] The educational policy of the society was concerned with the elementary schooling of its entire body of converts and inquirers. Sir Harry Johnston estimated that 200,000 of these had been taught to read in a single generation.[14]

Two visitors to East Africa, famed in affairs of state, commented on the results. Theodore Roosevelt wrote:[15]

Even a poorly taught and imperfectly understood Christianity, with its underlying foundations of justice and mercy, represents an immeasurable advance ... Where, as in Uganda, the people are intelligent and the missionaries unite disinterested ness and zeal with commonsense, the result is astounding.

Another observer, the young Winston Churchill, noted the pitiful welcome his party had received in more primitive parts of Africa, and contrasted it with his experience of entering Uganda, 'another world' of 'clothed, cultivated, and educated natives.'[16]

In the Congo, the American Baptists were maintaining 109 schools with 3285 pupils, while their British colleagues reported slightly higher figures, between them a majority of the total of 10,471 scholars and 318 schools operated by the evangelical missions together.[17] The running start made by the Baptists was due to a series of evangelical awakenings beginning at Banza Manteke in 1886.[18]

In West Africa, the missionary societies were operating nearly a thousand schools between the Benin Gulf and the Gambia River, 40,000 pupils attending.[19] Wherever colonial government welcomed the advent of evangelical missions, the educational developments matched the church planting. Wherever penetration was forbidden or discouraged, the educational developments have lagged to this day.[20]

As at Lovedale, in 1872 a Week of Prayer was held at Yokohama with encouraging results.[21] This was recalled by James Ballagh in another series in 1883. An extraordinary evangelical awakening spread throughout the tiny Japanese churches.[22] Its greatest effect was felt in the colleges, for the whole staff and students of Aoyama Gakuin (University) were deeply moved. Similarly, the Week of Prayer begun in January of 1884 at Doshisha University in Kyoto could not be stopped, but ran on until March, and two hundred students were baptized. Awakenings occurred in other such colleges.[23] There were intense emotional upheavals, much confession and restitution, and continued joy.

Historians designated the period 'Rapid Growth, 1883-1888,' when the Japanese Protestant churches grew in total membership from four thousand to thirty thousand people. A period of retarded growth followed, due to the entrance of an anti-evangelical theology. Theological students dwindled in numbers from three hundred to a hundred.[24]

Until the beginning of the twentieth century, the outbreak of college revivals was rare or unknown in China and nearby Korea, there being few such collegiate communities.

After the Boxer Uprising, Timothy Richard proposed that Chinese authorities pay half a million taels of the indemnity toward establishment of a University in Shansi. Curriculum, faculty and administration of funds were placed in his charge for ten years.[25] Thus began the modern Chinese universities system, missionary colleges aligning themselves with it.

By 1911, there were 543 Protestant secondary schools in China, with 33,000 pupils, one-third girls; 33 colleges and universities, with 2000 students, one-fifth women, out of a total in China of 115 colleges and universities, and 40,114 students in all.[26]

Among these thirty-three colleges and universities were the Canton Christian College, later known as the Lingnan University; St. John's University in the great metropolis of Shanghai; the University of Nanking, supported by three of the Protestant denominations; the Shantung Christian University, supported by two denominations; and the Peking University, supported by three denominations, and later on merged into Yenching University. Out west in Szechwan, the West China Union University was founded. In Nanking also there was built a Christian college for girls, Ginling.

The medical missionaries, numbering in 1895 nearly a hundred men and fifty women, laid the foundation of a medical service which produced a number of medical schools, including the famed Peking Union Medical College, leading medical college in all of China until the Communist dictatorship.[27]

The virile evangelical forces at Yale University sent out graduates to found a 'Yale in China,' building in Changsha, provincial capital of Hunan, a hospital, a medical school, a school of nursing, a middle school, and a college.

Likewise, in Korea, missionary penetration in the 1880s was followed by evangelism and by education, from primary to secondary schools and to colleges. Mrs. Mary Scranton, a Methodist, founded Ehwa, to give women education through to the college level. The six major missions coordinated their educational projects.[28] The Union Christian College, in Pyungyang, was begun in the year following 1905.[29]

Protestant missions soon surpassed the earlier founded Roman Catholic, partly because of extraordinary Revival, and partly because of their stress upon schools and hospitals.

CHAPTER XIII

THE AWAKENINGS OF THE 1900s

The twentieth century dawned without mass premonition of disaster, either of war or revolution, and among ardent Christian people there was a hope that at long last the Kingdom of God was at hand. Spontaneously and simultaneously, the new century was greeted by prayer meetings, intreating another visitation of the Spirit.[1]

The fifteen years following 1899 proved to be years of great spiritual awakening around the world. The greatest such movement, without a doubt, was the Welsh Revival of 1904 onward.[2] Its leading figure was a 26-year old student, Evan Roberts,[3] who had enjoyed a remarkable experience with God before enrolling at Newcastle Emlyn College.

With the permission of his college principal, Roberts left his studies and proceeded to his home and church in the village of Loughor, not far from Swansea. Only seventeen people waited to hear his first message.[4] But he gave them four points—to confess any known sin to God and put right any wrong done to man; to put away any doubtful habit; to obey the Spirit promptly; and to confess faith in Christ openly.[5] The response was instantaneous.

Within three months, a hundred thousand converts had been added to the churches of Wales. Five years later, a book debunking the Revival was published, and the main point made by the scholarly author was that of the 100,000 added to the Churches, only 80,000 stood after five years.[6]

The influence of the Revival upon life in Wales was beyond calculation. Crime was so greatly diminished that the magistrates in certain counties were presented with white gloves, signifying not a case to try.[7] Drunkenness was cut in half, and a wave of bankruptcies swept the taverns of the principality.[8] Profanity was curbed, until it was said that the pit-ponies in the mines could not understand their orders.[9]

Throughout the Revival, and for many months afterwards, all the churches of Wales were crowded with worshippers, not only on Sundays but weeknights as well. Unprogrammed meetings were the rule, anyone 'moved by the Spirit' taking part.[10] Extraordinary conversions were reported, and most unusual instances of restitution of wrong.[11] There was such an improvement in public morals that local authorities met to discuss what to do with the police forces, unemployed on account of the Revival.[12] Many were the critics of the overflowing emotion of the movement, but all were agreed that the ethical transformation was tremendous.[13]

The Welsh Revival affected the mining valleys of South Wales as well as the quiet little towns of North Wales—among them historic Bangor, where all the churches were so moved that crowded congregations engaged in simultaneous, spontaneous audible prayer.[14] In Bangor was one of the three university colleges of Wales. At the onset of revival, a student in the commons lounge felt constrained to sing an old Welsh hymn, whereupon another extemporaneously offered prayer, and an unbroken succession of hymns, prayers and testimonies followed.[15] Lectures were cut as more than three hundred gathered for afternoon prayer, while in the evening the students marched en masse through the streets to the largest church in town, which was crowded.

This happened at the colleges in Aberystwyth and Cardiff. Not far from Aberystwyth, a great political rally had been arranged to hear a distinguished speaker.[16] The sponsors called upon a local minister to offer prayer, which provoked the huge audience to break out into a grand old hymn, whereupon a blind man offered fervent prayer, and the speaker was entirely overlooked in the proceedings—none other than David Lloyd-George, afterwards Britain's Prime Minister during World War I. Lloyd-George compared the movement to a spiritual earthquake or a religious tornado, predicting far-reaching social effects.[17]

Visitors flocked to Wales from other parts of Britain, from Western Europe, from Canada and the United States, and from Australia, New Zealand and South Africa. Within a short space of time, the same awakening was stirring the churches of all these countries, and mission fields besides.

The Awakening spread to England and the Archbishop of Canterbury called for a Day of Prayer.[18] Soon various parts of the country were experiencing crowded churches, while great torchlight demonstrations marched through the streets. Excursions trains were run to the cities and towns where unusual events were happening.[19] Student interest in things spiritual mounted in Durham University, as phenomenal movements were reported in the county towns.[20] The same was true in constituent colleges of the University of London, scattered throughout the metropolis, which was mightily moved by the Awakening.[21]

John R. Mott, the international evangelist of the World's Student Christian Federation, engaged in remarkably frutiful evangelistic campaigns at the Universities of Oxford and Cambridge in 1905.[22] British observers attributed the great response not only to Mott's personality and dedication, but to the spirit of revival abroad in the land, saying 'it is true that religious forces have been moving beneath the surface for a few months.'[23] Of 800 in the Oxford Town Hall, no less than 200 agreed to engage in daily Bible study. Mott also visited Cambridge in the afterglow of the Welsh Revival.[24]

Dr. R. A. Torrey and his song leader, Charles Alexander, were ministering to huge crowds at the Royal Albert Hall in those days, and Alexander, a winsome personality, visited Cambridge briefly, stirring the Cambridge Inter-Collegiate Christian Union. Torrey followed up with a campaign.[25]

In 1908, John R. Mott returned to Oxford and Cambridge. Sponsoring Oxford Inter-Collegiate Christian Union leaders rented the capacious Examination Halls, and rejoiced to see them crowded out:[26]

> The great examination schools were packed to their utmost limit. Never before could such scenes have been witnessed in Oxford . . . It is no exaggeration to say that the lives of many first took shape and form in those days and received an inspiration and a hope that will not fade away.

Mott spent six days at Cambridge, 'days of effort and strain,' said a sponsor, who saw halls crowded with unparalleled audiences in spite of impending end-term examinations. In one meeting, 1250 attended and 560 stayed for counsel.

It was the same in Scotland.[27] Such a movement developed at Motherwell that the streets of the industrial town were crowded from wall to wall, and, as the Revival subsided, eight churches and three public halls were crowded nightly. There were similar stirrings in Edinburgh,[28] where fully a thousand inquirers were given counsel in a single church. John R. Mott directed a thoroughly successful evangelistic campaign for the students of Edinburgh University also.[29]

Similar reports were made from Ireland, where in the North and around Dublin there were extraordinary stirrings of the Protestant population,[30] influencing the students at Queen's in Belfast and at Trinity in Dublin.

As usual in such movements, the student awakenings developed a missionary trend. In fifteen years, the Student Volunteer Missionary Union of Great Britain and Ireland had sent more than a thousand of its choicest graduates to the mission fields, a third of them to India; but, at the end of 1905, 1200 university students were preparing to go out.[31]

Under Albert Lunde—in later years, like Evan Roberts, a personal friend of the writer—an extraordinary awakening began in Norway, with spiritual and social results similar to the Welsh Revival.[32] Robert P. Wilder, a founder of the Student Volunteers, spent 1904 in Norway;[33] hence when the Awakening began, it affected the students immediately. In the other Scandinavian countries, there were evangelical awakenings of significant strength.

A general awakening occurred in Germany also, and a missionary conference followed at the University of Halle in 1905,[34] 'the largest, the most representative, and the most successful missionary convention ever held on the continent.' Similar reports came from Holland and Switzerland.

Australia and New Zealand were swept by evangelistic campaigns and congregational revivals between 1901 and 1905, and it was reported that fully one-quarter of the total of students of Australasia were members of the Christian Student Movement, one-sixth enrolled in Bible classes.[35]

Awakenings occurred in South Africa, beginning among the Afrikaners who had suffered defeat in the Boer War and continuing among English-speaking and Afrikaners during the campaigns of Gipsy Smith.[36] Students were revived.

In 1905, the news of the extraordinary Welsh Revival was featured in almost all the American religious press, and in many secular newspapers also. Conferences were held by the various denominations to discuss the possibility of a similar awakening.[37] Before the end of 1904, 'outbreaks of revival' were occurring among the Welsh settlers in the mining valleys of Pennsylvania.[38] Then the movement in the churches became general.

The editor of an official journal in Methodism,[39] then the largest Protestant denomination, declared unequivocally that 'a great revival is sweeping the United States. Its power is felt in every nook and corner of our broad land . . .' as additions to Methodist church membership doubled in 1905. The Baptists issued similar reports.[40] Although immigration reinforcing three-to-one the Roman Catholic Church was in its full flood of more than a million a year, the Protestant denominations increased 150% as fast in the Awakening.[41] Of this, until the present writer's researches, nothing at all has appeared in church histories, general or particular.

The Awakening in the Churches soon communicated itself to the academic community. It affected not only Christian colleges, but secularized and state universities and colleges. The World's Student Christian Federation declared 12th February 1905 as a Universal Day of Prayer for Students. As in the 'Week of Prayer' first instituted by the Evangelical Alliance in 1860, its implementation became the fulcrum of many a movement of spiritual awakening, for spontaneous outbreaks occurred that month on campuses far apart.[42]

The Universal Day of Prayer for Students was implemented in college after college by prayer groups meeting in rooms and in special prayer services, the burden of some being that 'revival may spread until all the colleges in the country are reached.'[43]

In March 1905, John R. Mott, whose personality clearly dominated not only the North American constituency but that of the World's Student Christian Federation, reported very sympathetically upon the Welsh Revival.[44] The Y.M.C.A. had already proclaimed the rise of an 'unparalleled interest of men in spiritual things.'[45] That this applied to young men in universities and colleges became apparent.

Throughout New England, despite the lack of any great evangelistic campaign, the churches—it was reported— were obviously in the midst of a revival of greater power and extent than New England had known since 1857, for the additions to the churches were larger than for any month in many a year.[46] The movement was characterized by an intense sensation of the presence of God in the congregations, as in the Welsh Revival. Despite the lack of organization or follow-up, the movement was deemed most effective as compared with organized evangelistic campaigns.

Awakenings were reported in Maine, New Hampshire and Vermont, in Massachusetts, Rhode Island and Connecticut. In the Boston metropolis, there were church revivals and evangelistic campaigns.[47] Student organizations showed the impact, for at the Massachusetts Institute of Technology— for example—the noonday prayer meeting doubled.[48]

At Bowdoin College, with a select enrollment of about three hundred registered in the historic Maine institution, the voluntary Bible study class doubled as a result of the revival.[49] This represented a typical New England college.

The Connecticut Awakening of 1905 was felt at historic Yale University where more than three thousand men studied. There the faithful Henry B. Wright, a Y.M.C.A. secretary recently become a full faculty member, was overwhelmed by seekers after God. He shot off a letter to John R. Mott, one dated 25th March 1905:[50]

I come to you with a very insistent message from Yale . . . We want you and Speer to come to Yale for a series of meetings (April 9 to 12) directed especially to making Christians out of church members. The Spirit of God is with us here in power . . . I have never known a time when there were so many inquirers . . .

Alas, Mott was leaving for Oxford and Cambridge. So the faithful faculty and student evangelists were thrown upon their own resources. A memorable series of group meetings was begun in the spring and winter of 1905 among some intimate friends who were deeply concerned about the religious need at the University.[51] Four years later, Professor Wright was still reporting, 'The group is having wonderful meetings.'

The Awakening of 1905 was especially powerful in New York City churches, 'a sight never duplicated' occurring in Calvary Methodist Church there when 364 were received into membership on a single Sunday,[52] while in the Baptist Temple in Brooklyn five hundred waited for counsel.[53] The movement was even stronger in upstate New York, for the various churches of Schenectady were swept by a revival which captured the attention of the secular press.[54]

The Awakening was so strong at Cornell, with 3000 men in residence at Ithaca, that in 1907-08 the Bible study groups doubled their numbers to 350 students, meriting an article in the national organ of the Christian Associations.[55]

On the Jersey coast, there was such a revival in Atlantic City that—it was claimed—not more than fifty unconverted people remained in a population of 60,000.[56] Town after town in New Jersey experienced a reviving of church life and work. Such was the revival at Rutgers University, in the town of New Brunswick in New Jersey, that 111 of the 220 men engaged in study there entered voluntary Bible classes —a 400% increase in enrollment.[57]

Late in 1905, a great awakening was reported in Newark, in which 'Pentecost was literally repeated . . . with its strange spectacle of spacious churches crowded to overflowing and great processions passing through the streets' during the height of the revival.[58] Nearby, in Princeton, the average attendance at the weekly evangelistic meeting was more than a thousand, out of 1384 men registered there. In the Seminary, attendance weekly exceeded registration.[59]

By early spring, the Methodists alone in Philadelphia were claiming ten thousand additions, 6101 on probation— indicating recent conversion.[60] The Philadelphia Awakening of 1905 was regarded as the greatest ingathering since 1880 when Moody reaped a harvest.[61] The University of Pennsylvania was enjoying the effects of a great campaign. The smaller colleges of Pennsylvania, the Normal Schools at Indiana and Edinboro, and Juniata College in Huntingdon, all reported movements in early 1905 resulting in converts. At Juniata, a year later, more than half the students were enrolled in missionary study classes, meeting voluntarily each week to prepare for service in the field.[62]

Late in 1904, the Atlanta newspapers reported that fully a thousand businessmen united in intercession for a spiritual outpouring. At the time of great meetings under the direction of Dr. J. Wilbur Chapman, stores, factories and offices with unprecedented unanimity closed at noon for prayer.[63] Much the same happened in Louisville in Kentucky.[64]

By spring, 1905, it was reported that marked spiritual awakenings were occurring in Virginian institutions of higher education—Randolph-Macon College, Emory and Henry and the smaller colleges being singled out.[65]

One of the most remarkable awakenings ever experienced in Virginia occurred at Randolph-Macon Academy in Front Royal, a college with less than two hundred students.[66] The immediate causes of the revival were the steady work done in Bible study and the observance of the Week of Prayer. The meetings owed nothing to visiting evangelists, being conducted by senior students, and gatherings were characterized by a deep anxiety on the part of Christians and a strong conviction of sin on the part of non-Christians. The thoroughness of the work done was especially noticed by the members of the teaching staff.

'A revival of very great power' swept the student body at Trinity College in Durham, North Carolina, almost one-third of the two hundred men there professing conversion. 'In fact,' it was reported, 'there are left only about twenty-five students in the college not professing Christians, and special prayer and personal work are being undertaken.'[67]

It was the same in South Carolina. Observers in Florida reported that the revival was 'still rolling' over the state, a prominent evangelist in the awakening being Mordecai F. Ham,[68] afterward famed as one who captured Billy Graham. Conversions[69] were reported from the State University of Florida at Gainesville, a small campus with a hundred men. An unusual revival was reported from Stetson University, commencing (it was said) as the gentle rain, but becoming showers of blessing, continuing with the sound of abundance of rain.[70] The movement had begun with a circle of but three students, but soon encompassed the whole academic family; yet the only agents were students and professors. Florida had few institutions of university level.

Emory University and Mercer University in Georgia had benefitted from the revival wave, for the vast majority of their registered students were enrolled as members of the evangelical Churches.[71] It was the same in Alabama. 'The Spirit of God is being graciously poured out in many places of our country, but not more anywhere than in our colleges,' reported the Methodists, rejoicing in a revival at Meridian. Probably every student at the Mississippi A. & M. College (or more than 800) attended the evangelistic meetings run by the students. Of the 360 average attendance, some sixty men professed conversion.[72]

Louisiana shared similar reports. Across the state line into northeast Texas, an extraordinary awakening occurred in Paris.[73] Farther south, 'a tidal wave of spirituality . . . rolled through the city' of Houston, reviving the churches and cleaning out the gambling dens.[74] The churches of Waco were moved by the Revival, and an extraordinary upheaval shook the Baylor University campus.[75] It began in meetings for prayer, continued in confession of sin, resulted in many conversions, and enrolled the majority of the students in classes for missionary preparation.

Weekly attendance at student meetings exceeded student registration at Ouachita Baptist College in Arkansas.[76] The stirring was felt in Oklahoma. Arizona and New Mexico had little or no higher educational facilities in those days.

The growing city of Los Angeles received much benefit from the Awakening of 1905. One night, despite torrents of rain, four thousand people marched at midnight to the Opera House, attracting a host of bleary-eyed brawlers, besotted drunkards, blatant scoffers and women of 'easy virtue' to a midnight meeting. Not only were there revivals in the local churches in Southern California, but Dr. J. Wilbur Chapman conducted vast evangelistic services, 180,000 in aggregate attendance—notable in those days—with 4264 inquirers.[77]

As a result of the Awakening, the volunteer missionary band at Occidental College in Los Angeles, a college of 135 students, enrolled the second largest number thus pledged in all the Presbyterian colleges in the country. Other small but growing colleges in the area enjoyed the same sort of spiritual stirring.[78]

The Bible Institute of Los Angeles, now Biola College and Talbot Theological Seminary, rose from the impulse of the 1905 Awakening.[79] So also did the Baptist City Mission Society;[80] while, farther north, the Pacific Coast Baptist Theological Union founded the Berkeley Baptist Divinity School, at a time when an awakening was stirring churches in Oakland and San Francisco.[81]

The University of California at Berkeley returned no statistics in 1906 because of the devastation of the April 18th earthquake around San Francisco Bay. The University, originally a Christian college, possessed a student body of 1450 in 1905, a tenth of whom enrolled in Bible classes. In fraternity Bible groups, many outstanding men were won, including the captain of the Varsity football team, the private secretary to the university president, and the popular Varsity football half-back. The awakening added a hundred to these Bible study groups.[82]

The spirit of revival at Stanford University carried on through the disastrous earthquake of 1906, when most of the campus buildings were destroyed.[83] Of a student population of a thousand, 200 belonged to the Christian Association and two out of three attended weekly Bible studies.

In a report entitled 'Portland's Pentecost,' describing the religious enthusiasm in the Oregon city, it was said:[84]

... for three hours a day, business was practically suspended, and from the crowds in the great department stores to the humblest clerk, from bank presidents to bootblacks, all abandoned money-making for soul-saving.

McMinnville College, now Linfield College in the town in Oregon named for a Scotch-Irish settler, was founded in 1857. In 1905, with ten faculty, it boasted of 177 students who paid $30 a year in tuition.[85] The 1905 Awakening affected the faculty and students, L. W. Riley (afterward its president) writing that he 'saw something . . . never witnessed before, the president and all of the faculty on their knees together praying together for the unsaved students under their care,' a daily occurrence.[86] That year, forty students confessed their faith in believers' baptism. The impulse continued for years to come.

There were several factors in the McMinnville revival. A Day of Prayer for Colleges was held in February. A very recent graduate, K. S. Latourette, later a China missionary and a famous Yale church history historian, challenged the students.[87] A Methodist evangelist, C. W. Ruth, under whose ministry in Oregon more than five hundred had been converted in the Awakening, visited McMinnville and this was followed by a revival in the Baptist congregation.[88] And at the Oregon Baptist Convention, the McMinnville College was remembered in a special session of prayer.[89]

There was also an awakening at Newberg, described as 'the greatest meeting in the history of Newberg Baptist Church,' in which a Baptist evangelist, H. Wyse Jones, was ministering. The students at George Fox College, a Quaker academy at which Herbert Hoover received his training, were moved in the community-wide revival.[90]

Just as churches in the Oregon towns were moved, those in Washington State were stirred.[91] And in Seattle, there was voiced a unanimous approval of the great evangelistic series conducted by the Chapman team. 'Mighty processions' of witnessing Christians marched through the streets.[92]

Late in 1905, Seattle Pacific College—supported by the Free Methodists, and destined to become one of the best private colleges in the Northwest—climaxed 1905 thus with an extraordinary movement of the Spirit:[93]

On the night of December 18, in our new Chapel at Seattle Seminary, we had a most glorious meeting. A large congregation gathered in the Chapel and from the beginning God manifested His power and glory... At times, the Spirit was so outpoured as to make it impossible to describe the scene . . . Wave after wave of blessing, billow after billow of divine glory rolled over the entire congregation. A number of our choicest young people felt that God was calling them to the missionary work and identified themselves at once with the movement . . . So great was the power of God that the unsaved were unable to resist and a number of them broke down and commenced to seek the Lord. The meeting continued in power and interest until long after midnight, and a number were saved.

On Friday, 20th January 1905, a Day of Prayer was proclaimed in Denver.[94] At 10 a.m., the churches were filled; at 11.30, almost all stores were closed, at the Mayor's request, four theatres being crowded for prayer at noon, 12,000 folk attending the services of intercession in all seriousness. All schools were closed. Six months later, it was said that 'the influence of the revival is still being felt.' University Christian Associations reaped some benefit.

Reports from Iowa showed that the Revival of 1905 and its evangelistic outreach made great progress. Burlington's stores and factories, for example, closed for prayer.[95] The university and college students shared in the Awakening. Iowa College, in Grinnell, reported conversions occurring. Of the twelve hundred men students at Iowa State College in Ames in 1905, 616 enrolled in Bible classes arranged by the students of the Christian Association, which had about two hundred members.[96] At the end of 1905, the Christian Association at Drake University in Des Moines, reported a Bible classes enrollment of one-third the student population, or nearly three times that of previous years.[97]

Awakenings were reported in St. Louis and Kansas City, and during March of 1905, 'a spiritual awakening of real power' took place in many of the higher educational schools of the state of Missouri, paralleling the extraordinary revival in the town and country churches there.[98]

The Awakening began in prayer meetings in Chicago, and was felt in many parts of the nearby states, immediately. Such was the religious interest at Northwestern University in Evanston, Illinois, that two-thirds of the men students had enrolled in the Christian Association, and fully one-half of that total were engaged in Bible study.[99] At Northwestern College in Naperville, there was such an awakening that 80% of the student body or more than 200 became members of the Christian Association, 109 enrolled in Bible classes and 104 studying missions.[100]

There were tidings of revival from other Middle Western states, Minnesota, Wisconsin, Indiana, Michigan and Ohio. At Oberlin, the students translated their revival into a concerted drive for the conversion of outsiders, reporting more than fifty 'decisions,' for conversion or restoration.[101]

112

A Baptist foundation, Denison University in Granville, Ohio, experienced a noteworthy awakening as 'study rooms became prayer rooms.'[102]The following year, 300 of the 320 men registered there had become church members.[103]

There had been some spiritual decline during the autumn of 1904 in Upland, Indiana at Taylor University, whose name acclaimed one of the most successful Methodist evangelists who extended the 1858 Awakening over four continents. On 6th January 1905, President C. W. Winchester preached on the Baptism of the Holy Spirit. This created a burden for the active Christian students, leading to a spirit of conviction upon those not yet committed to such a degree that all academic and social exercises were abandoned for a week. Taylor residents reported 'the greatest revival ever known' on the campus.[104]

A school of similar background, Asbury College in the town of Wilmore in Kentucky, was 'practically closed' as its classes became services of prayer, confession, reconciliation, restitution and dedication, even of conversion.[105]

The Awakening was especially powerful among Baptists and Methodists in Michigan.[106] Adrian College shared in an awakening in town unheard of for years. A movement was manifested in Kalamazoo likewise.[107] There were approximately 3600 students at the University of Michigan in 1905, and 2400 of them packed University Hall in Ann Arbor on occasion to hear the Word.[108]

The 1905 Awakening affected the life of minority groups also. In the year following, registration of young men at Tuskegee Normal School in Alabama increased from 900 to 1000; membership in evangelical churches rose 50% from 600 to 900.[109]

In a remarkable religious awakening at Topeka Industrial School, a Negro institution, all the students—with the exception of two—were won to the Christian life. A Christian Association was organized which included in its membership every man in the school.[110]

The Christian life was revived at Cherokee Academy and Bacone College, spreading to the related communities of American Indians in the Southwest, and reaching even the recalcitrant Apaches.[111]

An awakening began in a Baptist church in Wolfville, in Nova Scotia, in which large numbers were converted, two-thirds of the converts baptized being students at Acadia University, where 115 men were registered and 175 was the average weekly attendance at devotional meetings.[112]

At McGill University in Montreal, student registration increased by fifty to 1000 in 1906, while membership of the Christian Association rose from 333 to 615. Of University of Toronto's 2000 men registered in 1905, 518 entered the Christian Association voluntary Bible classes.[113]

First Baptist Church in Winnipeg was packing into its new sanctuary two thousand worshippers and turning away another two thousand during the Awakening. In the nearby Brandon College, the registration was 134 and the average weekly attendance at devotional meetings was 160.[114]

The Awakening of 1905 was felt across the prairies and over the Rockies, to the farthest parts of British Columbia. The manifestations of the movement in Canada were the same as in the United States, prayer for revival, concern for the outsider, ardent evangelism and instant response— and the academic community was affected likewise.

It is apparent that the year 1905 was a year of spiritual awakening in the colleges and universities of North America, and it can be added that, if until now the story of the 1858 Awakening in colleges has never been written, the story of the 1905 Awakening seems not to have been suspected.[115]

CHAPTER XIV

THE 1905 AFTERMATH

The Awakening of 1905 was nation-wide—indeed, world-wide—and it made an almost immediate social impact. In Philadelphia, for example, the Methodists reported upon the events transpiring in that city, when its citizens arose in righteous wrath and overthrew a regime of corruption in a 'Revival of Social Righteousness':[1]

> We are in the excitement and enjoyment of a great civic righteousness revival . . . To a delegation of businessmen at City Hall on June 1, our mayor John Weaver said 'the hand of the Lord is in it.'

A leading journal,[2] reviewing the 'Great Twelvemonth' of 1905 throughout the United States, noticing in particular the social influence of the Awakening still going on, readily affirmed that throughout the Republic there were signs of the revival of the public conscience which, in many states and cities, had broken party lines, rejected machine-made candidates and elected Governors, Senators, Assemblymen, Mayors, and County Attorneys of recognized honesty and independence. The 'father of the social gospel,' Washington Gladden, conceded there was a moral revolution going on.[3]

It is worthy of note that many of the early advocates of 'the social gospel'—for example, Walter Rauschenbusch and Washington Gladden—were sympathetically active in the cause of personal evangelism.[4]

One significant outcome of the student awakenings of 1905 was the widespread adoption of an 'honor system' in college examinations, an idea already tried out. As a result of the recognition of a higher code of ethics prevailing in student societies, several prominent universities now deemed the 'honor system' practicable.[5] The Awakening had achieved results in personal honesty and veracity.

The mainspring of the continuing influence of the 1905 Awakening was the voluntary Bible class on campus. The rising interest in continuing Bible study became so pronounced that the Collegiate Y.M.C.A. claimed that (in one state with 11,000 student population) 2790 were members of Christian Associations, 1660 engaged in voluntary Bible classes and 312 in missionary studies.[6]

Examples could be taken from the North and the South. At Emory and Henry College, in Virginia, a marked spiritual awakening was followed up by a Bible study canvass of the students, with the result that all but six students on the campus enrolled in voluntary Bible classes, and at the end of the year, three-quarters of them were so engaged.[7]

In 1905, of five thousand students enrolled in Virginian university and colleges, fully one-fifth were enrolled in the voluntary Bible classes arranged by the students of local Christian Associations.[8]

Similar interest in Bible study occurred North and West. Such was the impact of the 1905 Awakening at Cazenovia Seminary, a liberal arts college with a hundred students in Cazenovia, New York State, that every man in the residence building not already a Christian made public profession, and all but six of the student population enrolled in Bible study.[9]

One of the most interesting developments in the student awakenings of 1905 was the growth of Bible study groups in the fraternities.[10] A score of campus groups reported 800 engaged in regular Bible study within fraternity houses, the Greek letter men contributing their quotas in converts and missionary volunteers.

It would be next to impossible to assess numerically the growth of Bible study groups and membership. Such classes operated in three very different situations: first, the interdenominational Christian Association (Y.M.C.A. affiliated) on state and secular campuses; second, the active Christian colleges, with their chapel services and integrated society; and third, the newly-emerging denominational fellowship on state and secular campuses. Statistics were compiled for the first constituency only, and could be calculated for the latter two only by investigating whatever records remain for certain colleges and nearby congregations.

In 1902, the Collegiate Y.M.C.A. (in 642 Associations on campus) served a constituency of 126,841 university and college students, of whom 58,762 were members of various evangelical churches.[1] Active members of the Y.M.C.A. on campus numbered 27,926, while an aggregate of 643,454 attended religious meetings apart from church services.

Two years later, before the Awakening had begun, the Collegiate Y.M.C.A. served a constituency of 130,827 college men in only 505 associations, an increase of little more than three per cent, evangelical church membership showing a rise of only one-and-a-half per cent, or 870 students.[12] The active Y.M.C.A. membership had now risen to 28,051, this representing a gain of only 125 or one-half per cent, but attendance at campus religious meetings increased.

Thirty-six new Associations were organized on campus in 1905, reaching a total constituency of 137,256 students, while membership of evangelical churches reached 67,814, and active Y.M.C.A. membership 29,660, 754,588 attending religious meetings on campus in the year of revival—the beginning of steady growth.[13]

Two years after the commencement of the Awakening, there were 667 Associations, serving a student constituency of 169,945, an almost 25% increase through expansion, while membership in the evangelical churches reached 70,156, of whom 29,660 became active members, a more than 15% increase. Attendance at religious meetings on campus now numbered 929,539 aggregate (a more than 23% increase), and later passed the million mark.[14]

Thus active membership in the Collegiate Y.M.C.A. increased one-half per cent in the two years before the 1905 Awakening, but 15% in the two years after it, more than 20% including the year of revival. Student membership in the evangelical churches increased one-and-a-half per cent in the two years before the Awakening, three-and-a-half per cent in the two years after it, nearly 20% including the year of revival. The figures indicated a considerable number of nominal church members being converted.

The State Colleges, though not religious foundations, had great benefits to cause rejoicing—increased membership of Christian Associations being 200%, Bible classes 130%.[15]

117

Just before his death, W. Rainey Harper, erudite president of the University of Chicago, expressed his opinion that no matter how liberally private institutions might be endowed, the future (in the West) lay with State Universities.[16]

At the end of the decade, a committee of the newly-formed Northern Baptist Convention declared:[17]

> ... of the first six universities in America numerically, four are state schools, all of them in the Middle West—Michigan, Minnesota, Illinois, Wisconsin—outranked only by Chicago and Columbia; of the twelve largest universities in America, only two are classed as other than state or non-sectarian.

The increasing secularization of higher education had not as yet resulted in 'godless' state universities. In 1905, chapel services were held in seventeen out of nineteen state universities, with attendance required in at least nine.[18] The Collegiate Y.M.C.A. supplied much spiritual fare.

In 1904, the Michigan Baptist Convention appointed a full-time pastor at the University of Michigan, choosing the Rev. Allen Hoben, afterward president of Kalamazoo College. In 1905, he was succeeded by Dr. Warren P. Behan, serving three hundred Baptist students.[19] In 1905, Rev. C. J. Galpin became Baptist university pastor at the University of Wisconsin.[20] Thereafter, the idea spread to other campuses.

In early 1905, during times of spiritual revival at Ann Arbor, the Rev. J. Leslie French was called as the first Presbyterian student pastor, a well-trained man.[21] In the same year, Presbyterian pastorates were begun at the University of Illinois and the University of Kansas, after which the idea spread from state campus to campus.[22] The Congregationalists had also made tentative beginnings, but in 1906 they appointed their first full-time student pastor, Rev. Richard H. Edwards, at the University of Wisconsin.[23]

On 19th November 1905, a dozen students met with a sponsor to organize a Lutheran church at the University of Wisconsin.[24] Later, the Rev. Howard R. Gold began work.

Just as the interdenominational Christian Associations arose in the 1858 Awakening, so the denominations founded their student pastorates in the times of the 1905 Revival, to meet the changing situation.

The 1905 Awakening was accompanied and followed by a surge of evangelism. John R. Mott, who (upon the death of Moody) committed himself more and more to the ministry of evangelism in colleges and universities, spent the winter of 1904-05 in student evangelism in Canada and the States.[25]

At the University of Toronto, where three quarters of the students were nominal members of evangelical churches, Mott campaigned in meetings that evidenced earnestness. Active membership in the Association increased 20%.[26]

Philip E. Howard, afterwards well-known in evangelical circles, and father of a famous family, reported that John R. Mott 'struck hard at sin' in his University of Pennsylvania campaign in the winter of 1904-05, making his points with 'sledgehammer facts—physical, psychological and spiritual.' Of the active members of the Christian Association, three fourths attended its religious meetings for the year.[27]

At the University of Michigan, John R. Mott held three meetings drawing fully a thousand men. In his last meeting, which was mixed, three thousand attended and nearly two hundred remained as inquirers.[28] The Christian Association numbered four hundred, and to this interdenominational total the new denominational student pastorates added quite a few.

At Iowa State College at Ames, an evangelistic campaign in 1906 won thirty men to a public profession of faith.[29] Two hundred active group members in 1905 became 325 in 1906. Likewise, the Awakening of 1905 was followed up in 1906 by an evangelistic campaign on Pennsylvanian campuses, more than seventy men publicly professing faith.[30] Organized efforts seemed less fruitful than spontaneous revival movements.

In Illinois, in 1907, A. J. Elliott conducted evangelistic campaigns in two of the leading institutions. At the Urbana University of Illinois campus, his first meeting attracted a thousand students; the last session lasted two hours, more than fifty inquirers professing faith. At Evanston, Northwestern University students were greatly moved, many converted. Clayton Cooper visited Pennsylvania State College, where 900 gathered in Sunday morning chapel, 150 inquirers receiving counsel at vespers, 130 publicly professing faith. These instances could be multiplied in state after state.[31]

*   *   *   *

The World's Student Christian Federation met in Tokyo in 1907, and its General Secretary reported that the movement had grown both extensively and intensively during the past four years. Christian Associations or Unions had been planted in at least 225 universities, colleges and schools scattered throughout the national territories. Membership increased by 35,000, to reach a total of 138,000 students and professors in 2060 associations. The demand for evangelistic missions, apologetics lectures and evangelistic Bible classes far exceeded the apparent supply.[32]

The college revivals of the early nineteenth century provided volunteers for the missionary societies that they themselves provoked into action, and continuing revivals supplied a steady stream of missionaries to India, South Africa and the Islands of the Pacific.

The awakenings of 1858-59 provided volunteers for the existing missions and the new, interdenominational 'faith' missions that carried the Good News and good works into East Asia, other parts of Africa, and Latin America—as well as the earlier-opened fields. Subsequent awakenings on campus and in quadrangle supplied a veritable torrent of thousands of missionaries for overseas service.

It is not surprising that the student awakenings of 1905 accelerated the movement, providing volunteers by the hundreds annually for all the mission fields of the world, a recruitment more remarkable in the retrospect of history— just before the onset of war and revolution that kept the world in turmoil for threescore years.

In discussing the ideals of missionary volunteer bands, C. H. Fahs insisted that:[33]

Student missionary uprisings, like college revivals, when traced to their sources are shown to have started almost invariably in a group of individuals associated for prayer ...

The missionary impulse was felt on campuses far apart, north, south, east and west in the United States, in Canada, in Britain, Scandinavia, and other parts of Europe, in South Africa, Australia and New Zealand, and on the mission fields themselves. In Beloit College, Wisconsin, forty of the 175 students enrolled in missions studies in 1905; the Baylor

University Christian Association (later B.S.U.) reported no less than 160 students thus engaged; Princeton Theological Seminary in New Jersey noted 70 students taking voluntary missionary training, 40% of the student body; Occidental College in Los Angeles raised a record-making mission band.[34] It was the same in Canada, where 40 of the 55 young men in the Anglican College (Wycliffe) in the University of Toronto were engaged in missions study.[35] One sector only of Christian students, 275 Associations, reported more than 7600 students engaged in missions studies in 1905.[36]

Considering the whole of the Evangelical constituency, in 1896, there were 2000 students enrolled in missionary study classes; in 1906, 11,000 engaged in this concern of their hearts and heads.[37] In 1891, 680 students attended the Student Volunteer Convention in Cleveland; in 1894, 1325 attended in Detroit; in 1898, 2221 again in Cleveland; in 1902, 2597 gathered in Toronto; and in 1906, 4188 met in Nashville between 28th February and 4th March, convened to discuss the expansion of the missionary crusade.[38]

The evangelical awakening in universities and colleges showed its effect upon the numbers of students volunteering for missionary service abroad. In 1902, 211 sailed for the mission fields;[39] in 1903, 219; in 1904, 293; and in 1905, more than 300—a total of 3000 in twenty years. Y.M.C.A. editors published annual lists of names made known to them. During 1905, among 214 student volunteers sailing from the United States and Canada were two outstanding missionaries known to the writer—T. J. Bach of the Scandinavian Alliance Mission (later Director of the Evangelical Alliance Mission), and Paul C. Metzger of the American Baptist Congo mission. In 1906, 254 university and college students sailed for the foreign mission fields: to Africa, 24; to China, 85; to India, 47; to Japan, 18; to Korea, 9; and to Latin America, 26. Otis Maddox and his wife Effie sailed for Brazil, where they raised a family for service with the Southern Baptists. And in 1907, 275 student volunteer missionaries sailed for the fields of their calling: to Africa, 28; to China, 75; to India, 36; to Japan, 25; to Korea, 23; and to Latin America, 33. In the long list, the name of Eli Stanley Jones is noticed, a product of the Awakening at Asbury College.[40]

The Asbury awakening of 1905 occurred during blizzard weather that afflicted the whole of the northern hemisphere. It began in confessional prayer, and continued in dedication, It was not long before the movement took a missionary turn.

A talented student from Maryland was completing studies at Asbury College at the time. He had a friendly disdain for those rougher-raised Kentuckians and Tennesseeans who made up the majority of students there, and in particular he felt much superior to the 'shouting Methodists' whose feelings seemed to lie so close to the surface.

Prayer meetings multiplied in the colleges everywhere. Young Jones attended again an unofficial prayer meeting of a few fellows in a dormitory room one evening. Nothing unusual was expected, but no doubt their friends were also praying for the boys at college. Suddenly 'the Holy Spirit fell upon them,' transforming their dutiful travail into a tryst with God on the threshold of rapture. Jones was overcome by emotions never hitherto expressed.

Next morning, he and his companions were amazed to find that the regular chapel service had given place to spontaneous intercession, spreading throughout the school and the town. In the midst of overwhelming feelings being vented by young and old, Jones was possessed by an uncanny sense of quiet. His storm had passed, and he heard a still, small voice. It showed him that emotion was not indispensable, he said.

Subsequently, Jones was asked to address a missionary meeting of students, and, 'feeling utterly inadequate, sought the help of God.' In prayer, he had an unshakable conviction that this, his first missions appeal, would issue in at least one hearer volunteering for mission service. He was tempted not to tell his fellow students of his conviction, but did; and as he concluded his message, no one was more amazed than he when the Voice told him, 'You are the one!'

On graduation, Jones had the alternatives of teaching or evangelism placed before him, but volunteered for mission service, and the same Voice confirmed clearly his 'call to India.' It is no exaggeration to say that Dr. E. Stanley Jones became the best-known missionary to India in the twentieth century, one who held the affection of India's leaders from Gandhi to Nehru, yet faithfully preached the Gospel.[41]

Less dramatic but just as fruitful was the experience of Kenneth Scott Latourette, thrust into the revived Christian groups at Yale in 1905, after seeing the results of the local revival at McMinnville College in Oregon: [42]

> In my final year, I was made Bible study secretary of Dwight Hall . . . That year we had about 1000 undergraduates enrolled in these groups. At the same time, Henry Wright had his freshman class in the life of Christ, with an average attendance of about 100. I attempted to know every man in the classes of 1909, 1910, and 1911 . . . From the class of 1909, which I knew throughout its four years, with possibly one exception, came more missionaries than from any other class in the history of Yale College.

Latourette, of course, went to China as a missionary, was invalided home, became a member of the faculty at Reed College in Oregon, then Denison University in Ohio; finally he became one of Yale's most distinguished professors — but not until he had passed through a spell of agnosticism. In 1948, Latourette became the president of the American Historical Association, the year that the present writer met him when Oxford granted the historian an honorary doctorate — and Latourette became an encouraging friend in research.

Another life shaped by the Awakening of 1905 was that of William Borden, a young millionaire converted in times of revival.[43] He threw himself into the evangelical activity at Yale with abandon. With Charles Campbell and John Magee, Bill Borden founded the Yale Hope Mission, a skid-row project.[44] Borden volunteered for missionary service with the China Inland Mission, and proceeded to Egypt to master Arabic, useful in China's great northwest. There he lost his life, but his challenge lingered on to recruit men and women for China and other missions abroad.

So great was the response to the student volunteer call that a Laymen's Missionary Movement was founded in 1906 to undergird the newer missionary drive focalized by the quadrennial convention of the Students Volunteers and by a centenary celebration of the Haystack Meeting at Williams College, the student beginning of American missionary outreach abroad, with its significant by-products.[45]

CHAPTER XV

COLLEGIATE AWAKENINGS OVERSEAS

In 1905, as the wave of spiritual awakening arose around the world, it was claimed that[1]

> Never in the history of universities have there been so many genuine spiritual awakenings among students; in fact, some of the remarkable revivals have taken place in undenominational and non-Christian universities.

When the early nineteenth century revivals began in the American colleges, there were parallel movements in the British and European universities—though of a different sort—but none in mission colleges abroad, for the simple reason that no such mission colleges had been founded.

When the mid-century awakenings began in 1858, there were revivals and awakenings in Christian colleges and in secular universities in North America and Europe alike; but college revivals overseas were limited in number, just as mission colleges were limited in number, in India and in South Africa. African tribal society was far removed from higher education, and ready for only the most elementary instruction. In India, the missionaries had concentrated on elementary education, and only recently switched to higher forms. So there were revivals in places like the Lovedale Institution in South Africa, and in the Scottish colleges in India which were handicapped by an insufficiency of truly Christian personnel, in faculty and students alike.

At the beginning of the twentieth century, a different kind of situation prevailed. Over Asia, Africa and Latin America, mission colleges had been planted, staffed by the cream of the crop of university graduates supplied by the Volunteers, not only eager educators but ardent evangelists. It was to be expected that genuine college revivals and community awakenings would occur in non-Western territories.

Thus in the early twentieth century college awakenings became commonplace on the mission fields of the world. A new day had dawned for evangelism in education.

The Boer commandos had fought bravely against overwhelming odds, and were finally defeated in the South African War. As they were being shipped overseas to prisoner-of-war camps in Bermuda and St. Helena, India and Ceylon, the British and Foreign Bible Society agents with tears supplied them with the Scriptures in their language of worship.[2]

Extraordinary evangelical awakenings occurred in every camp.[3] One such leader in St. Helena was Ds. A. F. Louw—with whom the present writer had cordial fellowship at the University of Stellenbosch, where Louw wrote his account of his 'first ninety years.'[4] At St. Helena were two Student Volunteers, already prisoners for a couple of years.[5] They deplored the past neglect of pagan Africa within easy reach of enlightened South Africans, and affirmed their conviction that Afrikaner missionaries were needed to work in Bantu territories to the north. A missionary interest developed.

Two hundred Boer prisoners of war, converted in the same kind of awakenings in British military camps in India, Ceylon, Bermuda and elsewhere, volunteered their service for foreign missionary enterprise and were constituted into a training college at Worcester, up-country from the Cape.[6]

In 1903, another awakening occurred at Lovedale among Bantu students, attendances averaging six hundred in eight days of meetings, conversions numbering 242.[7] Many Bantu students followed the example of William Koyi in offering their lives for service to other less-fortunate tribes.

In 1906, in the wake of the Welsh Revival and its South African reverberations, John R. Mott directed a conference at Lovedale which resulted in the reconciliation of English- and Afrikaans-speaking ministers, and another movement of revival among the African students.[8]

In the first decade of the twentieth century, there were evangelical awakenings in Central Africa, East Africa, West Africa, and even North Africa. But the effects of these were felt less in higher education, and more in primary schools. This was not true of the other continents of missionary outreach, where extraordinary college revivals occurred.

In the last decade of the nineteenth century, the Empire of China suffered humiliation after humiliation at the hands of foreign powers. In 1900 came the Boxer Uprising, which was encouraged by the Imperial Government. The Empress ordered all foreigners executed, and a blood-bath ensued.

In the spring of 1900, an awakening of great power swept the North China College at Tungchow, with all the intensity of feeling in confession and dedication for three weeks.[9] The classes were suspended while the students toured the district and moved multitudes in Peking, Paoting and Tientsin. It proved to be a baptism for future suffering, for forty of the students were done to death in the Boxer Uprising. At the same time, an awakening occurred in the Anglo-Chinese College in Foochow, described by the Rev. Llewellyn Lloyd as without parallel in China. A high proportion of students there professed conversion to the Christian faith.[10]

In 1905, a remarkable awakening was reported from the Chinese seaport of Foochow, where 80% of the students were non-Christians from the better families. There were three hundred present in the final meeting, 80 or less already of Christian profession, 100 or more who had become converts in the series, and another 100 who made public profession in Bishop J. W. Bashford's final meeting.[11]

This second wave of revival affected not only South China but North China. At Union College in Weihsien in Shantung, 196 students out of a total of two hundred professed their faith in 1906.[12] In 1907, an extraordinary awakening occurred in Japanese colleges among Chinese students, a church being formed to care for 250 Chinese converts in one place.[13]

In 1908, Jonathan Goforth—a product of the Canadian college awakenings of 1887—became the leader of a third wide movement in China.[14] Again there were college revivals, one at the university in Peking being outstanding.[15] The most significant feature of these Chinese awakenings was their raising up of Chinese student leaders for the movement.

Again the missionary interest manifested itself. Sixty Peking university students offered themselves for mission service to their own people.[16] One of China's great evangelists was Ting Li-mei, a student volunteer. Leland Wang, a Navy officer, became another great missionary.

There were similar awakenings in Korea.[17] The most phenomenal, spoken of with awe to this day, occurred in the city of Pyongyang in North Korea in 1907 and swept Korea, adding 79,221 to the churches. Nine-tenths of the students of the Union Christian College in Pyongyang professed conversion.[18] The moral transformations occurring in Korea were without precedent in the peninsular country.

There was an indirect result of the Awakening in education in Korea. Illiterate adults becoming Christians were required to learn to read Korean in a simple phonetic alphabet. A further inducement arose. Korean patriots had taken to the hills to challenge the Japanese occupation of their country. Pro-Japanese collaborators imitated the Japanese conquerors in closely-cropping their hair, patriots still wearing the top-knot. The guerrillas executed collaborators found with western-style haircuts, which Christians also affected.[19] To avoid killing patriotic Christian Koreans, the guerrillas challenged their prisoners to recite the Scriptures. In a short space of time, almost 100% literacy among the Christians was achieved.

Already, student movements had swept the campuses of Japan. In October 1901, fifteen hundred young men, of whom a thousand were students, professed faith in the meetings of the Student Volunteer leader, John R. Mott.[20] Subsequently, Japanese student teams engaged in a student evangelistic drive all over Japan. These days of 'Taikyo Dendo,' as they were called, were great days for the Evangelical Churches, who (by 1909) were teaching a hundred thousand pupils in a thousand Sunday schools, four thousand in boarding schools, eight thousand in day schools, and four hundred in theological colleges.[21] These were Christian projects.

The contribution of the missionaries to state-sponsored education in Japan, Korea and China has already been noted. Unlike Africa, these Asian countries adopted western educational ideas into their already-operating national systems. Yet the missionaries had something to offer. In China, they formed the Educational Association of China; by the time of the Revolution in 1911, half the missionary force was engaged in educational pursuits.[22] In Korea, the missions fully coordinated their educational systems.

The first part of India to share in the Welsh Revival was the hill-tribes area of Assam, where Welsh missionaries were working among head-hunters.[23] The effect was astounding. The Khasis, the Garos, the Nagas, the Mizos and other peoples turned towards Christianity in an ever-increasing stream, until they became as Christian as any nation of the West. Half a century later, the twenty tribes of Nagas numbered 420,230; the Khasi and Jaintia tribes, 389,969; the Mizos of the Lushai Hills, 224,180.[24] The overall percentage of literacy in Assam, including the Hindu plains and Christian hills, was 27.36%, but typical hill-tribe literacy was 44% for Christians and animists, as high as 86% for the Christians. The total number of Christians in the tribal areas of Assam was 567,049, which represented the highest percentage in all of India, and literates among them were 474,189. Many of the primary schools among the tribes were run by the local churches, which by mid-twentieth century, were completely indigenous and self-supporting.[25] The religious and cultural and educational revolution among them posed problems for the Government of India whose bulk of population lagged far behind. Autonomy rather than independence was granted to them.

The Awakening of 1906 in Andhra Pradesh began in the Christian schools of Nellore and Ongole.[26] Quarrels were settled, restitution made of things stolen and wrongs done, and students started saving rationed grain to share with the victims of famine.[27] This occurred on a Baptist missionfield. It was the same among the Anglicans in Tamilnad.[28] An extraordinary awakening occurred at Dohnavur, where the saintly Amy Carmichael operated a complex of schools. The famous Kottayam College in Kerala (Anglican) experienced revival. The Mar Thoma Syrian Church embarked on educational and evangelistic projects.[29] There were school awakenings in the Kannarese countryside.[30] The most extraordinary awakening occurred in Maharashtra, at the Mukti schools operated near Poona by the famous educationalist, Pandita Ramabai.[31] Nicol MacNicol, her scholarly biographer, reported transformation of the whole community.[32] Throughout India, college after college experienced awakening, and indeed the chief vehicle for the spread of the Awakening in the North was the students.

CHAPTER XVI

VOLUNTEER OBJECTIVES OVERSEAS

In recent years, a poll was taken of students from the emerging African republics currently studying in the North American universities. It was discovered that two out of three came from a background of Christian missionary primary schools. Fifty per cent of more than a thousand thus surveyed claimed secondary education likewise.[1]

This high percentage of Africans owing an educational debt to missions is far out of proportion to the numerical strength of Christians in Africa. It is more commonly recognized by educational experts in the field than by others, for one such declared that, despite past deficiencies,[2]

> The great debt that Africa owes to missionaries is that in a situation in which the forces of trade, colonial government, and the missions themselves were creating cultural havoc, it was only the missions that began to rebuild. Whatever any individual Westerner may think of the missionary edifice, every African knows that it is to missionaries that they owe the beginning of the African educational system.

United Nations statistics of data make it clear that the highest percentages of African children in school came from countries in which missionaries initiated and maintained the only African school systems in the nineteenth century. The middle third of percentages were recorded in countries in which the missions were delayed in initiating educational projects by handicaps of one sort or another. The lowest percentages came from countries in which the missionaries were restricted or prohibited during that initiating period.[3]

It is even more remarkable to consider that education was only a by-product of missions, and that the recognized good works of social service were not the major reason for missionary enterprise.

Indian friends, from acquaintances high in the echelons of Government to students low on the academic ladder, have expressed to the writer with diffidence or vehemence the suggestion that if missionaries had concentrated on social uplift and disowned every attempt at evangelization, their work would have met with uniform praise.

This suggestion ignores entirely the historical fact that, in nearly every case, the social reform proposed by missionaries met with passionate opposition. And it also ignores a religious fact, that the social concerns of the missionaries stemmed from their evangelistic burden. It has been said:[4]

> Every missionary will claim that the mission school in India has a definite purpose . . . that the function of mission schools in India is to lead boys and girls to Jesus Christ.

The dynamic for social action, according to the obvious motivation of missionaries past and present, is not sociological enthusiasm but theological evangelism. Missionaries have known, of course, that copyists and competitors would repeat their good works without the evangelism, and this has occasioned them no distress; but the fact remains that the original motive for all Christian social activity is evangelistic —not that the missions would have refused to do good works to all and sundry apart from evangelistic success.

What was the motivation of the missionaries? It was obvious that they did not go out to India for health or wealth. India's climate was not as deadly to Europeans as that of West Africa, 'the white man's grave,' but neither was it as congenial as that of South Africa.

Was there a mercenary motive? To this day, missionaries of high qualification serve on sub-standard salaries, doing for a lifetime what the young Peace Corps enthusiasts do for a limited period. They also face sadder family separations.

Was it the intention of the missionaries to set up educational systems for Indians? This was certainly not their primary objective. No doubt they took peculiar pride in contributing so much to the welfare of the people of their adopted land, and in observing how their charges from among the lower castes bettered themselves beyond all belief. They took it for granted that Christian education was a boon.

But the objective of the missionary, over-riding every other objective, was (from the beginning of the missionary era) to make Christian believers of the people. They were first willing to use education as an adjunct to evangelism and a help to inquirers and converts; then because it achieved some good in the country, they developed it, and extended it until it became a system, their philosophy being summed up neatly by an evangelical humanitarian: 'The State should do it, but does not. The Church of Christ must!' [5]

A distinguished missionary of the American Board, Dr. D. O. Allen, summarized missionary objectives thus: [6]

> In commencing their operation, missionaries have generally seen the propriety and importance of establishing schools. One reason for them is to educate the minds of the people, so that they may be more capable of understanding and appreciating the facts and evidences, the doctrines and duties of the Scriptures.

It is not long before people in the district served by the missionaries learn the advantages of procuring for their children a good education.

> Another reason for them is to increase the influence of the missionaries with the people, by communicating some advantage which they can appreciate and by showing that Christianity rests on an intelligent perception of its doctrines, and contains reason for the performance of all its duties.

Missionaries everywhere faced a recurring difficulty, that of obtaining access to the people. In this circumstance, schools become important in communicating not only with the children but with parents and their relatives, becoming places of social intercourse as well as chapels for worship:

> Another reason for such an education is in its procuring means and opening ways of access and opportunities of preaching to the people.

The objectives of the missionaries in adopting educational projects were recognized by many non-missionaries in India and elsewhere, often of other faiths. Nurullah and Naik, educational authors, commented: [7]

> The first and foremost object of the missionaries was to convert people to Christianity and one could not expect them to start educational institutions or to work as teachers.

Once the missionaries had won their converts, it became necessary to educate them. Naturally, the majority of converts came from the lowest castes and were generally illiterate. To read the Bible became their first objective. As they flocked to schools, the missionaries were compelled to publish books for reading and writing, and to establish printing presses so to do. It was a short step to establishing vocational schools to equip the converts for employment under state agencies that were 'varna-blind' regarding caste. Hence, the missionaries found themselves only beginning their work with such conversions. They continued with the improvement of the economic, social and cultural condition of their charges. This preoccupied much of their time.

This work of the missionaries proved to be so successful in the long run that its operations have continued to this day. One has met Indians high on the ladder of government office or business enterprise or educational system who had found their place through the educational zeal of the missionaries for uplifting the lowest castes, who had nothing to lose in accepting Christianity.

The arrival of Alexander Duff brought a new philosophy of education into missionary minds. He was not at all satisfied to win only the outcastes and low castes and orphans to the faith. He completed a survey of activities, and proposed to win the Brahmins by educational projects, feeling that the conversion of the leaders of society would result in the winning of the great masses. He also proposed that Bible teaching should be given openly and boldly, instead of optionally or surreptitiously.[8]

Duff was supported in his advocacy of English by the liberal Hindu, Ram Mohan Roy, and the veteran missionary William Carey, rather than the main body of missionaries. But in his proselytizing objectives, he soon began to influence the whole missionary cause, especially as a few choice converts were made among the Brahmins of Calcutta, potential leaders for the Christian churches.[9]

Duff made some of the greatest contributions of all time to the Indian educational system—but his main thesis was proven unsound, for the Hindu upper castes accepted his educational benefits, absorbed many Christian values into the sum total of their pantheistic Hinduism, but in the majority of cases rejected his educational evangelism. Supporters of this point of view had forgotten that apostolic Christianity had won its multitudes in the catacombs rather than in the Roman forum, which provided the select few.[10]

From the beginning, Protestant missions put great emphasis on the operation of schools. In these was given a predominantly Western type of education, in which the missionaries were the pioneers. By the mid-century, the missionaries had almost a monopoly of primary schools of the Western type, and about half the enrollment in institutions of a higher grade was being instructed in Protestant mission schools.

Within the missionary body, differences of opinion and of operation existed. Some missions for a while declined to fit into the government scheme of things; others maintained schools only for Christians; but a majority encouraged the enrollment of non-Christians, usually with a hope of evangelizing them.

Where Alexander Duff considered education as a means of winning the higher castes and of destroying Hinduism, William Miller of Madras Christian College thought of it as a means of permeating Indian society and winning it over to the Christian way.[11]

The Indian Government authorities extended generous financial assistance in the way of grants in aid, not because the schools were Christian but because they were schools in great demand. As a result, the missionary societies in India undertook educational projects much more than in China, although (in 1914 for example) the total missionary strength and general population were greater in China than in India.

The missionaries in the nineteenth century shared the ideas and convictions of the imperial powers regarding their trusteeship of colonial territories, without indorsing the exploitations. And yet their educational system, which did not challenge colonialism, encouraged in the second or third generation its Indian graduates who did, as in Africa.

Alexander Duff's old dream of converting India by means of progressive higher education faded. Noted was the failure of such higher educational projects to win many converts from the higher castes, not because the seed of the Word was unsuited, but because the soil was not fitted to receive it.

According to expert opinions, the real reason why converts were not being made in Christian colleges as they once were was because of movements within Hinduism itself, grafting Christian truths on ancient Hindu philosophy and religion.[12] Christian colleges themselves helped occasion this new development in Hinduism.

Remolding of Hindu thought continued into the twentieth century, a prime example being Sir Sarvapalli Radhakrishnan, a student first in a couple of Christian colleges in India, who became an advocate of a Hindu view of life obviously much influenced by Christian ideas and language. The capacity of Hinduism for embracing divergent ideas was demonstrated often during the rise of Indian nationalist leaders.

In the 1920s, the number of missionaries engaged in educational work rose to five thousand, with more than 27,000 out of 54,000 national and foreign mission workers helping.

In India, there were fifteen thousand schools (recognized and unrecognized) maintained by the Protestant missions in 1927.[13] That same year, the Government noted more than twelve thousand recognized mission schools operated by Roman Catholic and Protestant missions.

There were no Christian universities. But a considerable number of colleges, high schools, middle schools and primary schools were being operated by the missions:[14]

Schools	Mission	& Pupils	All-India	& Pupils
collegiate	55	16,018	307	82,760
teacher	100	4,104	597	24,060
high school	291	92,031	2,515	747,527
primary	11,158	421,182	184,829	8,017,923
other	257	8,945	8,583	290,073
totals	12,282	595,725	204,163	10,086,048

Mission schools provided 6% of both the institutions and scholars in all of India, the highest proportion of students being in colleges (20%), no less than 17% in teacher training, and 12% in high schools, the lowest (5%) in primary schools.

To the missionary colleges was attributed the deepest influence on students themselves, and the strongest corporate spirit and the greatest ability and devotion, especially noting the greatest earnestness and most marked success in the general improvement of conditions of living among the students, moral and physical.

By 1931 there were forty-two colleges maintained in India by the Protestant mission societies, not including Roman Catholic colleges or Anglo-Indian and European student bodies.[15] Five of them were theological colleges of degree standard, the remainder Arts colleges, of which three were women's colleges.[16]

There were more than 12,500 students therein. A quarter of the students in Christian colleges in the Madras Presidency in the south were of Christian profession, whereas hardly more than one in twenty in the north was a Christian. In the south, there were thirteen Christian colleges serving a population of more than 52,000,000, and in all the rest of India there were only nineteen Christian colleges, though two of them had more than a thousand students each, mostly non-Christians. It was difficult to maintain the pro-Christian atmosphere of a college where 1026 of the 1063 students were non-Christians, a majority of the teaching staff likewise.[17]

Of 833 teachers in Christian colleges, foreign and Indian, half were non-Christian, 30% or less Indian Christian.[18] The Government contributed $800,000, the overseas missionary constituency $400,000, student fees $600,000, $200,000 came from other sources, a total of $2,000,000, or $160 per student.

Far from being institutes of evangelization, the Indian Christian colleges showed their longer-range purpose by default—for there had been no more than a dozen conversions or baptisms in the three dozen colleges in ten years.[19]

Educationalists considered the view that 'all religions are the same,' that everything in Christianity is already contained in Hinduism. This view was categorically rejected as depending in the last resort upon an entire failure to understand the significance of a religion based upon history. The Christian colleges therefore greatly stressed the studies of history, economics and science, and felt that the climate produced by such studies was congenial to Christian faith.

Teacher Training Colleges were reduced in number but improved in academic quality. More than forty agricultural settlements and institutes were operating in the 1960s, headed by the great Allahabad Agricultural Institute—a significant contribution in view of India's agricultural backwardness.[20]

Christian High Schools increased in number, more than three hundred being listed in India without Pakistan, which was included in the pre-Independence statistics. Such Christian schools tended to multiply in areas of Christian concentration, where folk movements into Christianity had built up huge Christian communities. For example, the Lutheran community of 200,000 in the Chota Nagpur area (tribal converts) had one high school in 1939, but has added a dozen.[21]

Christian village and urban day schools have been maintained, though (with India's rising rate in elementary education) showing as a dwindling percentage of the total. Missionaries have faced many arguments against the 'school approach.' Undoubtedly, maintaining school immobilizes the missions. When a shortage of funds or personnel occurs—the schools take priority over evangelism.

Dr. Donald A. McGavran, missions expert, stated:[22]

> It is the adults who must be taught . . . teaching children who go back to a community of untaught and unchanged adults is largely a waste of effort . . .

In this respect, a great difference existed between mission enterprise in Africa and India. An African chief in Zambia once told a missionary teacher, 'We adults are committed to our fetishes and to our tribal gods. We are polygamists. We cannot become Christians; but take our youth, put them in schools. They will become Christians.' In India, it was the opposite with Hindu parents. They said, in effect, 'Educate our children for us. Our system has failed thus far. But do not dare convert them or us to Christianity.'[23]

Africa was able to adjust to the absorption of Christianized youth from the schools; Indian society, which was built upon caste, resisted change; and the major problems facing India today lie in the same utterly frustrating resistance to change which provoked nationwide riots over sacred cows but allowed animal pests to eat a quarter of India's total grain crop.[24]

Missionary effort in Africa produced much of the disintegration of tribal societies. Chiefs who, for reasons of personal or tribal benefit, had welcomed the missionary, seldom foresaw the inevitable result of the founding of a church—the transfer of loyalty to what appeared to be a better way of life and the depreciation of the old ways. Even though the missionary was an alien, the sharing of spiritual fellowship produced a spiritual kinship with him which the impact of less kindly Europeans could not destroy.

Missionary education produced a younger generation that soon felt itself superior to its elders, reversing an age-old and natural relationship.[25] The African student became an inhabitant of two worlds, the world of Western thought and technology and the world of his ancestors, parents and elders, and most of his age-group. Of his own volition, he admired the first with respect and fear while he despised the other with friendly familiarity and contempt.

In the areas of European settlement, the rise of an elite body of educated Africans disturbed the status quo. The first generation of educated Africans attempted with enthusiasm to enter the world of Europeans. They were not welcomed, except as inferiors.[26]

> The determination to prevent Africans from infiltrating into European jobs was accompanied by a fairly general prejudice against the educated African.

Therefore, the second generation of African students entered vocational training and became nurses, orderlies, carpenters, bricklayers, agriculturalists, technicians and printers, and also teachers, a skilled working class.

This was far from satisfactory to the elite. As Buell said, 'The African intellectual is probably the most sensitive[27] . . . in the world.' The third generation, reaching for higher education, channeled their frustrations into political activism and emerged as revolutionary leaders.

The missionary minimum in social reform was to make Christians of hearers, and leave the action to their developing Christian consciences. The missionary maximum included loud protests against social injustice, as they saw it. It was their hearers who carried it to its logical conclusion.

CHAPTER XVII

DECLINE OF A GREAT MOVEMENT

The First World War dislocated the operations of many an organization, especially those of a nation-wide scale, but the signing of peace between the nations in 1919 allowed them to take up where they had left off in 1914. The Student Volunteer Movement held its North American Convention in Des Moines in 1920.[1] From nearly a thousand universities, colleges and seminaries, 6890 students attended the various sessions—the peak of numerical success.[2]

Likewise, the year that followed produced the greatest number of newly enrolled student volunteers—2783 in all, and 637 sailed for foreign service in 1921. Little did anyone realize that, within twenty years, the number of volunteers would have dropped to 25, with actual sailings a handful.

A reading of the records of the Student Volunteer Convention held at Des Moines in 1920 has presented a picture of missionaries, veteran and novice, tackling the task of the evangelization of the world in their generation.[3] No inkling of the mood of the student delegates is given.

Observers realized that most of the student delegates were possessed by no great missionary purpose. It was felt that many were not even professing Christians.[4] The issues of the war had made students understandably concerned with the problem of peace, for, since the previous convention, ten million or more of the world's young men had died.

Another convention was held at Indianapolis in 1924. The post-war generation was predominant, and its concern was with economic and social problems, which they tackled with the zeal of uninformed inexperience, reaching no practical conclusions and making no great impressions.[5] Conventions followed in 1928, 1932, and 1936 at Detroit, Buffalo, and Indianapolis, and in 1940 only 465 delegates attended the Toronto Convention,[6] not considered a full convention.

By the time of the outbreak of World War II, the Student Volunteer Movement had almost ceased to be a decisive factor in the promotion of missionary projects throughout the denominations.[7] But the decline could not be attributed only to the onset of war.

Upon the conclusion of hostilities in 1945, there was a vast uprising of missionary interest, caused in part by the vision of servicemen returning from military duty.[8] New societies were formed, and 'twenty-five unbelievable years' followed.[9] The Student Volunteer Movement was untouched by the renewal of zeal, and while evangelical organizations proliferated, the S.V.M. was merged with the United Student Christian Council and the Interseminary Missionary Alliance in a union of weakness, forming the National Student Christian Federation, which in turn allied itself with the Roman Catholic National Newman Student Federation and other denominational organizations in 1966 to form the University Christian Movement.[10] Before the end of the turbulent 1960s, the general committee of the U.C.M. announced that—as a national organization[11]—the Movement had ceased to exist. Having lost its momentum as well as its power, it died in a whimper of futility.

Some signs of decline, even in 1920, were reflected in the statistics of the supporting Student Young Men's Christian Association, which showed a total of about 200,000 young men studying in higher educational institutions served by the Y.M.C.A. student organizations.[12] A little more than half of the total professed a nominal affiliation with a Protestant denomination, but no more than 30% were active members of the Christian Associations. These percentages were in keeping with those of the period of revival of fifteen years before, but the record of activities was changing.

Bible class attendance was declining, to about one in eight of the student population. Mission studies were attracting one in sixty. Throughout the United States and Canada, the Collegiate Y.M.C.A. won scarcely more than four thousand converts to vital Christian faith. In many states, the student associations reported no spiritual results. It was clear that the movement was living on its capital rather than on gains being made within a new generation.

One of the well-remembered privileges of the present writer was to study in graduate school under the direction of Dr. William H. Beahm, of the Bethany Biblical Seminary in Chicago. Beahm's doctoral dissertation concerned the factors in the development of the Student Volunteer Movement for foreign missions.[13]

The marks of the Movement's decline, averred Beahm, were paralleled by internal strain, confusion and change. The resignation of John R. Mott as director of the movement deprived the leadership of a steadying hand and perceptive eye, for Mott was first-rank in intellect and spirit.

Beahm proposed ten factors in the tragic decline of the great missionary movement. Its many changes of leadership broke the continuity of its life; there was an increasing difficulty in financing its operations; its direction tended to become top-heavy; its emphasis upon foreign missions seemed to overlook America's glaring needs; its leaders were undecided whether to stress its historic missionary commission or follow the shifting interests of students; missionary education had deteriorated from a base of information by experienced missionaries to one of discussion by inexperienced students; discussion of race relations, economic injustice and imperialism supplanted the earlier concern for Bible study, evangelism, call to service and missionary obligation; the arising of indigenous leadership overseas reduced the need for western personnel; the distinction between the unevangelized portions of the world and Christian homelands was blurred by the rise of the social gospel; 'revivalism' and its assumptions had given way to uncertainty regarding the validity of the Christian faith, especially its claim to exclusive supremacy.

Undoubtedly, there were many secular factors causing the decline of the Students Volunteers, the disillusionment of the War, the demoralization of the Roaring Twenties, the distresses of the Great Depression, and the discouragement of the international situation. The major spiritual factor is discovered in the history of the Y.M.C.A., which underwent vast changes in theological conviction, and—to all intents and purposes—abandoned its primary purpose in order to concentrate upon its secondary reasons for being.[14]

In the standard history of the Y.M.C.A. in North America, it is clearly recognized that the movement had operated from an evangelical position for the first half-century of its existence.[15] C. Howard Hopkins, its historian, suggested that from the mid-1880s—when, it must be remembered, the Student Volunteers emerged—a 'new theology' began to appear, capturing the loyalty of a few leaders in the mid-1890s.[16] It was not until the 1920s, however, that the whole Movement shifted its loyalty to what was described as the modernist viewpoint.

The nineteenth century and the first decade of the twentieth century found Protestants largely united in two great loyalties: the authority of Scripture and the unity of the Body of Christ —both generally taken for granted.[17]

In the same period, Protestant forces were engaged in two great enterprises: evangelism and social action. True, those who emphasized the social implications of the Gospel had begun to advocate a 'new evangelism,' one which aimed at 'redeeming' societies rather than individuals. But a majority recognized evangelism's priority without denying their social responsibility.

Just as the western world's populations were divided into two opposing camps which finally pitched into open warfare, so also Protestant constituencies were being polarized. Modernism rose to dominate denominational leadership, and fundamentalism rose to challenge it.

The modernist was weak in the doctrine of the authority of Scripture but strong on the unity of the Body of Christ. The fundamentalist was strong in the doctrine of the authority of Scripture but weak on the unity of the Body of Christ.

The modernist was weak in the primary task of the Church, evangelism, the winning of men to personal faith in Christ, but strong in the social work of the Gospel, even making it the primary message of the Church. The fundamentalist was strong in conventional evangelism, but often weak in social action, more so when propounded by the modernist.

This tragic polarization divided almost every Protestant denomination ideologically. It split or alienated many inter-denominational organizations, and affected the Christian testimony in the universities and colleges immediately.

Interdenominational witness and fellowship on campus in the first quarter of the twentieth century was largely under the direction and control of the Y.M.C.A. When leadership in the parent movement was taken over by its convinced modernists, the Collegiate Y.M.C.A. continued to operate with many advantages given it by its past leadership; but dissatisfied Evangelicals began to organize other campus fellowships, some cooperating loosely within the League of Evangelical Students,[18] later supplanted by the Inter-Varsity Christian Fellowship, a much more dynamic organization.

Strange to say, those denominations which most loudly proclaim their ecumenical enthusiasm most readily oppose interdenominational movements at the grass-roots level— regardless of theological affinity. The success of Christian Endeavor Societies provoked many denominations into organizing similar youth fellowships under strict denominational control. Undercover warfare against the Y.M.C.A. on campus diminished its operations.

Denominational witness and fellowship on campus followed the direction taken by denominational leadership—Baptist Student Unions in the Southern states remaining strongly evangelistic in the Southern Baptist Convention fashion; Wesley Foundations following the general Methodist trend in stressing the social gospel.

Denominational colleges either became secularized— resulting in a dissolution of the denominational connection— or continued to operate in the theological direction of their sponsoring denomination, stressing evangelism or social action, seldom both. Some evangelistic colleges became, in an evangelical context only, much more interdenominational in spirit, which was true of most of the Bible institutes.

Evangelistic colleges in their corporate life approximated the historic institutions in which evangelical awakenings had occurred a century before. The post-1920 period falls within the memory of the present writer. One never heard of an evangelical awakening of the phenomenal sort beginning in an institution where neither faculty nor administration were committed to the evangelical collegiate purpose—that of winning the unbelieving student to vital Christian faith, of strengthening the believer in the same.

Thirty years after the Evangelical Awakening of 1905-06, the writer visited all the States of the United States and all the provinces of Canada.[19] At that time, 140 Associations on campus were affiliated with the Y.M.C.A., reporting more than thirty thousand members.[20] Three-quarters of these collegiate associations reported more than a quarter of a million aggregate attendance at Bible classes or religious group discussions which may or may not have involved the study of the Scriptures, which (divided by the usual forty weeks of the bi-semester academic year of that time) gave a weekly attendance of more than six thousand, better than 20% of membership.

Unfortunately, there seemed to be no way of comparing the statistics of 1935-36 with those of 1905-06. The Y.M.C.A. in its more evangelistic days recorded attendance at Bible classes, cottage meetings, open air meetings, prayer and praise meetings, song services, jail and hospital visitation, and the like. In the 1935-36 statistics, there were only two categories cited resembling the foregoing—the number of religious interviews, and the number led to unite with the church.[21] Less than five thousand additions to the churches through Y.M.C.A. agency were cited for the whole movement with its million members in the United States.

There is likewise no comparison to be made between the reports occurring in the intercollegiate organ of the Student Y.M.C.A. of 1905-06 and 1935-36.[22] Apart from references to evangelism in India and China, experiencing awakenings in the 1930s, made by Indian and Chinese contributors, one found not a whisper of the word evangelism—rather page after page of propaganda for peace which seemed strange at a time when Hitler was beginning to incinerate helpless Jews in Germany. Thirty years earlier, the odd paragraphs and the major reports spoke of crowded meetings, converts by the hundreds, commitments for service, volunteers for overseas ministry, as well as hopes and plans for bettering the world. It could not be said that evangelism was dead in the campus Christian Associations, but whatever manifestation of it occurred was kept an organizational secret. The reports of evangelism and awakenings came from outside— in collegiate bodies of unquestioned evangelical loyalty.

For example, a Methodist minister of Norwegian birth, Abraham Vereide, reported from Seattle in late 1935:[23]

> I reflect, with much gratitude to God, upon Orr's ministry and especially the way in which he presented the message to three different groups—first, the business executives at the Athletic Club, after which he led a young millionaire to Christ: second the Metropolitan area business executives at the breakfast in the Olympic Hotel. The Holy Spirit spoke through His servant, and He is not letting His work return unto Him void.

> And it was a singular thing to meet on the University campus with that fine body of University students to hear Orr's fearless presentation of God's plan of redemption through Jesus Christ, given with a clarity, tenderness and power which gripped the hearts and led students to a decision. . . The revival is on. It has begun in my own heart . . .

The reviving in Abraham Vereide's heart was extended through his work with the civic leadership of Seattle, then that of the Pacific Northwest, and finally that of the United States, Vereide becoming the confidante of the Presidents from Roosevelt to Nixon, founding fellowship groups in the Senate and House of Representatives, inaugurating the annual Presidential Prayer Breakfasts, and effecting the extension of the movement to various countries overseas.[24]

The president of the University Christian Union at the University of Washington was Sterling Keyes, who reported on the results of the lectures and open forums on campus referred to by Abraham Vereide. Keyes explained that the University of Washington Christian Union 'desired to test "the power of God unto salvation" on this nationally-known atheistic campus,' for atheism was entrenched there.[25]

Lest this opinion sound alarmist, it is of interest that seven years later the incumbent Governor of Washington told the writer (his guest in the Olympia Mansion) that the atheists had so succeeded in excluding even the academic discussion of Christianity from the Washington classrooms that the only way to restore fair play would be to declare atheism a religion and exclude it from the classrooms also.

Sterling Keyes by his report gave an insight into the state of affairs on university campuses in those days of spiritual dearth:[26]

> Frankly, there was a number of students taken by surprise when they realized the nature of the meetings.
> A speech class came out in mass, upon the suggestion of the professor, to criticise. Of course, this was merely part of the speech assignment, but is was significant that the teacher did not understand the type of the meeting he had asked them to attend. Another group of students came for the sole purpose of causing disturbance . . . 'that every mouth may be stopped and all the world become guilty before God' . . . was marvelously fulfilled. A few, we found out at the next U.C.U. meeting, did become converted and we have the names of others who were convicted. We are now meeting twice weekly to pray for their conversion.
> With God's leading, we plan for evangelistic campaigns in the near future, hoping also to sponsor more lectures by men . . . who can authoritatively speak as a messenger of God.

It cannot be overemphasized that the University Christian Union represented a very tiny percentage of the 10,000 young people studying at the University of Washington. Throughout the United States, the Evangelical cause on campus was in a sorry state, due to the desertion by the Y.M.C.A. collegiate organization of its Evangelical commitment. The evangelist whose ministry stirred the Christian Union in Seattle also visited other campuses, with similar evidences of unusual interest, but likewise reaching only a tiny fraction of the student population.

There were ten organized Protestant groups in 1936 at the University of Washington.[27] A Campus Christian Council coordinated their efforts, with committees on religious education, social and economic problems, recreation, worship, publicity, world fellowship, and program. Evangelism was missing. The fall emphasis was on world affairs; the winter on philosophy and theology; the spring on social and economic problems—again, no evangelism. Retreats often attracted between fifty and seventy students out of 10,000.

During the writer's first visit to the universities of the United States, there were approximately three-quarters of a million students attending the sessions of the universities and four-year colleges therein.[28] A little over 5% declared no religious preference, and somewhat more than 6% gave no information thereon. Roman Catholics accounted for 113,428; Jews, 31,052; Christian Scientists, 10,840; Latter Day Saints, 8,914; Unitarians and Universalists, 4,144. The remaining half-million were nominally associated with a nominally Evangelical denomination—66% of the total.

One in twenty of these nominally Evangelical students supported the work of the Collegiate Y.M.C.A., but less than one in a hundred attended its weekly religious discussions. The standard Y.M.C.A. history explained it thus:[29]

> The purpose of developing a vital Christian faith had taken the place of the desire to win men to Christ, wherever the latter was narrowly interpreted. Similarly, Bible study underwent not merely a transformation, but virtually disappeared. At the beginning of the decade there were almost thirty thousand students in Bible study classes; by its end, only four thousand.

Personal evangelism came to be looked upon as 'the art of helping men in their quest for a complete life through the processes of friendship.' The evangelists of the new gospel were Henry Pitt van Dusen, Harry Emerson Fosdick, Kirby Page, Sherwood Eddy and Reinhold Niebuhr—'a far cry from the appeal of fifty years earlier'—undoubtedly—'but . . . equally effective'——! Membership dropped and so did contributions.[30] A. J. Elliott, whom the writer encountered during his travels of the thirties, maintained his standard, as a student witness 'at least one man who is associating himself with at least one other man who through prayer, sharing their Christian experience, Bible study, and other means, are seeking to influence men within the groups where they live, play or work, to become disciples of Jesus and to pervade those groups with His ideals.' 'Dad' Elliott, who had seen the days of power in the 1905 Awakening, itinerated throughout the country until he retired in 1935. His was a voice in the wilderness.

Reference should be made to a movement which arose during these years of decline of the worldwide, evangelical, student Christian organization—the Oxford Group, latterly the Moral Re-Armament movement. This controversial movement began as a student movement, but lost its specifically student character; it began as an evangelical movement, but lost its implicitly evangelical postulates.

Frank Buchman was born in 1878, of German stock, and received his schooling in Pennsylvania, where he was influenced by the Schwenkfelders, a somewhat mystical sect with an emphasis upon 'the inner light.' Buchman became a Lutheran minister, but seemed to himself and his friends to be defeated in life until he was challenged in a meeting in 1908 in a little church at Keswick in England, addressed by the Marechale, General Booth's daughter.[31]

From 1909 until 1915, Buchman served at Pennsylvania State College, after which he began to travel as far afield as China. Biographical data, even when supplied by himself, has been found so full of petty contadictions that no clear chronology of events has been reconstructed, but the year 1921 found him at Cambridge, and then at Oxford where he spent six years in student person-to-person evangelism, or group meetings. It was during a visit to South Africa in the late 'twenties that his team was named 'the Oxford Group.'

The Oxford Group stressed confession of sins, which recurred in collegiate awakenings, as a regularly practised feature, and guidance, which took on Schwenkfeldian emphasis at the expense of Scripture. Buchman used both to maintain a remarkable inner-circle discipline. Where the Oxford Group's challenge was accepted by thoroughgoing Evangelicals, it resulted in thoroughgoing conversion. The writer knew thoroughly committed Christians who gladly credited the Buchman team with their conversion to God.

A. J. Russell, editor of a London newspaper, was moved by the Oxford Group and wrote a best-seller about the work. In 1935, he found that his guidance ran counter to 'Frank's' in a personal matter, and he was dropped abruptly, for a while attaching himself to the writer's informal team and journeying around the British Isles together. Russell's book helped make the Oxford Group world-famous.[32]

In 1934, an evangelical awakening began in Norway, the preaching of Frank Mangs of Finland having a powerful effect. This was followed by an invasion of Norway by the Oxford Group team, with extraordinary impact. Where the Group was somewhat suspect in British Evangelical circles, it was welcomed by Norwegian Evangelicals, such men as Albert Lunde and Arnold Øhrn acting as interpreters and (noticeably) giving the message a more evangelical tone. The writer ministered in Albert Lunde's Assembly and in other Oslo churches in early 1935, and observed something of the national impact of the movement, which used group meetings as its method to reach the elite.

It is difficult to decide where and when the Oxford Group movement switched from its specifically evangelical to a generally religious basis of fellowship. Its principles of 'absolute honesty, absolute truthfulness, absolute purity and absolute love' became its message, calling for life-changing within any religious context (such as Hinduism) and without any necessary connection with the person of Christ.

Dr. Buchman had difficulty living down an indiscreet but passing remark of appreciation of the potentialities of the 'leadership principle' after a visit to Germany, magnified out of proportion by his critics and Hitler's enemies. The movement adopted the name, Moral Re-Armament, and so continued after the death of its founder at a ripe old age. Whatever it was in the beginning, it ceased to be specifically evangelical. Its methods were evangelistic, but its fellowship was religious in the broadest sense. It called for conversion, but its 'life-changing' was no longer the New Testament experience, though (paradoxically) two of the choicest Christian scholars known to the writer in Britain and the United States—one an Oxford principal and the other an Evangelical theologian of highest rank—both professed to have been changed by the Oxford Group.

CHAPTER XVIII

A SLOW EVANGELICAL RECOVERY

Wheaton College, situated in an attractive town to the west of Chicago, was founded in the wake of the great 1858 Revival.[1] Several years after the 1905 Awakening, its able president established semi-annual evangelistic services.

Unlike many other institutions, Wheaton College moved to strengthen its evangelical position in the years of decline following World War I. This was not done at the expense of scholarship, for, in numbers of doctorates earned, Wheaton College was surpassed only by six major universities in the state of Illinois, and itself surpassed more than forty other Illinois universities and colleges in that respect, while only ten colleges comparable in size in the whole country— Swarthmore, Carleton, Amherst, Oberlin, Grinnell, Knox, Occidental, Beloit, Antioch and Middlebury—were ranked above Wheaton in percentage number of earned doctorates.[2]

In the autumn of 1935, a team of students from Wheaton —including C. Adrian Heaton, who became president of the American Baptist Seminary of the West—visited Toronto where they heard of the revival challenge presented by a young Irish evangelist whose meetings had been moved from the auditorium of Canada's largest congregation to the great Massey Hall.[3] They started prayer meetings at Wheaton.

On 13th January 1936, the Irish evangelist addressed ten thousand or more at the Christian Business Men's rally in the Chicago Coliseum. That morning, he also addressed Wheaton's chapel assembly of about a thousand faculty and students, pleading for another campus awakening.[4] A senior (Don Hillis) told him that student prayer meetings were going on until midnight. He was advised that revival would come when Christians got right with God. The meetings multiplied, and the college journal predicted: 'We are on the eve of a spiritual awakening,' warning careless Christians.[5]

Three weeks later, a choice Christian educator, Robert C. McQuilkin, president of Columbia Bible College in South Carolina, arrived in Wheaton for the mid-winter series of evangelistic meetings, upon which much prayer and many hopes were focussed.[6] Alas, Dr. McQuilkin was confined to bed with acute tonsilitis; and Wheaton's president, J. Oliver Buswell, was off-campus on important business; so the song leader, Homer Hamontree, presided over the addresses of a series of substitute speakers.[7] It seemed that hopes were sure to be disappointed.

A medical man, Dr. Walter Wilson, addressed the chapel on Thursday, again speaking of the need of revival, both in general and particular. The praying students had become spiritually impatient with all the talk about 'revival.' One such passed an unsigned note to the chairman, declaring his lack of satisfaction, and asking for counsel. A senior, and one of the real spiritual leaders of the students, he followed it up by arising and making a public confession of his shortcomings. Another and another followed suit, until a student from the gallery suggested that everyone kneel in prayer. More than a thousand faculty and students remained in the chapel from 10 a.m. until daylight faded in the evening. The dining room was neglected. Hundreds of students made wrongs right.[8] Scores dedicated their lives to missionary service. Not a few professed new-found faith. The work carried over to the weekend, when Dr. McQuilkin seemed sufficiently recovered to bring a final word. And President Buswell telegraphed the Irish evangelist, then ministering in Texas, that a 'remarkable revival quite independent of human instruments' had swept Wheaton College.[9]

There were several factors of great significance in the Wheaton Revival of 1936. First, the students developed a burden of prayer which contrasted with the pessimism of the Christian community. Second, they seemed conditioned to expect the answer to their prayers in the visit of a fine evangelist. Third, they were forced to look directly and only to God. Fourth, the outbreak came through confession of sins, and not through preaching—of which they had heard their share. Fourth, the effects were lasting, traceable in movements of national significance in the 1970s.

Twenty-five seniors revived in the Wheaton Awakening of 1936 became outstanding missionaries in Europe, Asia, Africa and Latin America.[10] James Belote went to China and became Secretary for Far East Asia in the Southern Baptist missions. Don Hillis went to India, and became Associate General Director of the Evangelical Alliance Mission, world wide. Kenneth Hood proceeded to Costa Rica, becoming a professor in its national university as well as a missionary. Wilbert Norton went to the Congo, and returned to become professor of missions at his alma mater. Among younger students were (Professors) Carl F. H. Henry and Harold Lindsell, first and second editors of the leading Evangelical periodical in North America. Young Samuel Moffett became a leading missionary in Korea, and his brother Howard an outstanding hospital director in the same country.

A number of Wheaton students experiencing a renewal of missionary interest in the 1936 Revival attended a summer conference of fifty-three students, including some from the Columbia Bible College, who met at Ben Lippen Conference grounds near Asheville in June 1936.[11] Great concern was expressed over the lack of missionary emphasis on every college campus. They consulted with Robert McQuilkin.[12]

It was decided to start a new movement, and plans were presented at the New Jersey Keswick Conference. And so the Student Foreign Missions Fellowship came into being, chapters being founded on campus after campus. The first Acting Secretary of these new student volunteers, Joseph McCullough, later General Director of the Andes Evangelical Mission, was a senior from Columbia Bible College. The first part-time National Secretary was Wilbert Norton who became a key figure in later developments. The first full-time General Secretary was Kenneth Hood. Within five years, there were 2628 members in thirty-six chapters of the Fellowship.[13]

The Student Foreign Missions Fellowship operated on the campuses of Evangelical liberal arts colleges, theological seminaries of evangelical orientation, and Bible institutes. It soon entered into an arrangement with the Inter-Varsity Christian Fellowship which was operating chiefly on secular university campuses.

155

Dr. Robert McQuilkin returned to Columbia, alerting all his student constituency to the possibility of an awakening, urging prayer and expectation.[14] The Monthly News Letter of Columbia Bible College, 20th February 1936,[15] requested prayer for an outpouring of the Spirit during the Spring Conference, but March 24 News told of an earlier answer:[16]

For some time our students here have been praying for spiritual quickening, and there were evidences of God's working. So we were prepared for the visit of the young Irish evangelist who is touring the world when he came on February 24.

The Irishman came from a preaching engagement in the city of Atlanta with the Rev. Peter Marshall,[17] later famed as chaplain of the United States Senate, and from a visit to the University of Georgia, where a limited awakening had occurred on campus.[18] McQuilkin reported:

There was an atmosphere of spiritual power in the morning meeting; at night, the Tabernacle on the Bible College grounds was filled, with over 400 present. Following the message, confession of sin and prayer began and continued till 10 p.m...About 175 remained, including the 145 students; this meeting continued till midnight, with the evident presence and power of the Spirit. Chapel the next morning began at 9, and went on through classes in the Spirit-guided prayers until the closing message at 11.30.

There were 75 such Bible Colleges and Institutes in the United States at that time, differing from arts colleges, for in the words of Dr. McQuilkin:[19]

The Bible College is different from the secular college in that practically all the students are not only saved, but are devoted to the Lord. But a great uplift in spiritual life came with this revival. An immediate result was a quickening of faith in the Christian service, and the directors reported that there were more decisions for Christ within the next week than in the two or three months previously.

As at Wheaton, the impact of this awakening produced its effects long afterwards, the records so indicating.

During his first visit to the United States, the writer had occasion to visit Eastern Nazarene College in Wollaston, Massachusetts.[20] As in colleges committed to advocacy of a 'deeper experience,' Eastern Nazarene faculty and students expected revivals in every student generation.

In the late spring of 1930, Eastern Nazarene College had experienced 'the greatest revival in its history.' The unusual outbreak began on campus without any human planning. No special services had been planned and no evangelist had been called, and, in fact, there was very little preaching during the movement. But classes were canceled as classrooms were transformed into prayer meetings. At mealtimes, the dining hall was often nearly empty as the students prayed and fasted. Spontaneously, as soon as the assembly had been gathered in the college chapel and had been opened in song, there was a rush of students to the altar to pray.

Students and chaplain continued praying day and night for an even more sweeping movement before the end of the term, to bring every remaining student to a profession of faith. The revival movement had been in progress for three weeks when commencement activities began. Baccalaureate Sunday fell on 8th June that year, Pentecost in the sacred calendar. In the course of the baccalaureate service, a scripture lesson was read from the second chapter of the Acts of the Apostles, and while it was being read, 'the Holy Spirit fell' upon the assembly and more than a score 'prayed through to victory.' As this commencement made academic history for the college in its first-time granting of degrees, it was an unusual experience. President Nease thought that the 1930 movement at Eastern had surpassed even the memorable awakening of the year 1913 at Pasadena College in California.

Although two student generations had passed, it was not surprising that, on 10th March 1936, another renewing was experienced. President Wayne Gardner reported that the chapel service, which began at 9.30 a.m., lasted well into the noon hour, and that the days following were marked by prayer meetings in various classes and about the campus. A similar reviving occurred that week at Gordon College, where classes were abandoned and confessions made, with lasting transformations of life and character.

The rise of the Cambridge Inter-Collegiate Christian Union and of its counterpart, the Oxford Inter-Collegiate Christian Union, in the wake of the 1859 Revival in Britain and the great campaigns of D. L. Moody, has been noted.

These Christian Unions, and similar organizations in the other British universities, were well content to operate as fellowships within the Student Christian Movement of Great Britain and the World Student Christian Federation, for the American as well as European constituent members shared their Evangelical origin, purpose, methods and convictions. Robert Wilder had been welcomed as an evangelist, and so had John R. Mott. Luther Wishard and Donald Fraser were likewise evangelical and evangelistic.

The whole of the World Student Christian Federation had shared in the blessings of the 1905 Awakening. But by 1909 there were tensions arising, due to a change of theological and methodological persuasion in the directing leadership of the movement—away from evangelical conviction and from evangelistic action. Douglas Johnson observed:[21]

> It did not help matters that some of the new elements were derived from those major deviations from biblical principle which have chiefly been responsible for altering the course of Church history away from the simpler faith of the apostles. A great principle was at stake. More and more there were apprehensive questionings and a feeling of dismay . . .

It was in 1910 that neo-Protestant and Anglo-Catholic interests chose to enter the ecumenical movement, till then engineered and directed solely by Evangelicals, cooperating in the Edinburgh World Missionary Conference. They had already moved into places of leadership in the student work. Tissington Tatlow, general secretary of the Student Christian Movement, abandoned his attempt to persuade the C.I.C.C.U. to accept a more inclusive basis and advised disaffiliation.[22]

The First World War had a more drastic effect on the life of the Christian Unions in Britain than in the United States, but the work was never completely closed down, and in 1919 those Christian men who had survived the war began re-assembling at Oxford and Cambridge and other British Universities—only to find things further changing.

158

Among the returnees at Cambridge were Godfrey Buxton, Norman Grubb and Clifford Martin. The C.I.C.C.U. revived, and faced the problem of the wider associations promptly. Norman Grubb has told the story of his encounter with the new theology. His Cambridge professor explained that when the prophet Elijah ordered the people to soak the altar of sacrifice with water before the fire of the Lord fell, the wily Hebrew really persuaded them to douche the altar with natural petroleum from an oil well nearby, and that after getting the people to bow in prayer he ignited the fuel.[23]

Upon more serious theological grounds, the C.I.C.C.U. decided to maintain its witness separately, cooperating only when conscience permitted. The revived Oxford Union men followed suit, and so did the Unions in London's medical faculties.[24] It was the last-named that provided a surprising quota of leaders to the Inter-Varsity Fellowship of Christian Unions, which was formed in 1928.

Douglas Johnson, a medical man, was chiefly responsible for the consolidation of the I.V.F. in British universities. Scientists and scholars, such as Sir Ambrose Fleming and Sir William Ramsay, Prof. J. J. Thompson and Prof. Daniel Lamont, lent their support, as did leaders prominent in the affairs of Church and State.

In the United Kingdom, during the between Wars period, there were stirrings among young people, resulting in the emergence of a number of British-born evangelists who gained a worldwide usefulness—J. Sidlow Baxter, J. D. Blinco, Bryan S. Green, Howard Guinness, Roy Hession, J. Edwin Orr, Alan Redpath, T. B. Rees and Ian Thomas.[25]

Bryan Green engaged in university evangelism for seven years, under Christian Union auspices. A mission held at Trinity College, Dublin, produced lasting conversions, as did another at University College, London. As chaplain of the Oxford Pastorate, 1931-34, he was in touch with a third of the undergraduates in any given term; he was the chief missioner at Cambridge's triennial mission.[26] After World War II, Bryan Green became an international evangelist and rector of St. Martin's in the Bull Ring in Birmingham, his position moving left to that of liberal-evangelical, bringing him wide interdenominational support in his evangelism.

Another Anglican Evangelical friend of those days, F. D. Coggan of Cambridge, went on to become Bishop of Bradford and Archbishop of York. His account of the growth of the Christian Unions in Britain in the 1920s and early 1930s appended the names of three hundred graduates who had sailed for overseas service in a very few years.[27] Inter-Varsity was sharing the burden of the Student Volunteers.

Howard Guinness, a medical graduate, was the son and grandson of the famous missionary educators, Dr. Harry Guinness and Dr. Henry Grattan Guinness, whose Harley College had prepared 1300 missionaries for the field. He was charming and debonair, an effective evangelist.[28]

Dr. W. Bell Dawson, Principal of McGill University in Montreal, and others in Canada appealed to the Inter-Varsity leaders in Britain for an envoy. At the end of 1928, Howard Guinness left for a five months' tour before continuing in medical practice. He stayed away for thirty months, and opened up the student field around the world.

Commencing in the invigorating Canadian winter, Howard Guinness visited Montreal, Toronto, Vancouver, Edmonton, Saskatoon, Winnipeg and Toronto, seeking out contacts. In the spring of 1929, he visited universities of the Maritimes, and in September he convened the first Inter-Varsity conference at Kingston, Ontario—and only six showed up, 'a failure,' reported the pioneer. Guinness retraced his steps, revisiting Toronto, Montreal and the Maritmes, Winnipeg, Saskatoon, Edmonton and Vancouver. The Inter-Varsity Christian Fellowship which he helped found became a sturdy organization, the parent of the American organization which replaced the League of Evangelical Students, whose Chicago conference Guinness visited late in 1928, finding it rather intellectually bound.[29]

Guinness, more than six foot tall, was succeeded in the Canadian work by Kenneth Hooker, six foot four; and Noel Palmer, six foot eight, succeeded him. When he resigned, Canadian I.V.C.F. friends held their breath—but in 1934, a director of normal height but abnormal energy, C. Stacey Woods, an Australian graduate of Wheaton College, took up the task.[30] A graduate of the University of British Columbia, Wilbur Sutherland, became Canadian director in 1952.

Howard Guinness crossed the Pacific and helped found a vigorous Evangelical Union at the University of Sydney in 1930.[31] There were similar developments in the University of Melbourne. It was not until 1936 that the Inter-Varsity Fellowship of Evangelical Unions was constituted. Guinness found indigenous evangelical groups in Auckland University College and its counterpart in Dunedin, and in 1936 there was formed the Inter-Varsity Fellowship of New Zealand, which was greatly strengthened by Dr. John Laird.

Howard Guinness also visited India, to which he returned two years later in 1936. It was not until after World War II that a permanent Inter-Varsity work was established. Dr. Norton Sterrett, with training in both Wheaton and Columbia Bible College, became director of the pioneer Indian work, the Union of Evangelical Students of India, later directed by a Malayali, P. T. Chandapilla. In 1936, Howard Guinness campaigned in South Africa, guest of the S.C.A.[32]

Between his overseas tours, Howard Guinness conducted evangelistic meetings in the British Isles, in St. Andrew's, Glasgow, Belfast, Dublin, Aberystwyth, Cardiff, Newcastle, Leeds, Sheffield, Liverpool, Manchester, and other ancient and modern university colleges between 1931 and 1932. He teamed up with Bryan Green again in 1933.[33]

The Inter-Varsity work at Queen's University, Belfast, gained great momentum from a powerful revival of church life and service which followed the ministry of an Irish-American evangelist, W. P. Nicholson. This was also true of Magee College in Londonderry. This movement was still effective in Northern Ireland forty years later, when the writer was guest of the major Irish denominations, and met converts of the 1922 movement in places of leadership.[34]

In 1934, a conference between Scandinavian and British students was held in Oslo.[35] Its real leader was R. P. Wilder, whose ministry had helped begin the Student Volunteers, but who was deeply concerned over the drift of the movement into something less than New Testament Christianity. He had retired to the homeland of his Norwegian wife. He and Howard Guinness represented the older and younger strands in the movement which was soon to become worldwide. The resurgence of Evangelical Christianity was inevitable.

Meanwhile, in the United States, while there was vigorous evangelical life in certain Christian colleges, there was no inter-university movement comparable to the Inter-Varsity Christian Fellowship to the north in Canada. The earlier evangelical movement had spent its force. The League of Evangelical Students was far from strong, and independent Evangelical Unions found little support from the wider and wealthier church constituency.

It was after the stirrings of 1936 that American students appealed to their Canadian friends for guidance and help. Stacey Woods made several forays from Toronto into the nearby States, and in 1938 helped transform a local group at Ann Arbor into the University of Michigan Christian Fellowship. Charles Troutman, who had experienced the Revival at Wheaton in 1936, pioneered the movement in the State of Michigan, and became Associate General Secretary of the Inter-Varsity Christian Fellowship of the United States of America, Stacey Woods being its director until 1960, being succeeded in that office by Troutman, who had meanwhile served in World War II and in the Australian I.V.F. In due course, the American Inter-Varsity became the largest of the national organizations in the International Fellowship of Evangelical Students, formed as a result of international conferences in 1934, 1935, 1937 and 1939, and finally at the Phillips Brooks House in Harvard University in 1947.[36]

It is worthy of note that Wheaton College experienced yet another awakening in 1943, during the visit of a Michigan Baptist pastor, Harold P. Warren. All classes were suspended for a day of prayer requested by President V. R. Edman.[37] The president of the student council was a young North Carolinian named William Franklin Graham, who recalled many years afterwards being deeply moved.[38] Student teams carried the challenge to other communities.

> Sunday morning, a packed house listened to Billy as he put aside his sermon notes and talked about the revival . . . Before the meeting was over, many made public confession of sin in their lives. Even more listeners thronged to the evening service to hear more special music and an evangelistic message from Graham (who was assisted by Al Smith).

More than forty seniors went forth from Wheaton's 1943 Revival to the mission fields, though at that time World War II had closed many an operation[39] However, those wartime years witnessed the rise of a movement aimed at reaching the teenagers whose fathers and brothers were serving in the Armed Services[40] Two Wheaton graduates, already in the ministry in Illinois, Torrey M. Johnson and Robert A. Cook, took over the direction of a rapidly expanding work— Youth for Christ, which gathered multiplied thousands of young people on Saturday nights in rallies in city after city throughout the country and Canada. Within a short space of time, the movement was operating in four hundred cities. Billy Graham, graduated from Wheaton College, became the leading Youth for Christ evangelist. The movement was a high school age project, wholesome evangelism at its best, spiritual variety entertainment at its worst. Its effects upon wartime youth were incalculable.

Throughout the United States, college students entered the military forces of the country with high morale. At the Jefferson Barracks near St. Louis, for example, thousands of college graduates and undergraduates were processed as air cadets in basic training. In 1943, an Irish-American chaplain experienced a kind of campus awakening among the men in uniform, the area chapel becoming so full that it was necessary to hold services in the Wing Bowl, attendances rising to more than 100% of available manpower—where the others came from was a subject of wonderment and a matter of conjecture.[41] The special services officer complained to the post commander that the chaplain's Sunday evening services were disrupting the operation of the post movie theatre.

Overseas, many servicemen were developing a missionary vision, leading to a great resurgence of evangelical zeal in churches and colleges as soon as hostilities were over. There was no missionary-minded Student Christian Association or Student Volunteer Movement to capture or channel their interest, other than the newly risen organizations that continued in the evangelical tradition and those evangelical colleges still wholly committed to their founders' purposes, the winning of the world to Jesus Christ.

CHAPTER XIX

MID-CENTURY RESURGENCE

The writer hitch-hiked 24,000 miles westwards from Tokyo to Oxford at the end of the war, to enroll as a postgraduate student in the ancient university,[1] and as honorary Warden of Northgate Hall, used by Oxford Inter-Collegiate Christian Union members for their organizational meetings, and as a member of the St. Catherine's chapter of O.I.C.C.U., gained a rare opportunity of observing university Christian life in the post-war years.

Oxford, like Cambridge and the other universities, was flooded with servicemen returning to complete an education. In the historic colleges, most of the O.I.C.C.U. members were youngsters who had come up through the historic 'public schools.' St. Catherine's,[2] then a collegiate society, was full of men matured by war—Battle of Britain pilots, survivors of the death march to the River Kwai, veterans of six years of overseas service, and the like. Between them and the incumbent leadership of youngsters, under the influence of a godly summer-camp evangelist, there was a certain amount of tension—as between military veterans and Boy Scouts.

The youngsters snubbed several senior men among them, including Howard Guinness, ex-R.A.F., who had become the Anglican chaplain of the Oxford Pastorate at St. Aldate's. The older students and faculty such as C. S. Lewis and Sir David Ross lent him aid in his projects.[3] The youthful executive also voted not to invite to speak an American (Billy Graham, visiting the writer), though twenty years later some of them as Oxford clergy ardently supported the Regent Theatre T.V. hookup of his Earl's Court Crusade; and without doubt their appreciation of Guinness and others of experience increased with their maturity.[4] An I.V. weakness, recognized by high authority and later corrected, was that students are often unfitted for initiative and responsibility, without training.

Upon completion of doctoral studies, the writer crossed the Atlantic again, first residing in Illinois before moving to Southern California as a family home. Starting with an evangelistic series at Wheaton, opportunities arose for one series after another at the University of Wisconsin, Iowa State University, McGill University, and various churches. Generally speaking, the campus sponsors were chapters of Inter-Varsity Christian Fellowship, everywhere enjoying a new lease of life due to the post-war flood of students and student interest in things spiritual.

In 1949, the London organ of the Keswick Convention in England published an article by Norman P. Grubb, of the Worldwide Evangelization Crusade, describing his post-war visit to the United States.[5] Norman Grubb did not hesitate to say that the most remarkable of his experiences there was a conference of ministers held at the Pacific Palisades Presbyterian Conference Grounds in Los Angeles by the Rev. Armin R. Gesswein, a Missouri Lutheran ordained but interdenominationally active minister.[6]

Fourteen weeks later, the same journal carried a report by Claude C. Jenkins, executive secretary of the Christ for Greater Los Angeles Committee, an organization of laymen of all denominations.[7] It was entitled 'First Signs of Revival: Unusual Stirrings in California,' and it proved all the more significant in view of the fact that (within six months) the same committee had sponsored an evangelistic campaign in Los Angeles that made history—the first of the nationwide series of crusades by William Franklin Graham, better known as Billy Graham.[8]

Jenkins's news report described a most unusual pastors' prayer conference held in the first week of March, directed by Armin R. Gesswein, who had flown in J. Edwin Orr from a university campaign at McGill in Montreal and Harold J. Ockenga of Park Street Church in Boston to be the principal speakers on the subject of Evangelical Awakening:[9]

> More than 400 ministers and their wives attended, and half of these continued in penitence and prayer until the early hours of the mornings. There was a great moving of the Spirit, with the spirit of Revival being carried out from the conference to many areas.

As a result of this conference, a tide of expectancy began to rise in Southern California. Many churches reported an increased attendance at mid-week services for prayer, then an increased attendance at Sunday worship services, leading in many cases to the adoption of double and even treble hours of worship, or the building of new sanctuaries to accommodate the crowds.[10] Orr continued to minister throughout the area in churches of every denomination, urging them to expect another awakening. Ministers' meetings multiplied.

In Minneapolis, there was a similar conference of local ministers, known as United Spiritual Advance, co-chairmen Wallace Mikkelson (Methodist), Paul S. Rees (Covenant) and Victor B. Nelson (Moderator of the Presbyterian Synod of Minnesota), supported largely by Lutheran clergy.

Messrs. Gesswein and Orr engaged in a simultaneous campaign of spiritual deepening for fifty-five churches there in 1948, this being followed at the New Year by a Ministers' retreat at the Y.M.C.A.'s Camp Ihduhapi, addressed by Orr and Rees, the former declaring that a quickening among the students was imminent.[11] Hence, it was reported, with the goodwill of all these ministers but entirely on his own responsibility, Orr set aside the whole of the spring of 1949 to work on the campuses of St. Paul and Minneapolis.

An author, F. W. Hoffman, traces the beginnings of the mid-century college awakenings to a midnight prayer meeting of four younger men, William Dunlap, Jack Franck, Edwin Orr and Billy Graham, in the latter's office in Minneapolis. Without publicity, Orr began a series of lectures at Bethel College and Seminary (Baptist General Conference of North America) in St. Paul.[12] The meetings began in unemotional 'evidential evangelism,' with lectures on atheism and faith. There were lectures upon the history of Awakenings, and exhortations on the requisites for revival. It was urged that private sin should be privately confessed and public sin publicly confessed.[13] Controversies were examined in the light of the Scriptures and superficial conclusions avoided. Within a very few days, the seven hundred Bethel students were engulfed in a thorough awakening—all science, arts and theology classes being abandoned for meetings of prayer, confession, restitution and decision for life.[14]

President Henry C. Wingblade reported to the organ of the Baptist General Conference, 6th and 13th May 1949:[15]

> We have had a special visitation. The Holy Spirit has wrought a marvelous work indeed on our campus and we praise Him for it . . . I do not think we have had anything quite like (these meetings) in all the history of Bethel. There was confession of every known sin, and a cleansing of heart and the preparing of vessels to be used of the Lord for His glory.

The outbreak of unusual revival came at the conclusion of a prolonged chapel service, when a student uninvited and unexpected stood to his feet and asked the president's permission for a couple of days' leave to return to his home state to make restitution for money misappropriated. Dr. Wingblade reported:[16]

> I think none of us will forget that week, especially the climactic day, which was Thursday. The student body as a whole were on their faces before God in prayer, asking for His heart-searching, confessing before Him every known sin, and being willing to make any restitution that might be necessary. There have been many great meetings in the history of our school, but this was certainly one of the greatest experiences we have ever had. It is all by God's grace—we have nothing to boast about.

It was the advice of the visiting evangelist that the sooner the student body returned to the normal schedule of classes the better. There were no meetings after midnight, and the spirit of reviving was channeled into everyday activities instead of extra-curricular excitement. As a result, there was no reaction against the movement at Bethel College, which was described by the president two years later as 'utterly wholesome and lastingly effective.' [17]

At the height of the movement in Bethel College, the student body of the St. Paul Bible College, operated by the Christian and Missionary Alliance, visited Bethel campus for a missionary rally, and were stirred by the striking evidence of the local awakening. Early on the first day of classes next week, the director called the visiting evangelist and informed him that the college chapel had been filled by students since 5 a.m., a hurriedly called 'day of prayer' in prolonged chapel worship and group prayer meetings being the result, extended the week following in a series of student meetings on the plan of the Bethel lectures.[18]

It was different at a nearby seminary, where a number of students came under deep conviction and began to make the necessary restitution. The student body clamored for a week of special meetings, were discouraged by the faculty, but held their own series of vespers with limited blessing.[19]

At that time, the president of Northwestern College and Seminary was Billy Graham, who had reluctantly accepted the deathbed nomination by their founder, Dr. W. B. Riley. President Wingblade of Bethel College visited the faculty at Northwestern to tell of the Divine origin and continuance of the Bethel revival; and the president of the student body, an ex-U.S.A.F. squadron leader, Harold Christianson, relayed the news of the awakening to the Northwestern assembly. A series of chapel services were hurriedly arranged, broadcast over Station KTIS, except for the Thursday when all classes and even examinations were abandoned while spontaneous prayer meetings were in progress. In the absence of the President, the Dean remained in his office nightly till a late hour, dealing with startling cases of restitution.[20]

These student awakenings affected six college campuses, and more than two thousand students testified to personal quickening.[21] Evening meetings were held in First Covenant Church, seating 2000, packed nightly; and eighty meetings for students drew in all an aggregate attendance of 40,000.

Many ministers were baffled by the failure of Minnesota Christian Fellowship to cooperate in the movement, going on with a planned series of group meetings despite the pleas of their own members who had witnessed unusual stirrings. An international staff member told the writer that it was all due to an unfortunate chain of circumstances. During World War II, the chapter maintained itself by group Bible studies, but returning servicemen clamored for evangelism, finally carrying the day. Alas, they invited an obscurantist who gave out more heat than light, setting their cause back for about ten years. Other I.V.C.F. chapters in the area cooperated fully in the 1949-50 student awakenings.

In Southern California, serving as director of the Sunday School in the First Presbyterian Church of Hollywood, was a most remarkable woman, Henrietta Mears. She had built the organization until it had become the largest in the land. More significant was her work with college students of the greater Los Angeles area, hundreds attending her college Bible class. Perhaps her greatest work was done at Forest Home, a summer camp a mile high in the San Bernardino Mountains.[22]There, in 1947, began a student awakening that touched the lives of scores of young men, some destined to international usefulness in the Christian ministry—such as Richard C. Halverson, later director of the International Christian Leadership movement; and William R. Bright, later founder of an international student movement.[23]

These and others assisted Miss Mears in the 1949 College Briefing Conference held at the end of August, the morning and evening speakers being Billy Graham and Edwin Orr, with 'Dad' Elliott of the Y.M.C.A., Charles Templeton of Canada, and three Presbyterian ministers—Drs. Louis H. Evans of Hollywood, Robert B. Munger of Berkeley, and L. David Cowie of Seattle—sharing the direction of ministry. Five hundred students from a dozen western universities registered and became a thousand before September first.[24]

Graham's ministry followed an evangelistic line;[25]Orr's developed much as at Bethel College. By the middle of the week, there was repentance, private and public confession, restoration of backsliders and thorough revival of Christian students, together with conversions of the most unhopeful outsiders every day. An evening service, already lengthy, was followed by a score of after-meetings. Students were called from that conference to significant service in the missionfield and ministry, to business leadership and social action. Ten years later, Miss Mears was hostess to a select gathering of executives of no less than a dozen organizations resulting from, or expanded by, that Forest Home collegiate awakening. The faculty shared in the benefit, not the least Billy Graham, whose biographers all quote him as saying that he underwent a transforming experience there. In the stillness of long after midnight, he came to talk to one of his colleagues about total commitment.[26]

When Billy Graham sought a more perfect commitment of life during that startling awakening at Forest Home, he began his inquiry by mentioning that he had offered his life to God during the 1943 awakening at Wheaton College. His friend recalled discussing evangelism and revival when he had first met him at Trinity College near Tampa in Florida and at Lincoln College in Oxford,[27] where the conversation concerned a possibility of 'revival in our time.' Graham's transforming experience took place out in the woods, a mile high, alone with God. He saw the results within a month.

September was followed by the opportunities of October, Graham commencing his now historic campaign in the big tent in Los Angeles.[28] In October, a student awakening swept Northern Baptist Theological Seminary in Chicago, then a school accredited by the North Central Association, having 375 students.[29] Vespers, which were voluntary, were crowded until midnight. The evangelist was a Northern graduate. A further revival moved Northern in 1950, President Charles W. Koller reporting on this movement—which was reported also in the press and on radio:[30]

It was a most gracious visitation of the Spirit here at the Seminary, surpassing anything that any of us have ever experienced at Northern. At the time of our revival in February, many references were made to the work last October.

In the fall of 1950, Northern invited their evangelist for his fourth series there, and again there was an awakening 'more spontaneous than at previous times,' in the words of the student body president, Alastair Walker.[31]

In 1949, both Armin Gesswein and Edwin Orr addressed students at North Park College in Chicago on Awakening. In November of that year, a spontaneous revival lacking in human leadership began on that Covenant Church campus. A couple of hundred students gathered at mid-week chapel, engaging in ardent testimonies and continuing in a fervent prayer service in which confessions of wrongdoing were made. Prayer meetings sprang up in the dormitories where all but four of the unconverted residents professed faith. Teams of students went out to revive the churches roundabout and to evangelize all and sundry willing to listen.[32]

171

The college awakenings had been going on for ten months when they caught the attention of the daily and weekly newspapers throughout North America from Maine to California. It would be impossible to describe the local awakenings on the scores of campuses affected, but a sampling from north-central, east, west and south may give a fair picture—the campuses chosen being Wheaton College in Illinois, Asbury College in Kentucky, Seattle Pacific College in Washington, and Baylor University in Texas.[33]

Chaplain W. Wyeth Willard, a Marine hero in World War II and historian of Wheaton College, was assistant to the president of the college in 1950, and wrote from that vantage point about the awakening, its prelude and its sequel.[34]

What Chaplain Willard did not say was that there had been dissension at Wheaton in 1949, a dispute involving alumni, administration, faculty and students, with demonstrations of seniors that clouded the usually happy commencement. The faculty and students of Bethel College had communicated their good news to both faculty and students at Wheaton, but there was no immediate response. Willard referred obliquely to 'a certain amount of rivalry, clashing of personalities, and those daily irritations making life unpleasant,' 'roots of bitterness, deep in the hearts of many, . .'[35] Students began to pray earnestly for another visitation of the Spirit such as other colleges were experiencing, but others feared a 'washing of dirty linen.' In another report, Willard noted that, in the summer of 1949, an evangelist-historian had taught a course upon Spiritual Awakenings at the Wheaton summer school, emphasizing the need of revival on campus, and that much earnest prayer was offered.[36]

On Sunday 5th February, the Rev. Edwin S. Johnson, the pastor of the Mission Covenant Church of Seattle, began an evangelistic series of addresses. His inspiring messages were 'quiet, Biblical and unspectacular,' as desired. In the order of circumstances, Pastor Johnson had experienced a thorough reviving of heart at a ministers' conference just before coming to Illinois. His message was 'Neither know we what to do: but our eyes are upon Thee.' Tuesday was a day of prayer, in which divisions and classes met together to intreat Divine blessing.[37]

On Wednesday evening, President V. Raymond Edman opened the meeting for testimonies.[38] A few students arose to unburden their hearts. But when they had completed their brief confessions of sins and shortcomings, with affirmations of their new resolutions, others stood up to take their place. Neither preacher nor musicians found opportunity for their ministry. The testimonies kept on without letup—except for prayer—thirty-eight hours on end, until the whole campus had been affected. From 9 p.m. Wednesday until midnight Friday, faculty and students engaged in consultation in rooms set aside. Wheaton had its share of spiritual plagues and afflictions, 'but the revival brought immediate relief and cured the college of its spiritual diseases,' said Willard.[39]

The testimonies given followed the pattern of the initial Bethel College Revival, but there were several utterances of a hurtful kind given unwisely, provoking criticism off-campus. The college directors did not interfere, explained the president, because they were under rebuke themselves. This was in contrast to the Bethel movement, where faculty members put things right among themselves in advance.

The first twelve hours of the prolonged prayer meeting concerned professing Christians, but students rising before breakfast noticed with amazement that the lights were still glowing in the Chapel, and hastened to investigate, bringing an influx of unconverted or backslidden fellows and girls.

> The baptism of the Spirit in one mighty wave swept into the kingdom of God those stragglers on campus who had been slow to heed the Divine invitation.[39]

Immediately, students sought to make restitution to all and sundry, near and far. A member of the varsity baseball team visited his home town and paid for athletic equipment that he had stolen from a sporting goods store several years before while he was a high school student. The recitation of this incident kindled a reviving at his home church.

Chaplain Willard sat in the chapel all day Thursday and all the following evening. The delight of the occasion, said he, made the passing of time seem like a dream. In forty-five years living, he had never experienced such joy. He was convinced that the majority of decisions made were lasting.

Asbury College was founded by Dr. John Wesley Hughes in 1890,[42] and experienced extraordinary awakening in 1905. In early 1950, students were engaged in earnest intercession for another awakening. It came at a regular Thursday chapel on 23rd February, when the Rev. Dee Cobb was the speaker. A student arose to testify and was followed by others, but the chairman interrupted to call upon the speaker for his address.[43] Cobb was so overawed by a sense of the Divine presence that he cut his message short. 'It was as though an electric shock moved over the whole place, and there was such a sense of the presence of God... like a gentle breeze sweeping across a broad field of wheat. Everyone seemed moved... all over the auditorium young people were standing.' W. W. Holland, professor of philosophy, reported: [44]

So mighty was the presence of the Holy Spirit in that chapel service that the students could not refrain from testimony. Testimonies were followed by confessions, confessions by crowded altars, crowded altars gave place to glorious spiritual victories . . . Thus it ran for several days, wave after wave of glory . . .

The service that started at 9 a.m. on Thursday continued uninterrupted throughout the day and into the night. Few left the chapel, and hundreds prayed all night. Crowds returned after 6 a.m., and so it continued all Friday, Saturday and Sunday, when many attended the local Wilmore churches. After midnight Sunday, the dean requested the young ladies to retire to their dormitories, where group meetings went on; the young men stayed in the chapel. It was not until 7 a.m. on Tuesday 1st March that the chapel service concluded.[45] It had gone on for 118 hours. Throughout the rest of the week, capacity crowds filled the auditorium, and hundreds sought a spiritual experience of God. The basketball coach at Paris High School came to investigate and was overwhelmed by a sense of a supernatural presence upon entering the building. He felt impelled to announce his name and position, then his conversion and call to the service of God, adding 'If He will let me live until next September, I will give up my coaching and enroll at Asbury Seminary.' Jimmy Rose later became the Rev. James Rose, ordained by the Methodist Church.[46]

Far to the west, in Seattle, Dr. C. Dorr Demaray, pastor of Seattle Pacific College Church, engaged a senior student from Wheaton to come for an evening service in the church. Mr. Bud Shaeffer, now a veteran missionary, spoke also in a morning assembly period. This message, together with messages of other speakers, including Rev. Armin Gesswein, made the entire school realize that 'the Lord was working' even before a scheduled February Spiritual Emphasis week. There was no immediate breakthrough. The administration invited the speaker at the nearby University of Washington Religious Emphasis lectureship to address the school, and then to return for a week of late vesper meetings.[47]

Seattle Pacific College authorities reported in March:

There has been an unusual burden of prayer, much personal work, self analysis, confession and testimony. In one service with Dr. Orr, nearly a hundred students made requests for prayer on behalf of their own spiritual needs. As many as 150 went forward for prayer in a single service. Since Dr. Orr was tied up in evening services during the week in the local churches, it was necessary to have a late service at the college in order to have him with us in the evening at all. Four such services were held after 9.30 in the evening. Many times every one present sensed in a very real way that the Lord was working. The first evening, the service was held in the Marston Chapel. It was crowded out. On the other three evenings, the meetings were held in McKinley Auditorium.

The Rev. J. G. Bringdale, a Methodist evangelist, spoke twice a day throughout the week following, concluding three weeks of unusual experience on the Seattle Pacific campus. William H. Wrighton, formerly professor of philosophy at the University of Georgia, reported a similar awakening at the Simpson Bible College of the Christian and Missionary Alliance, then situated in Seattle. Classes were suspended, and evening services continued until midnight. One young man at the risk of federal imprisonment restored property stolen long before. There was not a hint of extravagance or hysteria.[48] At Northwest College, Assembly of God related, an awakening set classes aside for three days.

Baylor University, chartered by the Republic of Texas in 1845, soon experienced a 'glorious revival in which many students were converted and many united with the church' in 1858;[49] and since that date, the Baptist institution was moved in many an awakening—reports of which requiring careful analysis, for one Waco minister declared: 'We had a revival here last fall, but nobody got revived.'

Dr. George W. Truett, pastor of First Baptist Church in Dallas and a world-famous Baptist preacher, stirred the Baylor campus in 1939, hundreds of students being revived and hundreds converted. After the war, students organized a Waco Youth for Christ, which developed into the Youth Revival Movement among Southern Baptists in Texas.[50] The reports indicated that 'revival' was used as a synonym for evangelism, and rarely referred to a 'real revival.' Nevertheless, the movement demonstrated revival, evangelism and missionary outreach. A Nisei student, Reji Hozesaki, made a remarkable contribution, as did three young men, Jesse Moody, Buckner Fanning, and Howard Butt, the former two becoming outstanding ministers in the Southern Baptist constituency, the last-named an enterprising businessman who conducted great evangelistic campaigns, and established an impressive conference facility for laymen, directed by Bill Cody, yet another figure in the youth movement. Among the student leaders, Charles Bryan became an able missionary in tropical America, Milton Cunningham went to East Africa, Robert Harris proceeded to the Bahamas, Ronald Hill served in Thailand, and Wayne Oates worked in Peru. In early 1951, the organ of the Texas Baptists reported an evangelistic meeting reminiscent of the 'spiritual peak' of the Truett series, on the occasion of the visit of Billy Graham.[51]

As one on the campus begins to feel unmistakably this surge of revival, he must think back on a Baylor Religious Hour service in early December when Dr. Edwin Orr told 2000 Baylor students he wanted the Baylor campus to spark a... great revival throughout the Southwest.

The students accepted the challenge and a thorough-going renewal of spiritual life affected the Christian community on campus:[52]

176

Two students—a senior and a freshman—arose to pledge their prayerful cooperation in Orr's objectives for a world-wide awakening within this generation. Daily private prayers and the organization of prayer teams were encouraged . . . President W.R.White of Baylor then told the group that he had prayed for years for a spiritual awakening . . .

The Baylor correspondent noted that it was against this background that Graham came to the Baylor chapel. At least 3000 students packed into the Waco Hall auditorium, filling every available space for both standing and seating. Hundreds more were turned away. The evangelist delivered 'an old-fashioned evangelistic sermon' that brought 226 students to an adjoining auditorium for further talks.

The mid-century college awakenings became news to the whole country in February 1950. The national weekly news magazines and many daily newspapers from coast to coast carried reports and feature articles, long and short, written as objectively as secular journalists with little knowledge of evangelical religion could be expected to contribute. The photo-magazine LIFE[53] presented two pages of pictures; the news-magazine TIME[54] contributed two pages of reporting; NEWSWEEK gave generous space. Prestigious newspapers in cities like Chicago and obscure sheets in mining towns in Arizona all commented with amazement on the movement.

It was unfortunate that some imaginative reporter invented the term 'prayer marathon' to describe what happened at Wheaton and Asbury Colleges. A 'marathon' described 'any long contest with endurance as the primary factor,' and as such was applied to a dancing contest, a long distance run, or the like, involving competition and endurance. This was simply not the case at Wheaton or Asbury or any other such college. At Bethel College, the necessity of confession was met by dividing the whole assembly in classes and by sub-dividing according to sex; the school was able to return to its normal schedule within the day. Such a procedure adopted at Asbury or Wheaton would have achieved the same results. But, although the humanly unguided movements at Asbury and Wheaton were prolonged, there was utterly no thought of an endurance contest.[55] They did attract publicity.

On the whole, the press comment was friendly: 'It was not started by any shouting evangelist or fiery exhorter,' commented a Cleveland daily; 'None will smile at this remarkable manifestation of religious fervor,' added a Long Beach editor; 'There never was a time when mankind needed the redemptive and sustaining power of conversion to God more than it needs it today.' An Indiana daily observed that the awakening had 'more profound, constructive import' than other activities of students which captured public attention. A hard-boiled reporter admitted,[56] 'I went to Wheaton with the cynicism of my trade, and remained to be deeply impressed by the solemnity and seriousness of the students.' It was the same with reports of Lexington and Louisville newspapers investigating firsthand the Asbury movement.

A most telling comment was made by the editor of the local newspaper in Bisbee,[57] a small mining town in Arizona:

One often reads of student demonstrations—college students demonstrating against some cause, hurling stones or fighting among themselves: but at Wheaton College in Wheaton, Illinois, the students recently held a demonstration for God. This was a prolonged revival during which they prayed and confessed their sins, seeking God and His forgiveness.

The editor expressed his certainty that the movement would have a lasting effect upon most of the young people:

Naturally, being human, it will not turn them into saints, and some will drift back into paths of sin again. When one is young, temptations are great; but it is heartening to know that a group of young college students spent some time seeking God instead of Mammon.

The famous columnist, Walter Kiernan, expressed the typical journalistic viewpoint in his widely read column:[58]

. . . Looking back at it, that outburst of sin-confessing at Wheaton College may be one of the top stories of the year. The idea of 1500 people getting together and admitting they're wrong about anything is revolutionary. Some say it was hysteria, some say it was pure emotion, but it may be that even today the spiritual can meet the material and top it if given half a chance.

A secular newspaper editor, Edwin Leavens of Lexington, went to the Asbury campus out of sheer curiosity. It was an unfamiliar experience, but he was thoroughly convinced of its quality and reality. He commented to his readers in a pungent paragraph:[59]

> Fanaticism had no part in it. There were no great emotional or theatrical displays. Those who got up there in front gave vent to their beliefs. Sympathy and understanding of the audience was always with them. It was one of the most moving experiences I have ever witnessed.

The reflecting editor came away thinking that he had discovered the answer to the problems of the war-racked world, for those were the days of the Korean conflict.

College awakenings continued throughout the 1950s.[60] At Houghton College, near Buffalo, Dr. Dwight H. Ferguson of Ohio concluded a ten-day series of meetings without much apparent result.[61] That evening, 21st October 1951, revival began in the dormitories among the students, and by midnight the crowd was so large that it moved to the college church. Dr. Stephen W. Paine, president, went over to the gathering, found no faculty present, but recognized that it was orderly and sincere. More than five hundred students continued until 6 a.m. On two days, the morning classes were abandoned, and the rest of the week they were short. After the afternoon classes, many students took off for the nearby towns and cities to conduct evening services.

It would be wearisome to chronicle all the awakenings in colleges in the 1950s.[62] The religious press often gave short notices, but they were no longer newsworthy to the secular press. In the turbulent 1960s, the news was of riot, arson, assault, drug addiction, confrontation, promiscuity and the like—not on the campuses of Evangelical colleges or among Evangelical societies on secular campuses.

Again it might be thought that the college awakenings of the mid-century were exclusively American. The majority of Evangelical institutions of higher learning were situated in the United States, but there were some overseas, and in one and another of these there occurred awakenings. A few examples will suffice.

In 1952, Reavivamento Espiritual Brasileiro, an inter-denominational movement supported by Assemblies of God, Baptists, Congregationalists, Lutherans, Methodists, and Presbyterians, swept Brazil[63] The annual report of the American Bible Society observed that, while most of the growth of the evangelical movement could be attributed to the day-by-day witness of its members, special efforts also drew the attention of the people: [64]

> In a nation-wide evangelistic crusade that crossed denominational lines and drew the interest of the multitudes, a special evangelistic team went from center to center calling for repentance and dedication to Christ. Time and time again, the largest auditoriums could not seat the thousands who came to hear the gospel, and hundreds upon hundreds came forward to accept Christ as their Saviour.

The leading missionary journal (an international review) printed a report that the Brazilian evangelical churches were growing faster than those anywhere else in the world, many having been greatly stimulated by the preaching campaigns of an evangelist who used air travel to cover almost the whole land.[65] The American Bible Society added:[66]

> Some there were who compared this movement with the great nation-wide revivals which laid the foundation for Protestant growth in the United States, and there was a strong feeling that 1952 had been a crucial hour of victory in the winning of Brazil to Christ.

There are but few evangelical colleges in Brazil, but in several of them there was extraordinary awakening. In the Colegio Presbiteriana in the town of President Soares, 1500 people packed the auditorium, and 3000 knelt in the streets. Four churches, Baptist, Methodist, Pentecostal and Presbyterian, were crowded for aftermeetings, and then the main auditorium was filled again until midnight.[67]

The California-based evangelist ministered in the Baptist, Methodist, Presbyterian and other evangelical colleges in each state. The theological seminaries of Brazil, without a known exception, were evangelical also. And in these institutions also there were extraordinary revivals.

A German-Brazilian reported an awakening in a São Paulo theological seminary, one among several so moved:[68]

> . . . We have just had a marvelous revival in the Methodist Seminary, so marvelous that it has become the main topic of conversation in all our meetings . . . the Holy Spirit worked among us. All present confessed in sincerity and humility our sins and our failures, asking the prayers of our companions. It was a wonderful experience . . . many students fasted, remaining in their rooms in secret communion with God. Hearts and spirits were changed and now life in our Seminary is completely new.

The Moderator of the Presbytery of Recife, describing the meetings in the Seminary of the North, commented thus: 'Never in my life have I so felt the presence of the Lord in power as in the meetings we had during the week of Dr. Orr's visit . . .'[69] There are accounts of stirrings of students in other denominational seminaries in Brazil, including Rio Baptist Seminary, the Congregational Bible College nearby, and other institutions.[70]

It was a surprise to the writer to find that in India the Christian colleges were not generally Christian in their student enrollment. In one of the most famous, the Hindu students rioted and locked the Principal in his quarters for forty-eight hours, all because a Hindu student had been baptized of his own volition in a nearby town.

Consequently, the approach adopted in most Christian colleges was the same as in secular and non-Christian institutions, apologetics and evangelism of a discreet sort. In Bible colleges, however, the situation was different, there being a converted and sometimes committed student body, with a regular worship service.[71]

In one of these, the South India Bible Institute, a striking revival occurred sometime after the writer's visit. A senior student was assigned a reading of the accounts of awakenings in various parts of the world, and 'a fire was kindled in his heart.' Others joined him in fasting and fervent prayer—'Suddenly, deep conviction of sin fell upon the forty men students; some confessions were made and a burden of prayer continued for over an hour.'[72]

Next day, there was a spirit of expectancy throughout the school. Then the outbreak followed. Some confessions that were made were shocking to hear. Confessions of hypocrisy, stealing, and uncleanness were given.[72] The following day brought the restitution of items stolen. Breaches of school discipline were confessed to the proper authorites. When at last the catharsis was complete, the direction of the open testimonies took on a joyous note.

This movement at Bangarapet was wholly indigenous. It demonstrated the principle that evangelical awakenings can and do occur in evangelical collegiate communities without regard to cultural background.

There have been similar awakenings in colleges during the Indonesian Awakening of the 1960s. There have been movements also in African colleges where the student body was vitally Christian.

CHAPTER XX

THE EVANGELISM OF THE 'FIFTIES

The resurgence of Evangelical Christianity in Christian colleges in the 1950s was paralleled by a movement of vital evangelism in the universities and secular colleges of not only the United States and Canada, but other countries as well. One was related to the other, and a Christian college president insisted that 'the college revivals did much for higher education in America,' adding that since the meetings it had been easier to talk spiritual language and emphasize spiritual truth in higher educational circles than before.[1]

There was a sudden and definite upsurge of religious interest on the university campuses. The Religious Emphasis Weeks of 1950 on most campuses showed double the interest of previous years; and, five years later, secular observers were claiming that no less than 1200 of the nation's 1900 universities and colleges were sponsoring some kind of a Religious Emphasis Week of lectures.[2]

A young Episcopal layman, Robert Cummings, president of the Campus Religious Council, University of Washington, had visited Forest Home during the 1949 student awakening. He proposed the name of one of the Forest Home speakers to serve with a Jewish rabbi, a Jesuit priest and a scholarly Presbyterian minister as missioners in the 1950 Religious Emphasis Week.[3] He was strongly seconded by Dr. David Cowie of the University Presbyterian Church, afterwards president of the Council of Churches of Seattle.

It was strongly impressed on the mind of the Forest Home missioner to travel up to Seattle some time before these Religious Emphasis meetings were scheduled, to hold some sessions for the deepening of the spiritual life of Christian students. Word of mouth invitation was given, but few other than members of Inter-Varsity and the college department of University Presbyterian Church attended.[4]

183

The week of meetings for Christian students proved profitable. With dismay, they heard that the student who had been placed in charge of lecture arrangements was so out of sympathy with the evangelical message that he had taken it on himself to place the visiting rabbi, priest and minister in the Hub, the center of student activities, while the avowed evangelist was permitted to hold forth off-campus.[5]

Eagleson Hall was farther away from the lecture halls of the University than desirable, but on the first afternoon the place was crowded out, students sitting on floors, windowsills, standing in doorways and hallways, to hear a lecture on Science and Reasoning Faith.[6]

The attendance being ten times that of any other lecture, it became necessary to move to larger and larger lecture halls on campus, each one in turn becoming overcrowded. The student newspaper described the talks as 'Religion in easy-to-take doses,' and gleefully announced the crowded conditions provoked and the new venues chosen.[7]

In the evenings, after-dinner meetings were arranged in fraternity and sorority houses, sometimes going on unabated until 2 a.m. It became necessary to hold another week of meetings on campus for sceptics paralleled by a week of evangelistic meetings in University Presbyterian Church at which overflowing crowds of young people listened raptly, and a great number declared their faith publicly.[8]

The four speakers at the Religious Emphasis Week were cordial in cooperation. Not so all the campus chaplains. It happened that certain members of the Council opposed the adoption of the report of their own sub-committee upon the attendance at lectures, not for inaccuracy but because all records had been broken in one series, which could not be permitted to influence students in future series. Far better to have a score of students out of ten thousand attend languid lectures than a thousand hear the dynamic Good News.[9]

All the while, the missioner most concerned was busy in three other Christian colleges. More than 20,000 aggregate attended the meetings in this 'sane yet stirring revival of religion' among university and college students of Seattle, according to a report signed by three presidents of colleges and the president of the University Religious Council.[10]

184

Stacey Woods, director of Inter Varsity Christian forces, issued a call to the chapters of the nationwide Fellowship in an editorial entitled 'Revival or Ruin': [11]

God's insistent call to the Inter-Varsity Christian Fellowship this new academic year is revival and vigorous evangelism. Unless we are winning students to Jesus Christ we have no justification for existing.

Plans for a renewed and greatly increased evangelistic effort included four or five consecutive days of evangelistic missions on as many campuses as possible, overseas and Canadian and American evangelists to be enlisted.

The winning of students to the Saviour of the world must become the primary responsibility and occupation of every Christian man and woman in college and university.

A 'Year of Evangelism' was announced.[12] The Minnesota Christian Fellowship joined forces with the Westminster Foundation in presenting Billy Graham to the University of Minnesota during the first full week of the 1950-51 school year. The campus newspaper estimated that a total of 6000 attended four noon lectures in the Armory, where the Word was well received by attentive audiences. Professor Charles Hatfield followed up with a Bible study course for converts, who were also helped by their student friends.[13]

The Rev. Leith Samuel, a British Inter-Varsity speaker, crossed the Atlantic for a series of five-day campaigns on campus, tackling McGill University in Montreal, University of Toronto, University of Western Ontario, Northwestern University at Evanston, Wayne University in Michigan, University of Southern California, University of California at Los Angeles, University of California in Berkeley, University of Pennsylvania and Michigan State—ten campaigns in sixty days![14] After autumn campaigns in California and Texas, J. Edwin Orr conducted nine series of evangelistic meetings under Inter-Varsity auspices, including University of Chicago, University of Oregon and University of Manitoba —the latter during minus-forty degree weather. Without a doubt, in Samuel's meetings and those of the American and Canadian missioners, there was encouraging response.[15]

A Latvian emigre, Dr. Karlis Lejasmeyer, conducted a half-dozen campaigns, chiefly in the northern states. Dr. Robert Munger tackled Columbia University, Dr. Howard Sugden the University of Illinois. As usual upon secular campuses, decisions of students were more often made in the weeks following the campaign.

Student interest was as great in Canada as in the United States. The Rev. Maurice Murphy, an Anglican clergyman serving Inter-Varsity as director for British Columbia, flew down to Seattle to appraise the February meetings there. The President of the University of British Columbia chaired the first of a noon-day series of lectures, but more significant were the 7 a.m. meetings for Christian students— also crowded out.[16] Then the evangelism received impetus.

It so happened that a student columnist in the university newspaper delivered a blast at the Student Christian Movement, which represented a more liberal Christianity on the campus.[17] It referred to orthodox Christianity as a 'comic opera,' as 'unproven revelation of dubious interpretation.' It ended with the statement, 'We have got to find a better social philosopher than Jesus Christ.'

Inter-Varsity sprang to the support of the S.C.M. Their evangelist, with a certain measure of experience in the subject, tackled the columnist in a debate in the engineering lecture hall, which was utterly overcrowded by faculty and students who sat on the floor and stood in the corridors. The opposition declared that the social philosophy of Jesus Christ was difficult to decide, seeing that the Gospels were written four hundred years after He had died. His case was so weak that his challenger had to be doubly courteous to avoid a swing-over of popular sympathy to the underdog. No vote was taken, but a number of students professed faith in the next evangelistic meeting of I.V.C.F. The chapter reported by telegram to headquarters:[18]

Public meetings attracted good crowds, meetings for Christians resulted in real times of refreshing from the Lord, prospects at University of British Columbia brighter than for some time, the group being engaged in active follow-up of a large number who received help through the meetings.

Meanwhile, a significant new movement was emerging in Southern California. Dick Halverson, Bill Bright and other young men revived in the Forest Home awakenings of 1947 and 1949 were busy in evangelistic enterprises of various sorts.[19] Halverson served as a minister at the Hollywood First Presbyterian Church; Bright enrolled at Princeton and then at Fuller Theological Seminary.

William R. Bright had been raised in Oklahoma, where he married his hometown sweetheart, Vonette Zachary. He and his wife both owed their conversion to Henrietta Mears and both continued as her ardent collaborators.[20] In 1951, at midnight while studying for a Greek examination, Bright had an uncanny but real sense of the presence of God and felt sure that he had received direction for the rest of his life.

So strong was the impression that he was to devote his life to helping win and disciple the students of the world to Jesus Christ that he dropped out of seminary, even though he had only a few units of study to complete for graduation. One of his professors, Dr. Wilbur Smith, became his close adviser. He enlisted his personal friends, Henrietta Mears, Billy Graham, Dick Halverson, Dawson Trotman, Cyrus Nelson, Dan Fuller and Edwin Orr as honorary advisers.[21]

The Brights moved to Westwood to attempt an entrance to the University of California at Los Angeles.[22] First, they organized a twenty-four hour chain of prayer for U.C.L.A., then they began to recruit and train students as teams to visit the various fraternities, sororities and dormitories. To their amazement, as many as half those who listened remained behind to make 'the great decision.' Within a few months, 250 U.C.L.A. students, including the president of the student body, the editor of the newspaper, and a number of top-flight athletes, had 'committed their lives to Christ.'

The writer participated in those early meetings on the U.C.L.A. campus and nearby. As chaplain of the Hollywood Christian Group, in which famous movie stars met in one anothers homes, he found the Campus Crusade for Christ gatherings in comfortable drawing rooms very similar. The students sat on sofas, chairs, floor rugs, hassocks, stairs and the like—just as among the movie stars.[23] Fellowship was the penetrating influence.

It is of more than academic interest that the first series
of meetings off the U.C.L.A. campus in various universities
and colleges of Southern California to be conducted by the
Campus Crusade for Christ was under the auspices of local
chapters of the Inter-Varsity Christian Fellowship.[24] In the
beginning, Campus Crusaders envisioned themselves as an
evangelistic arm of the Church with a special calling to introduce students to Christ and to encourage them to become
active in local churches, Inter-Varsity chapters and other
similar groups. It soon became apparent that hundreds of
new Christians—later thousands—would require a special
kind of follow-up. This produced a varied program of Bible
studies, action groups, and correspondence courses—these
last-named catering to 75,000 at the time of writing.

The writer and his family left United States for Brazil in
1952, and rented his home at cost to the Brights and their
co-workers, who used it as headquarters, saying long after
that 'it proved to be ideal for this next phase of our U.C.L.A.
ministry.'[25] Little did one think that ten years later these
ardent university evangelists would purchase a property
appraised at $6,700,000 for their international headquarters
—and develop into a movement with three thousand staff
workers in half the major countries of the world.

One of the first U.C.L.A. athletes to be moved by the
awakening on campus was Donn Moomaw, an outstanding
footballer, U.C.L.A.'s all-American linebacker of 1952. Not
only did he lend invaluable aid to campus evangelism and to
national enterprises such as the Graham Crusades, but he
gave up professional football to study for the Presbyterian
ministry, graduating from Princeton and becoming pastor
of the influential Bel-Air Presbyterian Church.[26]

Campus Crusade had a runaway success with athletes on
the U.C.L.A. campus, touching such men as Rafer Johnson,
world decathlon champion. By 1954, nine of the eleven first
stringers on U.C.L.A.'s football team had become active in
Campus Crusade—Ellina, Davenport, Long, DeBay, Norris,
Heydenfelt, Villanueva, Palmer and Shinnick—and not only
had four of these received all-American honors, but U.C.L.A.
that year was the number one team in the country.[27] One was
engaged in conversation with Bill Bright when the coach of

the rival U.S.C. team came and quite seriously asked the student evangelist to come and 'convert' his team also. On other campuses, star athletes professed conversion, and of these a number formed an Athletes in Action team.

Bill and Vonette Bright added nine graduates to staff in 1952; by 1955, they had 44; by 1960, 109; by 1965, 469; and in 1970, 2029, including couples. Campus staff were college graduates, not a few seminary graduates also, as in Inter-Varsity, with a thousand workers, not including wives.[28]

In its regular weekly gatherings, Campus Crusade—like Inter-Varsity—attracted tens of thousands of students, but—unlike Inter-Varsity—enrolled no members. Inter-Varsity circulated an excellent monthly magazine; Campus Crusade provided a couple of quarterly newspapers, one for students and the other for laymen and students, a combined printing of more than a million, and a quarterly magazine, 150,000.

At the height of the student demonstrations at Berkeley, the president of the student body there, Charles Powell, made a commitment of his life to Christ and exercised his abilities to temper the militant mood of the campus, joining Campus Crusade staff, later serving in Europe. Ten thousand student radicals were rumored ready to invade another state university campus, boasting that they would burn down buildings and shut down the campus. Campus Crusade staff and following from round about joined forces in presenting a Christian solution to the problems of the individual and the world.[28] Their rallies were twice the size of the militants', who failed to reach their objective, while several radicals themselves professed conversion.

International Christian Leadership, which sponsored the annual prayer breakfasts in Washington, attended by Presidents Eisenhower, Kennedy, Johnson and Nixon, provided a student witness, inviting key student leaders to Washington or to state and civic gatherings to share in the Christian presentation of Good News in a civic setting.[29]

Another student organization emerged in the 1950s, the American Association of Evangelical Students, active on the campuses of Christian liberal arts colleges. By 1970, the movement had spread to forty colleges and universities with a total enrollment of more than 26,000.[30]

In 1931, a young layman named Dawson Trotman started a corps of young men, chiefly collegians, to minister in the high schools and junior colleges.[31] By 1938, he was giving at least equal attention to students and to servicemen, but in 1941, the resources of these Navigators were mobilized to meet the needs of the millions of men in uniform. Groups of Navigators (as they were called) met on battleship and on shore base for Bible study, Bible memorization and witness. Hundreds of the returning servicemen entered colleges and universities in the post-war years, with instructions from headquarters not to start Navigator groups on campus, but to work at winning and discipling fellow students for Christ, helping Inter-Varsity and any existing evangelical agency, and nearby evangelical churches.

President W. F. Graham requested the Navigators to begin work at Northwestern College in Minneapolis in 1949. In 1951, the Navigators assumed responsibility for follow-up work in the Graham Crusades. The Navigators also seconded staff members to the newer Campus Crusade and International Students organizations. The Navigators thus avoided unnecessary duplication of organization. But in the twenty years following the mid-century, the number of staff workers resident in university and college cities and towns increased, until, by the end of 1970, they were working on nearly two hundred university and college campuses in a score of countries.

It was the privilege of the writer to enjoy the friendship and support of Dawson Trotman, whom he encountered at home and far afield. On 18th June 1956, Dawson Trotman was drowned in a lake in the Adirondacks, giving his life to save another. Billy Graham said of him: 'I think Dawson Trotman touched more lives than any man I have ever known.'

Lorne Sanny, Trotman's eventual successor as Director of the worldwide Navigator organization, was himself one of the collegians recruited in Los Angeles in 1940. It could be said that, although the Navigator work began in the 1930s, it burgeoned in the 1950s. In 1970, the executive directors of Inter-Varsity Christian Fellowship, the Navigators, and Campus Crusade were meeting annually or oftener to share experience and to plan strategy.

A young Oklahoman student-athlete, Don McClanen, gave thought in 1947 to the idea of forming a Christian Athletes' Fellowship. It was not until 1956 that the idea materialized and quite a number of athletes enlisted in the venture, Donn Moomaw and Bob Davenport among them. Christian athletes found plenty of opportunity to witness to young people. Within a decade, summer conferences were drawing more than 4000 athletes and coaches; and more than 10,000 were attending rallies held annually.[32] Permanent staff numbered 25 in 1970.

Youth for Christ, aimed at high school populations, re-cruited collegians for staff and fed its converts into campus organizations. Young Life, another evangelical creation, continued its work of reaching teen-agers in high school and camp, and fed them into evangelical organizations likewise.

In 1950, Robert Pierce and Robert Finley as evangelists visited Korea and saw something of the revival that preceded the Korean War. Pierce was moved to found the worldwide service organization, World Vision; Finley started a notable work in the United States to reach the hundreds of thousands of foreign students in American universities.[33]

Within twenty years, International Students (based in the national capital) had placed its staff workers in more than twenty-five university cities and towns, reaching 15,000 foreign students in a constituency of 200,000 in any year. A significant number of such students professed conversion either in the United States or upon return home, the fruit of what director Hal Guffey called 'friendship evangelism.'

These organizations partly filled the vacuum caused by the demise of the Student Volunteer and Student Christian Movements. They shared a mixed blessing in being outside the stream of denominational life, lacking support from so many worthy congregations yet free of interference in the specialized ministry to which they were called. Despite the catastrophic slump of the '60s, they thrived in their work.

The student ministry of these various organizations, in a general sense, could be said to have begun or expanded in the outbreak or the aftermath of the mid-twentieth century evangelical awakening. So too began the ministry of Billy Graham in the great universities, not his main ministry yet by no means his least significant.

Between the ministries of D. L. Moody and Billy Graham in the universities, there were certain parallels. Although the formal education of the latter exceeded the former's by ten academic years, they shared a diffidence regarding their capacities for campus ministry. Graham was nearly as nervous about speaking to Cambridge undergraduates as Moody was. Yet both Moody and Graham attracted university students by the thousands, some out of curiosity but many in genuine interest. And after Graham had attempted to lecture on higher academic levels, he realized that straight-forward preaching of the Good News was what was wanted by many and needed by most.

Billy Graham followed up his 1950 University of Minnesota campaign with occasional campus engagements sandwiched between his city-wide campaigns. In October of 1954, he addressed a large gathering at Wayne State University in Michigan, for example. In the 1960s, he devoted more time and effort to academic ministry. In March of 1961, he spoke at the University of North Carolina, North Carolina State University and Wake Forest College, finding a great and open interest in the Gospel, followed by lengthy discussions with the students and much individual counseling. In July, nearly half the summer enrollment of the University of Minnesota crammed Coffman Union to hear his message. In September, he spoke twice at the University of Pennsylvania and met hundreds of seminary students nearby.[34]

In 1962, Graham ministered at the University of Chicago under the auspices of Inter-Varsity Christian Fellowship. He began 1963 by addressing a great crowd at Ohio State University and ended the year with meetings at Princeton and the Academies at West Point and Anapolis. In 1964, he conducted a week of meetings at Harvard University and Massachusetts Institute of Technology, assisted by Dr. Akbar Haqq, an Indian graduate of Northwestern University, and John Wesley White, an Oxford doctor of philosophy. He also tackled rallies at the University of Michigan and at Northwestern University in Evanston. In 1965, five thousand heard him at Andrews Amphitheater in the University of Hawaii in February, two thousand or so at the University of Houston in November with tens of thousands by television.

In 1966, Billy Graham visited both Oxford and Cambridge Universities in May. The Rev. Keith de Berry hired the Oxford Town Hall for his own flock, and packed St. Aldate's with students. Pickets passed out leaflets reading 'Danger! Psychologist at work. Before you attend this meeting, you are warned that it is incredibly easy to confuse a state of passing emotional excitement with revelation or deep religious experience.' 'Very sensible,' said the vicar, 'I quite agree.' More than two hundred students waited behind for counseling. An even larger crowd filled Great St. Mary's Church in Cambridge, and more than two hundred made commitments to Christ.[34]

In 1967, Billy Graham addressed great meetings at the University of California at Berkeley and the University of California at Los Angeles, with Campus Crusade as hosts. He had meetings at Columbia University and other schools. In November, Graham addressed a great crowd at Belmont Abbey College, a Roman Catholic school in North Carolina. He spoke at functions in various theological seminaries, including Fuller Theological Seminary in Pasadena, and in the military academies, including the Air Force Academy. In 1970, the Graham Crusade in Knoxville was conducted in the Neyland Stadium of the University of Tennessee, with vast crowds attending, including thousands of students and the President of the United States, who addressed the rally.

Graham was not a universities' missioner like John R. Mott. His campus ministry was incidental, yet (in the words of a national student leader) his drawing power on campus was exceeded by no one. It was part of a prophetic power over the multitudes. In recent years, it became his policy to try to reach the entire student population within a hundred miles of his crusade operations.

What were the results of his ministry? Despite the fact that student commitments are usually delayed actions, an encouraging number has sought immediate counsel in every major effort. Inter-Varsity, Navigators, Campus Crusade and hundreds of churches received an accession of students revived or converted. Many switched their major interests of study to the mission field, the ministry, and social service, for Graham preached with a social conscience.

In the years following 1951, the writer was ministering overseas, five years in all. Occasional visits to the home base in Southern California reinforced the impression that the mid-century awakening was still being felt on campus. After seven years of evangelical awakening, the editor of Inter-Varsity's magazine reviewed the times in 1956: 'The year ending seemed to mark, in North America at least, the zenith of Christianity's popularity during the 20th century.'[35]

Church membership stood at an all-time high, sixty per cent of the American population belonging to a church, and church giving, while not quite keeping pace, was setting new records, construction and purchase of new buildings having steadily mounted.[36] Record sums of money were being contributed by Americans for missionary work abroad.[37]

> One must go back to the late-nineteenth century to find any mass evangelistic appeal comparable to the continually expanding ministry of Billy Graham. Yet in addition to this meteorite there are many others—Hicks, Rosell, Vaus, Orr, Shuler, to name just a few—who have probably surpassed any records except Billy Sunday's between the two World Wars.

The editor, mistakenly of course, suggested that previous revivals of religious interest in this century seemed to by-pass the university student group—not so the contemporary. He quoted the secular journalist, Stanley Rowland, writing in one of the country's leading newspapers:[38]

> Educational and religious leaders report a surge of interest in religion among students in recent years, and to an extent among faculty members . . . Religion has become 'intellectually respectable.'

Nicholas McKnight, Dean of Students at Columbia in New York, was cited as saying, 'I've been in the dean's office here for more than twenty years, and never have I seen such a wide interest in religion among the students.'

The editor presented the antithesis—the prevalence of crime, divorce, hypocrisy, irreligion. He warned against the danger of disdaining the current revival of religion in America simply because of favorable conditions in American society in general and in the universities in particular.

Dr. Reinhold Niebuhr, late in 1950, was quick to declare that the evidences were not conclusive that there was a true revival of religion,[39] despite the popular conversions, the receptivity among intellectuals, the departments of religion in colleges, and manifestations of escapism. Dr. Martin Marty, in a penetrating analysis of American religion published in 1958, specified as periods of awakening the movements of 1730 onwards, the 1800 awakening, the movements of 1830, the awakening of 1858, and (omitting the widespread awakening of 1905) and gave consideration to the revival of the 1950s.[40] One of his main criticisms, well-taken, was the vagueness and generality of the 'revival of interest in religion.'

There is no doubt that the genuine revival of Evangelical Christianity which developed following 1948 was accompanied and, in a national sense, overwhelmed by a wave of sentimental 'mushiness' about the faith.[41] The film industry tried hard to capitalize on the religious interest, but presented less than Christianity in so doing, as was expected.[42] There arose a determined effort to subordinate the evangelical awakening to the less noble objectives of anti-Communism. A great deal of the revival of interest was superficial indeed.

But this was not to say that the evangelical awakening in its evangelistic outreach was any less genuine than any of its predecessors. Evangelical Christianity was no longer 'the establishment' in America. It was 'mainstream' in its line of descent from Whitefield, Dwight, Finney, Moody, Wishard, Wilder, Chapman, and Mott, but not in its predominance, which had been seized by a hybrid of humanism and Christianity. And when the 'fifties gave way to the turbulent 'sixties, the hybrid Christianity offered little resistance to the flood of crime, violence, profanity and adultery —whereas Evangelical Christianity maintained its stand, and even took the offensive against the debauchery.[43]

An Australian asked the writer why it was that New York was swept by the 1857 Revival, whereas the Graham Crusade of 1957 was more like a missionary foray. The answer was obvious—the New York of 1857 was overwhelmingly a city of Evangelical Protestantism, whereas a century later it was one-third Jewish, one-third Roman Catholic, and—with Harlem allowed for—only 15% of what it was in 1857.

CHAPTER XXI

THE UNBELIEVABLE YEARS

On 6th August 1945, the writer was one of many engaged in staging for an invasion of the island of Kyushu, where it was anticipated that there would occur a million casualties as the Japanese resisted on their sacred soil.[1] Then came the news of that hideous mushroom cloud over Hiroshima, received—as a letter home recalled—'with very mixed feelings, with real satisfaction that the war would soon be over and with real dismay in contemplating the sort of world that our children may have to grow up in.' [2]

The post-war world proved very different to the one for which so many millions had given or risked their lives. It saw a vast extension of the dictatorial power of the Union of Soviet Socialist Republics into Europe; it witnessed a vast assumption of dictatorial power by the Chinese Communists in Asia; it watched the emergence of liberated African nations as 'the winds of change' blew colonial governments away; it observed the transfer of power and accompanying turmoil in India and Indonesia; and it discerned an uprising of oppressed classes in Latin America and other parts.

The meeting of the International Missionary Council at Whitby in 1947 met the threat of closing doors with a brave call for church-based evangelism, but, five years later, the conference at Willingen betrayed its deep anxiety over the adverse conditions facing the Christian faith in every major field where its world mission faced 'other faiths of revolutionary power . . . in the full tide of victory.'[3]

The dean of church historians, Kenneth Scott Latourette, could not bring himself to admit the decline of the Student Volunteer Movement, in which he had played such a stirring part.[4] He died before its demise in 1969. But there were many who expressed the concern of Christian leaders about the future, including Canon Max Warren:[5]

At Whitby, in 1947, we hoped that the most testing days of the Christian mission, at least in our generation, lay behind us. But here at Willingen clouds and thick darkness surround the future and we know with complete certainty that the most testing days of the Christian mission in our generation lie just ahead.

The testing days expected by the capable and informed General Secretary of the Church Missionary Society proved no illusion. The West was in retreat almost everywhere; and Christian missions suffered through association. Yet in the twenty-five years that followed, undaunted by the apparent hopelessness of the situation in general and in particular, new movements of Evangelical Christianity soon arose, indigenous movements on the field and spontaneous movements at home, particularly in North America.

The North American Student Volunteer Movement had almost dwindled away by the outbreak of World War II. In the years that followed demobilization, servicemen by the thousand recalled their surprise and joy upon encountering native Christians in the lands of their military engagement; and not a few flocked to the universities and colleges to prepare to return as missionaries of the Good News. The Student Volunteer Movement of earlier generations no longer offered guidance and help. But a mid-century Awakening, appreciated by the secular press, welcomed by Evangelicals and depreciated by their ideological critics, began in North America, accompanied by yet another series of collegiate awakenings of sufficient power and intensity to attract the attention of sophisticated secular journalists.[6]

North American missionary strength, which had declined to less than 10,000 before World War II, expanded to more than 30,000 by 1970; other Protestant missionary strength, close to 20,000 in 1940, declined to little more than 10,000 in 1970.[7] By far, the greatest gains were made by thoroughly Evangelical agencies. It may be pointed out that the number of missionaries is no index of strength in the territories of the Younger Churches with their millions of church members. But it must also be said that the fields where the Faith was growing most rapidly were those in which the Churches were most evangelical and evangelistic, despite affiliation.

In the post-World War II years, the writer has visited every state in the vast territory of Brazil, and every other republic in Latin America; every state in India, and every other country in Asia; every province in Southern Africa, and every other country in Africa. On the basis of such an experience, one is prepared to assert that the pulse of overseas Protestant Christianity is strongly Evangelical.

Undoubtedly, there are 'younger churches' that maintain the most cordial relationship with their parent denominations in the 'home' countries' whose leadership is no longer as Evangelical as in the days of pioneering and church-planting. The cordial relationship without doubt stems from gratitude, sincere gratitude, although continued financial support is not ruled out as a factor. Generally speaking, however, the 'younger churches' have demonstrated far more evangelical and evangelistic sentiment and practice than the sponsoring denominations.

Take, for example, the Presbyterians. The fields of their greatest success are undoubtedly Brazil and Korea. It was the Brazilian Presbyterian Church which spearheaded in 1952 the Reavivamento Espiritual Brasileiro movement. In many parts of Brazil, the Presbyterian churches are full of evangelistic fervor. The Commission on Ecumenical Mission and Relations of the Presbyterian Church in the U. S. A. made a minute of record regarding the remarkable series of evangelistic campaigns 'resulting in a deep and widespread spiritual revival in the churches and thousands of conversions.' And yet, their Secretary for Latin America told the writer that he had been unable to persuade the national Presbyterian periodical even to mention the Brazilian Awakening. And very recently, the writer addressed a mid-week prayer-meeting in a Presbyterian church in Seoul attended by more than a thousand intercessors. Where in the United States would one find a thousand people in a Presbyterian prayer meeting?

The leadership in the American Baptist Convention's Department of Evangelism has been under fire for many years on account of its lack of evangelism in the historic sense. This is no secret. Yet in India and the Congo, the 'younger churches' are engaged in perennial evangelism.

The Anglican Archbishop of East Africa told the writer that, when the Mau Mau terror frightened multitudes out of Christian fellowship, the 'Abalokale' or evangelistic East Africans remained steadfast. Without a doubt, evangelism is more common among Anglicans in East Africa than in England.[13] East African evangelists regularly visit England and other English-speaking countries with the Good News which they learned through the East African Revival.

David Barrett, missionary expert in Nairobi, has shown convincingly that if the present trends in Africa continue, by the year 2000 the Christians will constitute 45% of the population of the continent, which 'for sheer size and rapidity of growth[14] . . . must be one of the most spectacular stories in history'—to quote a widely read American news magazine.

One has lectured in overseas Methodist seminaries where the national faculty and students requested the recall of an American professor who denied basic Methodist beliefs. It is a fact that the Reformed Church of certain Indonesian islands has enjoyed extraordinary evangelical awakenings while its parent Church in the Netherlands is in the doldrums.

To what must one attribute the comparative good health of Evangelical Christianity in so many countries of the so-called mission fields? The first factor must surely be the awakenings which have swept these Christian communities in recent decades. The second cannot be ignored. The vast bulk of the missionaries going overseas are still thoroughly Evangelical, and this applies to the historic denominational societies as well as the new post-war organizations.

In twenty-five years, the missionaries associated with the Division of Overseas Missions of the National Council of Churches of Christ in the United States of America have almost doubled, from 5,500 to 10,000 in round numbers.[15] In the same space of time, the missionaries associated with the avowedly Evangelical missionary organizations of the I.F.M.A.-E.F.M.A. axis have more than trebled, from 4,200 to 15,500. And unaffiliated missionaries, generally deemed Evangelical, have increased from 1,000 to 10,000. In percentages, the 25-year growth has been 82, 270 and 900!—a far cry from the nightmares of post-war pessimists or of the prophets of doom.

In view of the dwindling out of existence of the Student Volunteer Movement, where have the missionary societies obtained their recruits? One source has been the college revivals. For example, many of the leaders of the rapidly growing Inter-Varsity Missionary Conventions have been missionaries influenced by the Wheaton and other revivals of 1936 and 1950.[16] It is startling to learn that no less than a hundred graduating students affected by the Wheaton Revival of 1950 have served on the mission fields, some with great distinction—including Nate Saint, martyred by the Aucas. These figures must be multiplied many times over to allow for other colleges thus awakened in the 1949-50 movement.

Or take the Forest Home Conference in the mountains near Redlands in Southern California. A youngster told of visiting his brother at the Forest Home summer camp:[17]

I was just ten years old at the time, and it was there that I was challenged to dedicate my life to God for whatever purpose He might desire. When the invitation was given to go forward and to seal whatever commitment we had made, I turned to Paul for support and asked if he would go with me.

Paul readily agreed, said Dwight Carlson, and he subsequently reiterated his desire and willingness to serve, never forgetting his commitment. The slaying of Dr. Paul Carlson by the Simba rebels in the Congo provoked an international incident, and ended the career of a medical man who was a hero to the Congolese and a martyr to his faith.

The Student Foreign Missions Fellowship, associated in its activities with Inter-Varsity Christian Fellowship, not only acted as the arm of the movement on university campuses but maintained a strong witness in the Christian colleges.[18] At Wheaton College, for instance, attendance at the S.F.M.F. meetings averaged 300 to 500 out of 1500 there, and often attracted half the student body. The leader of the chapter was Jim Elliott, an outstanding scholar (graduated with highest honors) and a champion wrestler, who later was martyred on a lonely river in Ecuadorean Amazonia. More students went to the mission field from that campus during that post-revival period than at any other period. After 1951, student volunteers in the S.F.M.F. declined somewhat.

The first international missionary convention organized by Inter-Varsity Christian Fellowship and Student Foreign Missions Fellowship was held in 1946 in Toronto, where only six years previously the Student Volunteer Movement, representing thousands of campuses but limited in its outreach, had attracted only 465 delegates.[19] With a smaller but much more evangelistic constituency, the S. F. M. F. drew 575 student delegates.

In 1948, the international missionary convention was held at the University of Illinois campus at Urbana, a more central location, and the conventions were held triennially there in future, becoming known as the Urbana Convention.[20] The attendance in 1948 was 1,294; in 1951, 1,646; in 1954, 2,141; in 1957, 3,486; in 1961, 5,027; in 1964, 6,264; in 1967, 9,200;[21] and in 1970, 12,304—practically double the best that the Student Volunteers had registered in their heyday.

In 1936, Kenneth Scott Latourette, as the dean of church historians, had declared: [22]

> Our reading of Christian history has accustomed us to see Him break forth in unexpected places where souls have opened themselves to Him and have been made great by the touch of His Spirit.

Latourette insisted that the new movements which saved Protestantism and started it off on its great nineteenth-century career did not emerge from the intelligentsia who sought to defend the faith by logic-proof intellectual arguments, not that God shuns the well-known centers, for sometimes His great saints and prophets rise from them. But, prophesying himself, Latourette added:

> We believe that He will break forth again, even though it may be in most unprecedented quarters . . . We believe that souls will be found to respond to God and that tomorrow as yesterday new movements will demonstrate His power.

Strange to some, the turbulent 'sixties brought a surge of new life to the Student Foreign Missions Fellowship.[23] Many restless students were attracted to the missionary program, and in turn the two Evangelical missionary associations which between them represented more than a hundred missionary societies established student personnel commissions.[24]

The Missions Advanced Research and Communications Center, Fuller Theological Seminary, and Inter-Varsity Christian Fellowship circulated a questionnaire of ninety-nine topics to the nine thousand delegates attending the 1967 Urbana Convention.[25] Two-thirds returned the questionnaire.

Men were only slightly in the minority, reflecting the sex composition of the general population.[26] Almost two-thirds of the delegates came from secular university campuses, one-eighth came from Christian liberal arts colleges, and one-twentieth from theological seminaries. Less than one in ten were interested high school students. More than half were in the college age bracket, 19 to 22 years of age.

Baptists predominated, followed by Presbyterians and Methodists. One in eight were children of missionaries. The great majority paid their own way, transportation and tuition. Nine out of ten professed belief in a personal God, and an equal number believed in the deity of Christ. A high percentage believed in a judgment to come, and, for a large number, the primary motive of missions was to reconcile men to God. More than four out of five were members of churches, and attended at least once a week.[27]

These missions enthusiasts shared a clearly evangelical basis of faith and practice with the Student Volunteers of 1890 to 1920. A reading of the records of the international missionary conventions would have suggested that the S.V.M. had continued on into the S.F.M.F., with the 1924 Convention and its successors until 1940 representing the beginning of almost another movement which soon failed in its deviant or uncertain objectives.

In Campus Crusade, the missions interest was expressed rather in enlisting nationals of the 'younger churches' on the field, giving them a particular training, and supporting them from the home base or from a field constituency.[28] The International Students even more emphasized the role of the national on the field, stressing that the student from the country overseas was the match of the American missionary intellectually, and his superior in knowledge of the language and culture.[29] Navigators also established a work overseas, sending qualified specialists overseas to train the nationals. Youth for Christ enlisted many nationals overseas.

The development of student missionary interest in the 1950s and 1960s was only part of the resurgence of mission enterprise in North America. Another feature was the establishment of service organizations to assist the 'younger churches' and the older mission societies.

World Vision, with a vast program of social relief in the areas of greatest need as well as of pastors' conferences designed to help the national workers on the field, grew out of the personal concern of a Youth for Christ director, Bob Pierce of Los Angeles, whose 'heart was broken' by what he saw of human misery in Korea in 1950.[30]

Overseas Crusades, also a California-based enterprise, developed from the vision of Dick Hillis, who saw service in China before the drawing of the bamboo curtain. Instead of planting churches, Overseas Crusades assisted national churches and overseas missionaries on the field, in many different ways, but especially in evangelism.[31]

Wycliffe Translators, also rooted in California, stemmed from the experience of Cameron Townsend, who had seen the need of presenting the Good News in the languages and dialects of Indian tribes in Latin America. They became a world-wide enterprise after the mid-century.[32]

Missionary Aviation, again quartered in California, had its origin in the war experience of many pilots, including Grady Parrott. It joined forces with British Commwealth pilots who divided the mission fields between them, providing missionaries with emergency and scarce transportation.[33]

Space would fail to tell of all the service organizations that sprang up in the 1950s, such as the Far East Broadcasting Association, with its great radio stations in Manila, matching the program of an earlier project in Ecuador also broadcasting worldwide in many languages.[34] The writer met Russian believers in the Ukraine and Siberia who listened to his friends broadcasting from Monaco or Korea. Moody Institute of Science, California-based, produced effective films which combined up-to-date science and eternal faith in such as way that they were in constant demand even in schools of other faiths.[35] Gospel Recordings manufactured records presenting the Good News in the most obscure of human tongues.[36] All recruited student personnel.

CHAPTER XXII

EPILOGUE: 1970

Some Wheaton observers proposed the hypothesis that college awakenings on campus there occurred in a seven-year cycle.[1]   Certainly, there were major awakenings in 1936 and 1950, with a minor awakening in 1943—quite apart from excellent evangelistic meetings every school year.

There were no unusual awakenings in 1957 or 1964, but Wheaton campus news in the former year was dominated by reports of a campaign conducted by the Rev. Larry Love. Three weeks before these meetings, a student journalist supplied an article on the quiet bravery of a girl student who had been born without sight in one eye and had lost the sight of the other—completely blind, according to the doctor. During the evangelistic service on February 7, sight came to Muriel Arney suddenly, and next day the doctor confirmed 20:20 vision in her left eye.[2]

There was no awakening at Wheaton in 1964. Old friends of the college were grieved to hear of student recalcitrance and contumacy instead.[3] Wheaton's reputation for excellence had caused keen competition for a limited number of places, resulting in a raising of entrance requirements and tuition costs, so that the college was attracting sons and daughters of well-to-do laymen and intellectually bright youngsters.

A group of young dilettantes, dabbling in hobbies ranging from logical positivism to empirical humanism, formed a pressure group nicknamed 'the fabulous fifty,' and used their undoubtedly sharp intellects to harass the Christian faculty and to tear down the faith of the student majority. Capturing key positions in student life, they increased in numbers but there were instances of mental breakdown and even suicide. The turbulence of the world of higher education was affecting even the Eden of evangelical scholarship. The few friends aware of the problem engaged in anxious prayer.[4]

In the annual series of evangelistic meetings, compulsory morning chapel services registered 1800 in attendance, but, despite the fact that the evangelist was one of Wheaton's ablest graduates, voluntary attendance in the evenings was little better than 300.

Wheaton's President invited a universities' missioner with experience of apologetics lecturing to conduct the 1965 winter Spiritual Emphasis Week.[5] The visitor requested full freedom to conduct the meetings in a secular lecture style, beginning with 'atheism and agnosticism' in morning chapel and concluding in the evening with 'faith that makes sense,' tackling the topic of 'conscience' next morning and dealing with 'the playboy morality' in the evening. Attendances in the evenings went up from 500 to 1500.

In the concluding chapel address, the visitor spoke upon 'decision,' but surprised his sponsors by giving no invitation in the customary form. That evening, before 1500, he set aside preaching, and turned the meeting over to the students, asking them to respond to the week of ministry. It was evident, reported the President, that the visitor was 'guided by the Holy Spirit . . . particularly in the closing service . . . the climax of a week of spiritual blessing.' The leading Evangelical periodical reported the 'Campus Awakening,' the greatest stir since 1950:[6]

About 1000 students gathered every evening for services at which attendance was voluntary. So many students lined up to give testimonies on the concluding night that the meeting continued until midnight. The testimonies were punctuated with personal confessions of sin, recalling a larger spiritual awakening that swept the same campus in 1950.

The 'testimonies' were none of them trivial. Many of the leaders of the 'resistance' repented, and many serious delinquencies were made right. The altered atmosphere on campus continued until the end of the school year, and three times the student body petitioned the faculty for an 'open' chapel in which to tell of continued benefits.

There were sporadic college awakening occurring elsewhere during the turbulent 'sixties, generally in isolated pockets of evangelical enthusiasm.

The Pentecostal movement arose in the aftermath of the 1905 worldwide awakening, and within a generation or so, became the most rapidly multiplying sector of Christendom. Pentecostalism, with its own distinctives, nevertheless was part and parcel of the Evangelical movement, rather than a third force beyond Catholicism and Protestantism.

The fast-growing Pentecostal denominations, following the example of older denominations, began developing their educational facilities, transforming Bible schools into four-year liberal arts colleges and raising the standards of their theological training schools.

The pattern of academic life in Pentecostal colleges was very much that of the historic and continuing Evangelical institutions. The only difference noticeable to a visitor was the occasional glossolalia in chapel services.

It was not surprising that college awakenings occurred on Pentecostal campuses in the 1960s, even attracting the attention of the secular press. Evangel College, Springfield, Missouri, accredited by the North Central Association of Universities and Colleges, was one such institution. In 1969, for example, students carried on 24-hour prayer chains; in the prayer chapel, three or four young men began meeting for intercession, moving to the chapel auditorium a hundred strong; Spiritual Emphasis Week began 4th November with Willard Cantelon as evangelist, 700 students attending the voluntary evening service. Weary, the evangelist left after Thursday evening ministry, but the students stayed on, and at 11 p.m., there was 'an outpouring of the Spirit.'[7] There were 700 students in the chapel at 2 a.m. The students engaged in prayer all night, and classes were canceled all day Friday, the unusual movement continuing until Sunday. In the school year, revived students contributed nearly $20,000 to the Christian service organization—chiefly foreign missions including sending student interns to India, Malawi, Tanzania, French West Indies, and other countries.

It could be said of the Pentecostal colleges that they expected college revivals in every student generation. These movements achieved much in raising the educational qualifications of Pentecostal missionaries without diminishing their obvious spiritual zeal.

One of the more amazing developments of the post-war world has been the invasion of the historic Churches of Christendom by the new Pentecostalism, the 'charismatic movement.'[8]   That glossolalia—the speaking in tongues—and other charismata considered peculiar to Pentecostalism should break out among liturgical Anglicans and Lutherans caused great surprise, but that the same should occur in the tradition-bound Roman Catholic Church caused the utmost astonishment.

However, the agency of John XXIII and the ministry of David DuPlessis sent ripples out from different points of impact, and where they overlapped came the new 'Catholic Pentecostalism,'[9] most apparent on university campuses. In the historic Roman Catholic University of Notre Dame and in the innovating State University of Michigan, and in other universities, there are groups of zealous members of the Roman Catholic Church engaging in Bible study and in extemporaneous prayer meetings, experiencing 'outpourings of the Holy Spirit' in the Pentecostal style.

Visitors have told of ministering to groups of 500 at Ann Arbor, and of a steady attendance of 200 at South Bend.[10] A usual pattern in one of these 'Catholic Pentecostal' groups is to spend from 8 until 9 p.m. in Bible study, from 9 onward in a prayer meeting.   In March 1968, a conference on the renewal in the Holy Spirit was held at Notre Dame.   Fully a hundred were in attendance at the opening meeting, and the conference which followed was typically pentecostal while authentically Roman Catholic.[11]

While many Evangelical Protestants are puzzled, if not repelled, by the new developments, it is undoubtedly true that the historic Pentecostal denominations and the neo-Pentecostal movement in older denominations are being widely accepted.   To date, there has been no theological seminary or church-related college captured in its totality by the charismatic movement.   Hence, in Roman Catholic and Protestant colleges and seminaries—outside the truly Evangelical institutions already considered—there has been nothing as comprehensive as a college awakening thus far. But the toleration of charismatic groups within these schools promises much for the future Awakening.

In April 1969, the American Association of Evangelical Students held its convention at Asbury College, attracting a fair attendance of student delegates from Christian liberal arts colleges of the country.[12] The main speakers were Dr. E. Stanley Jones, Dr. Frank C. Laubach and Dr. J. Edwin Orr. The conference lasted only three days.

However, Orr addressed the delegates and local student auditors on the topic of 'Evangelical Awakenings,' in the course of which he referred to the Awakening at Asbury in 1905, a year of widespread college awakenings. A student asked politely what good it had done, whereupon the speaker called upon Stanley Jones, Asbury's most famous alumnus, to answer. Jones, who had graduated in 1905, was deeply moved as he recalled the visitation of that year.

Within a year, a series of college awakenings broke out on the campuses of Asbury and a score of colleges within the constituency of that conference, and far beyond, again attracting the attention of the nation's press.[13] The movement affected a surprising number of churches across the country. It raised the hopes of Christians after a decade of distressing demoralization.

As at Wheaton in 1950, there had been serious dissension at Asbury College prior to 1970. It was not of the students' making, but it depressed the spiritual tone and hurt the corporate life. Much prayer ascended to God, and when an answer came, it was manifested spontaneously among the students themselves.

A week of special meetings were held at the local United Methodist Church, where the soloist told of having been 'a professional religionist' specializing in church music until his home 'fell apart,' after which he experienced 'conversion' that transformed him and his home. So many were moved to respond that the sermon was omitted.[14]

During January 1970, a group of students rose about thirty minutes earlier than usual to engage in prayer and Bible study. On 2nd February, the entire faculty assembled. Tuesday's chapel service was given over to spontaneous testimony. Students readily confessed sin and asked for forgiveness.[15] All classes were closed down for that week, as the chapel service ran on, non-stop, for 185 hours.

A month later, the Rev. David Seamands, pastor of the Wilmore United Methodist Church, stated in retrospect:[16]

The spectacular is over but a wonderful spirit continues among students and townspeople . . . Many of the more hippie types, some of whom have been on drugs, are meeting for Bible study, sometimes in the place where before they were doping.

Teams of Asbury students fanned out over the country, as many as six hundred at a weekend, to recount the story of the visitation in churches only too glad to pay the cost of air travel for each team. Thousands of professed conversions were reported.[17]

Dr. Raymond C. Ortlund of Pasadena was the speaker at Wheaton's winter series in February. An outbreak of student testimonials displaced the sermon one evening and continued all night and next day. In analysing the happening, some of the faculty attributed the outbreak to the presence on campus of students from other colleges experiencing similar revival. Some students from the very beginning refused to admit the possibility of anything real in the services. Others thought that the movement was the event of their lives.[18]

In early February, Professor Gilbert James of Asbury Theological Seminary preached at Greenville College, also in Illinois, with unusual and disturbing effect. Some were inspired, but others were angered. Then news was received of the Asbury Awakening. Students began to confess publicly their wrong attitudes. The movement continued in night-and-day long scenes of prayer and praise, witnessing and singing. Even adults 'over-thirty' sought reconciliation.[19]

In Indiana, Anderson College experienced a remarkable movement, described by the campus minister, the Rev. James Earl Massey, as a 'phenomenon of integrity' in which a new spirit of concern for others supplanted preoccupation with selfish pursuits, competition and attitudes of rivalry. Noon day services dominated by college and high school youth 'happened' in the City Hall Auditorium.[20] In the South Meridian Church, 1200 crowded out the building. Hundreds of college students were affected by the revival. 'The old familiar cry of emotionalism is heard here and there, but most of the public services are in low key and subdued.'

At Taylor University, February 5 had been set aside as a day of prayer, and students responded beyond faculty expectations, the concluding services being marked by confession, conviction, and consecration. On the following Sunday, the preacher (Dr. Sherwood E. Wirt, of the Graham organization) was delayed by plane schedules, and the time instead was given to testimonies, a 'tremendous outpouring' of the Spirit ensuing.[21] A week later, a team of Asbury students visited the campus.

Graduates of Michigan's Spring Arbor College attending Asbury Theological Seminary returned to describe the local revival, and, as a result, the three-quarter hour chapel extended itself for five hours. Houghton College near Buffalo was in the midst of evangelistic meetings when an Asbury team arrived, and confession, testimony and prayer lasted long into the night. Students at Trevecca Nazarene College in Tennessee had already commenced prayer groups when the news of the Asbury revival reached them. The chapel service on February 9 extended itself, involving students and townspeople and visiting board members. At the Fort Wayne Bible College, a chapel speaker canceled his visit, hence the President opened the meeting for testimony, and the students took over until 5 in the afternoon.[22]

It is impossible to recount the details of all the forty or so colleges which reported unusual happenings in February 1970. One of the first to be moved was Azusa Pacific College in Southern California, where a chapel service addressed by an Asbury student went on for seven hours.[23] Students fanned out into churches in the Greater Los Angeles area, and on February 9 the afternoon classes were canceled again. Much the same sort of thing happened at Seattle Pacific, as classes were peacefully disrupted by prayer.[24] More than 800 students crammed into Gwinn Commons, a dining hall, for an impromptu service of Holy Communion. In Tulsa, at Oral Roberts University—an academic newcomer in Oklahoma—an extraordinary awakening began on February 9, during the visit of Dr. T. A. Carruth of Asbury.[25] A request for prayer was sent to Asbury from San Antonio, and as a result, the owners of a strip-tease joint were converted and closed it up 'for ever.'[26]

Among the many institutions moved by news of the 1970 Asbury Revival were theological seminaries. Prof. Charles Shaver described what happened at Nazarene Theological Seminary in Kansas City on February 10 (Tuesday) as the 'greatest church service I've ever been in in my life.'

The Rev. Paul Cunningham had come to report upon the movement at Olivet Nazarene College in Kankakee, Illinois. 'As he described what God was doing there, the Holy Spirit fell on the Seminary.' A score of students went forward to kneel at the altar. It is customary in such meetings for those who feel prepared to help to go forward and pray with the seekers, but none went forward this time—possibly because all felt their individual need.[27]

Students began going forward to the microphone instead, to confess their faults and to apologize. The spirit of confession and prayer was carried into the classrooms. When students stood in class for a prayer of invocation, they continued praying for the 50-minute period, without a lecture. In succeeding days, praise and singing took over.

Something less startling was reported from the Northern Baptist Theological Seminary in Illinois, where a course in the history of Awakenings had been taught.[28] In Southwestern Baptist Seminary, Fort Worth, Texas, the largest seminary in the country, planned and unplanned meetings on campus and nearby churches provoked the confession of sins and animosities and mended broken relationships. Some who confessed cheating were given opportunity to correct their mistakes and defaults. The meetings were often crowded out, and ranged in length from two to nine hours.[29]

Interestingly enough, the outbreak at Southwestern was preceded by two years of intercession for a visitation of the Holy Spirit. When it came, there was 'depth and warmth of honest emotion exhibited, but nothing that over-emotionalized or cheapened the experience.'

Sometime earlier in 1969, local church campaigns held at Irving and Pasadena in Texas by Evangelist James Robison had produced more than 1500 professions of faith among the young people. In Texas, baptisms had increased by 1687 in 1969, whereas they had dropped 4780 across the Southern Baptist Convention in the same period.

The attitude of the press to the Asbury and associated college revivals was, on the whole, cordial indeed. There was a newsman who heard good news for a change and described it as 'heartwarming.' 'I'm sick and tired of covering campus riots,' he said, adding, 'If those kids run out of something to pray for about two o'clock in the morning, ask them to pray for me.'[30]

The Asbury College public relations office waited fully twenty-four hours before making any kind of news release. By that time, requests for information were pouring in— an onslaught of reporters from newspapers and magazines, radio and television, and the regular wire services.[31] Daily, and then weekly, news releases were prepared. Television crews moved onto campus, but the college officials, though allowing them to move freely, did nothing to stage any scenes.

Inevitably, the issuance of daily reports involved the danger of sending forth some item of news which had not been checked and double-checked.[32] A year later, a college administrator complained to the writer that it had been wrongly suggested that the awakening which had broken out on another campus had been attributed to the visit of Asbury students, whereas it had preceded them.

Another noticeable feature of the publicity accompanying the college awakenings—not the official Asbury releases— was the eagerness which which not a few interpreted the movement as the beginning of a nationwide movement of religious renewal.[33] This showed an ignorance of the extent of past awakenings in the United States, and of the depths of demoralization throughout the nation in the 1960s. It was true that a score of colleges were drastically shaken up for good, that another score enjoyed some times of renewal, and that numbers of sympathetic churches experienced the contagious reviving through the witness of college teams, and that hundreds, doubtless thousands, of individuals had been converted besides those who were revived. But the movement did not remotely compare with that of 1905, which upset the life of whole cities, or that of 1858, which stirred the nation through every state. The 1970 awakenings made up a minor visitation, not a major one. If so much good arose from a minor movement thus, what could a major one do?

CHAPTER XXIII

PATTERN OF COLLEGE REVIVALS

The main period of this study has been the century and a half between 1800 and 1950. There were college revivals recorded in the latter half of the eighteenth century, and such awakenings are still occurring in the latter half of the twentieth century. That there were no peculiar outpourings of the Spirit in academic communities in the sixteenth or the sixth centuries seems to be explained by the absence of specifically Evangelical Christian colleges.

The main territory studied in this research has been the United States of America, but the phenomenon of collegiate awakenings has not been confined to North America. In the United States, the Evangelical Christian institution of higher learning seemed to reach its greatest development. In the other English-speaking countries, apart from Bible schools and theological colleges, there appeared nothing remotely resembling the Evangelical college of American experience. The same could be said of other countries where the State controlled higher education, or where it was developed by a State Church. Evangelical Christian colleges were founded on the mission fields, but, apart from Bible schools and theological seminaries, they generally became something other than Evangelical communities of scholars.

Even in the United States, the phenomenon of Evangelical Awakenings occurred only in those colleges committed to an Evangelical Christian position. They were absent from the higher educational institutions of the Roman Catholic Church, rare in the less evangelistic denominations of Protestantism, once common but now rare in the colleges established by historic Protestant denominations which have abandoned their evangelistic educational motivation, but still persistent in the colleges of ardently Evangelical sponsors. And college faculties of highest academic excellence have shared them.

Within the United States, there has been no geographical peculiarity in the occurrence of Evangelical awakenings in collegiate communities. They were once recurrent in New England, but their rarity in that section of the country today cannot be attributed to any factor other than the rarity of Evangelical colleges there, thanks to the rise of Unitarianism, the influx of Roman Catholicism, the abandonment of evangelistic objective by Congregationalism, and the gradual secularization of the historically Evangelical universities and colleges. The continuing outbreaks of such awakenings in the Middle West, the South, and the Far West may simply be ascribed to continued operation of Evangelical colleges.

Seldom has one heard or read of a phenomenal college revival occurring twice in the same student generation—or within four years, though there have been renewals of zeal in years following one another. The historian, Frederick Rudolph, has noted that there was a revival at least every four years at Amherst College. He also stated:[1]

> No college could sustain a revival every year. A revival might be sparked by the day of prayer, or by a dramatic and especially effective sermon, or by the tragic sudden death of a popular undergraduate. Whatever the inspiration, its manifestations would be much the same, whatever the decade, whatever the college.

He could have added 'whatever the century, whatever the state.' But the word 'sustain' cannot be translated to mean 'organize.' College revivals were simply not organized. In 1970, several authorities assured the researchist that their college enjoyed a revival each and every year, but of course by this was meant a series of evangelistic meetings, not a revival in any logical or historical sense. In some such 'revivals,' apparently no one was revived.

It is significant that the years of the most widespread and most effective college awakenings were those of widespread or general revival of religion in the population—the outbreak of revival in the 1800s, followed by a renewal thirty years later; the extraordinary awakening of 1858, and its renewal through the ministry of Moody; the year 1905; and the mid-twentieth century movement.

There has been recurring discussion regarding the place of preaching and teaching in the college awakenings—indeed in all general awakenings. It was complained in the Welsh Revival that there was not enough preaching and teaching of the Word, but observers on the spot replied that the Welsh people had heard the Word over and over again, and that the great need was to obey what they knew.

It was the same during the college awakenings of 1950. Strange to relate, the first significant criticism was voiced in the organ of the National Association of Evangelicals two years after the outbreak of revival at Bethel College, by an anonymous correspondent quoting the opinion of a senior at a college which had a 'most publicized' revival. It recognized that much good was accomplished,[2] but also serious harm: 'The whole revival progressed with an almost complete lack of Biblical exposition—there was no doctrinal emphasis at all before or after the long meeting.'

President Edman of Wheaton replied that if the writer had reference to the 'deep moving of the Spirit' at Wheaton a year previously, his opinion was not shared by the majority of those on campus: 'for hundreds of us, life has never been the same since those days and nights of sitting in God's presence in Wheaton Chapel.'[3] But was there scriptural exposition during that long prayer meeting? Hardly. There had been scriptural teaching by Bible scholars in the series of meetings that preceded it, and throughout the year.

Alastair C. Walker, then president of the student body of Northern Baptist Theological Seminary, now an outstanding Southern Baptist pastor, took the trouble of writing to the president of each college reporting awakening, including Canada, and received in reply a flat contradiction of charges aired in the magazine:[4]

There was definite Biblical exposition and exegesis, doctrinal emphasis, and all was related to the person and work of Christ and the Holy Spirit . . . the spiritual level of our college was uplifted definitely, and, since the meeting, through the witnessing of the students and faculty members who have gone out, we have records of more than 20,000 people who have made definite commitments to Christ in a twelve-month period.

At the mid-century, the first of the college awakenings occurred at Bethel College in Minnesota, and the most widespread in its results was the Forest Home Awakening of 1949. At Bethel College, the awakening was preceded by lectures on the great doctrines of the Christian life, Dr. Wingblade (Bethel's President) commenting:[5]

I liked the way he dealt with controversial subjects in the light of the Scriptures themselves, emphasizing the heart core of the matter instead of controversial terms of superficialities.

As for Forest Home, fully seventeen years later, the biographer of Henrietta Mears stressed the Bible teaching that preceded the outbreak of extraordinary response:[6]

The emphasis was on the Holy Spirit, and the evening messages delivered . . . were central. There was a depth of presentation that has rarely been equaled . . . In classroom fashion, the doctrine of justification and sanctification were exhibited for even the most untutored mind to grasp. The meetings were not short, the lecture alone sometimes extending as long as two hours.

And what were the results, in David Benson's memory?

But such an obstacle went generally unnoticed as the Holy Spirit convicted young people of their sins, filled them with grace, and instructed them concerning their callings. Upon the conclusion of a lecture . . . blackboards filled with outlines and Scripture references . . . usually (came the) call for a period of silent reflection and quiet prayer . . . Sophisticated collegians stood one after the other to repent of evil deeds and thoughts and to confess Christ as Lord. Dozens of young men decided for the ministry or the foreign field.

And Billy Graham, facing the great crisis of his ministry, spoke of the 'logical development of the whole subject of full surrender and the outpouring of the Spirit' stirring the whole conference, evening by evening, and 'of tremendous blessing in my own life.'[7]

This preparation for spiritual revival by the simplest of doctrinal teaching was a feature in at least a score of the college awakenings of 1949-1950.

It may be safely said that college revivals do not occur in academic communities where there is little or no know- of the Scriptures as the Word of God. This also is true in evangelical awakenings among the masses. Either there is a familiar knowledge of the Word, or the Word is preached in great power. Where there is little knowledge or none, a turning to God may occur, but it is more likely to be in the form of a folk movement, without conviction of sin.

How can the intense conviction of sin which occurs in all evangelical awakenings be explained? For conviction of sin there is, and it seems to smite almost everyone within the sound of the human voice or within the sphere of influence. Indeed, it may be felt beyond the sound of the voice and away from physical lines of communication. At the very moment that the spirit of confession was poured out upon Wheaton's chapel assembly, a Wheaton College Glee Club was touring in Florida, when a student called out 'Stop the bus!'[8] When the bus pulled over at the side of the road, he unburdened himself of a breach of trust, and a chain reaction began in the membership of the choir so far from home. This kind of thing has occurred again and again in revival history.

Some may attempt a psychological explanation, but those who have been involved in college revivals—or any revival movements—seem content to accept a theological solution. Without a doubt, during organized evangelistic efforts of a more obviously human origin, self-appointed evangelists have been known to manufacture conviction of sin along the lines of their prejudices as well as convictions; but what can one make of a movement which, quite independently of any- thing that has been recently said, brings conviction to one hearer regarding cheating, and to another concerning petty theft, and to another about a lie told a thousand miles away, and to a member of the faculty sitting on the platform a sense of shame about his professional jealousy? All that can be said is that an unknown force has simultaneously set to work upon everyone's conscience.

The conviction of conscience appears to work upon all matters, great and small. Students have given themselves up to the police, or, on the other hand, confessed to giving a trifling excuse which now appeared to be a heinous lie.

Besides unusual prayer and preaching, and extraordinary conviction of wrong-doing, the outstanding and inevitable mark of the college awakenings has been confession of sin. This was true in the first half of the nineteenth century — as in the words of Frederick Rudolph — 'the fundamental individual response was the confession of sin and the profession of profound religious experience and conviction.'[9] It is equally true of the latter half of the twentieth century.

In any college history, it would be nothing to read of a student, who, after a night of drunken celebration, suffering the effects of a hangover, 'threw himself on the floor, and began to weep and moan and roll about, seemingly in great agony.'[10] Such remorse is understandable, even acceptable. But, when it is recorded in connection with the remorse that a college awakening provoked for a sinful life, there is the undertone of disapproval in the report.

So, the secular historian records the conversion of a student, David Coit Scudder, in a mid-century awakening in Williams College. And what happened to young Scudder? It is not said that he embarked for India, where he made his contribution to the achievements of the remarkable Scudder family, who initiated medical work in the Arcot district of Madras, and built the great Vellore Medical College and Hospital, one of the glories of missionary work in India — whose humble poor appreciated such glorious 'agony.'

There is also recorded an incident at Denison College in Ohio, the reading of which might provoke a pitying smile:[11]

> We had gone to chapel simply because it was duty, when in the dull routine, 'Little Kerr' . . . who was sitting back by the chimney, rose and asked us to pray for him! . . . In a little while seven or eight of as wild boys as were in the college, broke down, and sobbing, begged us to pray for them . . .

In 1858, 'Little Kerr' — John G. Kerr — was in Canton, where he became superintendent of the great Ophthalmic Hospital, and later was to achieve fame as the outstanding pioneer in the scientific treatment of the insane in China. What has sounded as superfluous sobbing in a collegiate awakening becomes something more than a trivial incident in a lifetime of noble service.

220

Throughout the whole of this research, the writer has not been informed of a genuine college awakening where it was felt that the results had not been lasting in character. Where it was agreed that the Spirit of God was at work, it was also agreed that the benefit was an enduring one.

Examples could be found in every state in the union, but one will be taken from a college well-known to the writer. Herbert Hoover, the 31st president of the United States, had received his early training at George Fox College in Oregon before proceeding to Stanford University, and he gratefully conceded that the Newberg college had shaped his character.

At World War II's end, the college was in poor financial as well as spiritual shape, and had weathered a leadership crisis. Facilities were limited, food was poor, and morale was low.[12] Conditions drove the students, not to riot, but to prayer, and a spiritual awakening was the result.

It began at the autumn Christian Emphasis Week and was marked by spiritual power. Many students were converted, and in the morning chapels for four years it was not unusual for conversions to occur. A 'great conviction of sin hung over campus' and students were often burdened to make public confessions and sincere restitutions. A student body treasurer, on one occasion, arose to confess that he had temporarily converted funds to his own use. His repentance was thorough, and he went on to become a certified public accountant and a strong Christian layman.

Many students who were reckless and hard-hearted found that they could not resist the conviction sometimes felt upon the campus. There was an occasion when a student rose up from the altar and reversed his repentance, declaring 'To hell with it!' Shortly after, he was killed instantly on an athletic trip, and great fear descended on the students.

Retrospect revealed that four out of every five graduates of those years were thoroughly converted during the special 'visitations of the Spirit.' Nearly half of these converted graduates entered full-time Christian ministry—pastorate or mission field. Half of the remainder were known to be strong Christian laymen, active in their local churches.

George Fox College is of Quaker foundation, but its local support and student enrollment is interdenominational.

In the mind of the writer, convinced Christians are fully justified in attributing the conviction of sin to the action of the Spirit of God. But some unthinking defenders—again in the opinion of the present observer—quite mistakenly attribute the expression of a confession to Divine compulsion. This would make Deity responsible for human foolishness and indiscretion.

For an example, once under the influence of the Oxford Group in the days of its founder, a deacon in Boston became so completely transformed from a grumbler to a radiant personality that the pastor invited him to give his testimony before a crowded congregation of two thousand.[13] He gave a stirring testimony of a transformed life—so far, so good. Then he unwisely added the details of a strong conviction of wrongdoing which had come upon him—that of preferring a foolish, adolescent, sex aberration to a normal relationship with his wife. The congregation was shocked; his wife was so ashamed that she could not raise her head. The couple absented themselves from worship for a while, and then moved to another town. That the deacon was convicted of sin by the Spirit of God, few Christians would doubt. That he was Divinely guided to rehearse the matter in public, few would believe.

The journal of the Inter-Varsity Christian Fellowship in 1950 carried an editorial on the subject of 'Sin—Confession and Restitution.'[14] Its wording, and the fact that the editor resided in the town of Wheaton, suggested that it was aimed at indiscretions manifested in the Wheaton Revival of 1950. It conceded that a revival is not staged, nor is it the result of human planning, and that (on such occasions) there is usually public confession of sin against one's fellows as well as against God alone—and even private sins confessed.

To whom then is this confession to be made? Always to God, sometimes to one's fellow-man. It has been correctly stated that private, personal sin should be confessed to God alone. Sin against another should be confessed to God and to that person. And where there has been the scandal of sin known publicly, then public confession before the scandalized world is necessary as well as confession to God.

This was in keeping with the teaching of the evangelist in the Bethel College Awakening of 1949, where—according to the President's report—it was made clear that 'private sin should be privately confessed and public sin publicly confessed.' And this was also made clear at Forest Home in 1949 in lectures afterwards published with an introduction by Billy Graham, who heard them:[15]

> Let the circle of the offense committed be the circle of the confession made. In other words, secret sins should always be secretly confessed, private sins should be privately confessed, and open sins should be openly confessed.

The Inter-Varsity editorial insisted that, as a rule, public confession of private sin is both unwise and dangerous, and the probability of unreality in 'mass-movement' confession of sin is ever present, presenting an element of competition. It deplored the permitting of 'the unbelieving world' to violate so sacred a moving of the Holy Spirit by photography and ignorant publicity. It stressed the need of restitution to demonstrate the reality of repentance.

At Bethel College, in the spring of 1949, and at Forest Home, in the late summer, as soon as the widespread conviction of sin had provoked spontaneous confession, the full assembly was broken up into group meetings—by class and by sex in Minnesota and by group and by sex in California. Thus the danger of unwise public utterance, women before men for instance, was limited; and the multiplication of meetings divided the time, making all-night sessions wholly unnecessary. Newspaper publicity, a mixed blessing, was missing. There were no photographs in national weeklies picturing unwise youngsters making unwise statements.

The fairest analysis of these college awakenings took note of the many obvious cases of genuine repentance and sincere reconciliation and thorough restitution which had occurred despite the sometimes unwise publicity. Far better to be over willing to confess faults than to discourage an uneasy sinner from putting his life right in the sight of God and of man. One has known of instances where confession of any kind was suppressed, and it was found that those responsible had been fearful of exposure of their own deeds.

From the records of the past and the reports of the mid-twentieth century, it can be concluded that the misery of conviction and agony of confession have always been followed by a sense of forgiveness and joy which completely eclipsed the travail of repentance. No one who was present at Bethel College in 1949 could ever forget the students, standing in long lines at the cafeteria, swept by joy and singing the songs of deliverance in harmony 'out of this world.' The days that follow a college awakening constitute a 'love-in' in the best and purest sense of that expression.

The records at Asbury College demonstrate most vividly the immediate burden of the students participating to testify. In the early 1800s, long distances and the limits of equestrian transportation impelled the revived students to letter-writing, a prodigious correspondence between colleges being exchanged. In 1970, within a week of the outbreak, 600 of Asbury's thousand students had fanned out over the states east of the Mississippi, and others were jetting to Seattle and Los Angeles in their enthusiasm.[16]

Such spiritual awakening is a very contagious thing. In academic communities of like mind, it seems to take but a contact of a personal nature to strike the spark that causes the blaze. It must be added that the skipping of preparation and searching of heart often makes the communicated revival less thorough and less lasting. Seldom does the news of a college revival affect directly a body of unsympathetic or unindoctrinated students. The testimony of revived students is converted into evangelism, which is something different. Yet the evangelism is not without advantage, for scoffers become curious to learn what has so strangely stirred up their fellow-students.

College awakenings have an almost immediate effect on the discipline and academic achievement of the students. In the early 1800s, college presidents welcomed revivals of religion as a valuable aid in administering fair regulations. In the latter half of the twentieth century, college officials commented upon the good effects of the awakenings upon both discipline and academic achievement. The majority of those replying to a questionnaire on revivals on campus readily asserted that discipline had been made easier.

In late autumn, 1949, the California Baptist Theological Seminary (now the American Baptist Seminary of the West) invited a missioner from the Forest Home Conference to conduct a series of meetings for their students simultaneously with a campaign in Temple Baptist Church, Los Angeles. In the Seminary, the vesper services went on until midnight, a news bulletin for November-December declaring: [17]

> The Holy Spirit has been manifested to our student body and the awakening has come. The good that He has done to the Seminary will be lasting and the results only an eternity will reveal. Students and faculty have met the Saviour face to face.

The following year, the Dean wrote to the missioner who had been involved to say that the whole tone of the Seminary had been improved, and that several students hitherto upon academic probation had restored their standing in school.

This wholesome impact upon academic discipline has been typical of college awakening, even during 1970.[18] An Indiana college president claimed that the movement in 1970 'had a beneficial effect upon discipline and academic work.' In a Lutheran institution, the awakening produced a 'good leaven.' An Illinois college reported 'discipline easier, more serious study.' A California college president reported that in every instance 'disciplinary problems were resolved and academic work improved.' One campus minister reported that some of the revived students tended to neglect their studies, but this was in a college where there was no general movement. There seemed to be no doubt that the evangelical awakenings on campus resulted in fewer breaches of discipline and in better application to study, despite the disruption of classes.

College presidents have told the writer that graduating classes in revival years and immediately following were of superb quality. The sampling of graduates provided by the administration at Wheaton College, currently the alma mater of twelve other college presidents, seems to confirm this. And yet, one has encountered college administrators and faculty who shied away from the idea of such an awakening for fear of disruption of class schedules. None of these, of course, had actually been involved in a typical movement, which appears to lubricate the whole academic machinery.

That capable historian, Frederick Rudolph of Williams College, though writing from a secular viewpoint, summed up the effects of a college awakening thus: [19]

> The really effective agency of religion in the life of the colleges was the revival, that almost unexplainable combination of confession, profession, joy and tears which brought many young men into church and into the ministry. Most college presidents and college faculties of this era felt that they— or God—had failed a collegiate generation if once during its four years there did not occur a rousing revival.

A prime outcome of college awakenings has been the call of young men into the ministry, at home and abroad. Every period of college awakenings has been followed by a definite upsurge of missionary volunteering. In ordinary years, a number of graduates choose the foreign field, not for just a couple of years to satisfy their yen for adventure, but for life. But in times of revival, a landslide of commitments to overseas service occurs. Those not involved may shake their heads and cry 'Emotionalism.' Yet many of the candidates represent the most scholarly students on campus.

One recalls discussing British missionaries in India with the governor of one of that Republic's largest states. He was a devout Hindu, but had studied at Cambridge University. He was amazed, he said, to find that some of the best men at Cambridge, who could have had the world before them, would quietly respond to a call of God and set forth for some far corner of the earth.[20] He remembered especially his room-mate, of a famous family, with an excellent record in university, quietly telling him that he had decided—not for the state or the law or the military or for industry—but to serve God in Africa. At first, he could not recall the name. Then, after a long pause, he said it was Alfred Buxton, but he had never heard what happened to him. Alfred Buxton! I assuredly told him that this scion of a famous family had become a modern missionary hero, helping C. T. Studd to plant a chain of mission stations across Africa. This was always true of the college awakenings. They supplied the missionary societies with first-class personnel and first-class talent for the task.

The historian quoted has been generous in recognizing the importance of college awakenings in the formative years of this great country. In his New England habitat, it seems easy to think of such revivals as things of the past. They are still a vital force throughout the country. Evangelical Christianity is not a negligible force in the churches and community, and it has a disconcerting way of renewing its vigor and strength when least expected.

Kenneth Scott Latourette was emphatic in insisting that the world-wide spread of Protestant Christianity was 'in large part an expression of a series of religious awakenings unprecedented in the history of Protestantism.' [21]

> In many quarters, the fires of this enthusiasm are burning low... Great bodies of youth have drifted away from the Church, or at best preserve only a nominal connection... In many circles in which Evangelical conviction was once strong, an easy-going liberalism now prevails.

Latourette noted that so many, even among the clergy, were seeking in a social revolution a substitute for the religious convictions for which their communions officially stand but to which as individuals they can no longer subscribe. Unless new revivals invigorate it, this kind of Christianity is doomed, even in its own strongholds. Latourette, as a prophet, predicted that God would break forth again, in the most unpredictable quarters.[22] Evangelical Christianity is making great impact on populations overseas, in Brazil, the Congo, Korea and Indonesia. It is by no means dead in the U.S.A. It is the only dynamic religious force in the U.S.S.R.

While Christian colleges, committed to evangelism as well as higher education, continue to exist, college revivals will occur. The greatest problem facing Christian colleges today is one of maintenance in competition with institutions supported by the State. An able educator, skilled in administration in both state multiversity and Evangelical college, has suggested that Christian colleges should move to state campuses, share their courses and libraries, provide what is lacking for a Christian education. There is no reason why, in such residential clusters of scholars and students, evangelical awakenings should not occur and recur.

It is not only an American phenomenon. The writer has been many times in the Philippines, in the 'thirties, during the Liberation in the 'forties, in the 'fifties and 'sixties and 'seventies. Many have been the choice experiences enjoyed there—exploring the remote island of Palawan, sharing in the liberation of Manila, preaching in crowded churches, and addressing thousands of university students. But the most refreshing was meeting in Manila, on the way to Vietnam, a famous Philippine evangelist, known from Japan to India— Max Atienza, of the Asia-wide mission broadcasting station in Manila—and, after thirty years or so, learning for the first time that he had been converted in a student awakening in Manila in which the writer had some small part.

One has met products of college awakenings in the far corners of the earth, in Latin America, in Africa, in Asia. Their colleagues held each in high regard, saying of them that they were wholly dedicated men. And the same is true in the ministry at home, among evangelists and pastors and teachers. Billy Graham is clearly the product of collegiate awakenings, one preparing him for the ministry and the other for a 'ministry of the century.' The best-known Canadian evangelist is Leighton Ford, likewise a product of the same campus but of later movements. The resurgence of historic Evangelicalism in the United States produced a scholarly periodical of widest circulation, and both its founding editor and its current editor—Carl F. H. Henry and Harold Lindsell —were students moved by successive revivals, who became scholarly professors before becoming able journalists. And in the pastoral ministry, hundreds of ministers are found who received their call in some college awakening. They may have been converted in some community evangelistic campaign, but their decision to serve the community as a servant of God so often was made on a campus in revival.

The subject is inexhaustible. Not only have products of the college awakenings gone into the ministry, but numbers have entered government, business, industry, teaching and the medical profession. Evangelical Christianity has the least of all emphasis upon a difference between ministry and laity, insisting that one is as clear a call to service as the other, but adding a challenge about stewardship.

CHAPTER XXIV

THEOLOGY OF COLLEGE REVIVALS

Evangelical awakenings in collegiate communities shared a firm theological basis with the movement of Evangelical Christianity in general, expressed in a doctrinal statement of the Evangelical Alliance of 1846[1] This Alliance united a very significant number of leaders in the Anglican, Baptist, Congregational, Disciples, Friends, Lutheran, Methodist, Presbyterian and Reformed denominations, although by no means officially committing these church bodies whose own statements of faith were—in general terms—concordant.

The colleges that enjoyed the revivals of the early 1800s, the colleges and university associations that participated in the 1858 Awakening, the student associations affiliated with the Y.M.C.A. between 1890 and 1920, the interdenominational student volunteers of the same period, the early denominational chaplaincies in the universities, the colleges that experienced the awakenings of the twentieth century, the Inter-Varsity Christian Fellowship, Campus Crusade for Christ, and kindred organizations, all shared in common the very same doctrinal basis. Theologically considered, the student movements in the half-century following 1920 that continued to use the historic appellations of Evangelical Christian foundations were aberrant, not mainstream.

The first point of the 1846 declaration of the Evangelical Alliance concerned 'the Divine inspiration, authority, and sufficiency of the Holy Scriptures, and the right and duty of private judgment in the interpretation thereof.' This statement, made fifty years before the rise of fundamentalism, was uncluttered with passwords of the modernist-fundamentalist battleground. It simply recognized the Judeo-Christian Holy Scriptures as the Evangelical authority in matters of faith and practice, and was very widely accepted by Protestant denominations, of conservative or radical reformation.

The second point of the Evangelical Alliance concerned the Godhead, the transcendence and immanence of God being taken for granted, but the Deity of Christ and of the Holy Spirit clearly stated. There was no room for pantheism.

The Evangelical Alliance, in its third point, described human nature as incapable of auto-salvation, using the term 'depraved' but not in its modern and popular sense. The image of God in man was not denied, but his incapacity for salvation by his own efforts was proclaimed.

The fourth point of the Evangelical Alliance concerned the incarnation of the Son of God, His work of atonement for sinners of mankind, and His mediatorial intercession and reign. The fifth point announced the justification of the sinner by faith alone. The sixth point acknowledged the work of the Holy Spirit in the conversion and sanctification of the sinner who received the Good News.

The seventh point predicted the resurrection of the body, the judgment of the world by the Lord Jesus Christ, the eternal blessedness of those justified and the eternal loss of the impenitent.

The Evangelical Alliance proclaimed a view of Christian unity that led to practice of fraternal fellowship having the force of a major dogma. This view seemed to undergird the convictions and practice of the collegiate communities which welcomed college revivals. It occasioned no surprise when an awakening which moved a Presbyterian college in turn was communicated to a Baptist institution.

The importance of recognizing the theological harmony of college awakenings cannot be overstated. On one hand, no such revivals were ever reported in Roman Catholic institutions. Nor did they occur in Unitarian colleges — and not in Harvard except in times of Evangelical resurgence. In state and secular universities, awakenings occurred only in proportion to the strength of Evangelical organizations on campus. And yet, there was more hope of Evangelical awakening on a state campus than in a church-related college which had abandoned its evangelistic purpose. A university would welcome an Inter-Varsity chapter, along with a Hillel Foundation or Newman Club. A church-related institution, generally speaking, would do neither.

Within the experience of revivals or awakenings, college or community-related, there were certain doctrines emphasized in preaching and practice, doctrines seemingly forgotten by the Church at large in times of complacency.

Foremost was the doctrine of repentance. 'Metanoia' was the first word in the exhortations of John the Baptist, Jesus Christ, His twelve disciples, the Apostle Peter at Pentecost, and the Apostle Paul throughout his ministry.[2]

To the average American, the word 'repent' means to feel sorry—a popular notion which conflicts with Biblical use, for the word means simply 'change of thinking.' But a change of behavior is implied, and a change even of feeling. How such a revolutionary word, 'to change,' ever became so diluted as to mean 'to feel sorry' is a matter of conjecture.

The intense conviction of sin, attributed to the Holy Spirit, is calculated to bring sinners to repentance, or a willingness to change. This results in conversion, or turning to God. The believer expects a genuine conversion to God to result in regeneration, or being born again.[3] Some Protestants in theory hold that they have been regenerated in infant baptism, but even among these the experience of conversion is regarded as a reality which transforms the life.

What of conviction of sin among professing believers who would claim that they are already converted? The New Testament teaches that such repentance will issue in confession of sin, already discussed as a practical issue. The teaching is clear: if believers confess their sins, God is faithful and just to forgive their sins, and cleanse them from all unrighteousness.[4] Christ Himself urged His followers first to be reconciled with their brethren before bringing God acceptable worship. And He urged innocent parties to initiate steps towards reconciliation with others.[5]

The Hebrew Scriptures already taught that confession should be specific and thorough.[6] The New Testament dealt with public confession of faults—not detailed descriptions of sins—in urging confession of failings to the fellowship, to obtain effectual intercession, to be delivered.[7] How much therefore should be confessed in the open meeting? Just enough to enlist the prayers of people right with God. The public confession of secret or private sin may be dangerous.

231

Without a doubt, in the course of many college revivals there have been unwise confessions made in public. The Scriptures discourage the discussion openly of sins of the flesh.[8] Open confession of pride, or hypocrisy, or unbelief, presents no temptation to the hearer. But human beings have glands as well as minds, and the confession of carnal appetites or practices may indeed present temptation.

The Hebrew Scripture enjoined restitution of wrongs. It is clear that confession without all possible restitution is a sham. The stories of college revivals are replete with the instances of costly restitution.

The impact of college revivals always included witness, immediate, and, in many cases, lifelong. The concern that revived students felt for their neighbors and acquaintances was based partly upon a warm-hearted desire for their well-being, and partly upon a fear for their eternal destiny. This seemed to be the fountain-head of the evangelism at home and the missions abroad that issued from college revivals. There was no place for universalism in their vision of the world. Missionaries of the nineteenth century, lacking the advantages of modern courses in anthropology, were often insensitive to the values in other folk's culture. Today, the missionary is better equipped than overseas businessmen and other representatives abroad to adjust to alien cultures. Most of those known to the writer—who teaches classes of graduates—work under the direction of leaders of another race or culture. But none of them holds the view that one faith is as good as another. They have learned to appreciate truth in all religions, but their conviction is shared with their predecessors in the Student Volunteers that they have Someone unique to offer.

So the student revived or converted in an awakening sets forth to share his faith with any who will listen. His record in social concern is nothing to be ashamed of—for he has already engaged in almost every good work attempted by the secular foundations and welfare corps. He has built schools and colleges, hospitals and asylums, orphanages and homes for the destitute. He has given his charges self-respect, often applied by them to achieve self-government. But he places obedience to God first in his program.

However, the student Evangelical is committed to change by peaceful persuasion rather than bloody revolution. This is even more the case where a Constitution exists which is pledged to justice for all in the promotion of the general welfare, a Constitution which needs to be implemented—or amended by enlightened action—rather than overthrown. And the Evangelical faculty member cannot condone the egging of capricious undergraduates to violence, which results in destruction, injury, bloodshed or violent death. In 1776, and in 1861, most Evangelicals condoned the use of force to overthrow militant injustice, but only by lawful authority of the representatives of the people, not by raging mobs.

Evangelical scholars are committed to the principle of academic freedom in state universities and colleges, on the grounds that no political party in power has the right to forbid the pursuit of truth in any direction, as is done under the dictatorships of the right or the left. However, it is but elementary right that money contributed voluntarily by the advocates of total abstinence for the promotion of temperance should not be diverted to advertising the sale of rum. And it is likewise fitting that money contributed voluntarily by devoted Christian people for the promotion of Christian higher education should not be used for the propagation of atheism. It would seem simple for a faculty member in a Christian liberal arts college, who has signed a statement of faith but changed his mind about it, to resign and seek a place in a tax-supported institution where Christianity as a philosophy of life has no preference over atheism—though in actual fact, there are many secular schools where the anti-Christian philosophies enjoy the obvious advantage.

Since the publication of Darwin's thesis in 1859, the subject of evolution has been a controversial one in Christian colleges. There are thousands of scientists of Evangelical faith who have sought for a harmony between God's Word made known in Scripture and God's Work discovered in Science. They and their colleagues in Evangelical colleges are usually committed to harmonies such as progressive creation or theistic evolution, rejecting medieval notions for scientific reasons and atheistic philosophy for reasons scriptural, but nevertheless dedicated to pursuit of truth.

It is inevitable that this treatise should present a theological conclusion. The writer's study of the great evangelical awakenings of the nineteenth century has led him to conclude that these movements constitute an integral element in that segment of Christendom known as Evangelical Christianity. Evangelical awakenings are based upon New Testament doctrine and experience, and have occurred and recurred since the days of Wycliffe at Oxford, seven hundred years ago.

Evangelical awakenings in collegiate communities are not aberrations, but are regular expressions of mainline New Testament Christianity. That they were not common before the eighteenth century is simply explained by the rarity of Christian liberal arts colleges before that time, and that they are not common in other countries with a Protestant constituency may be credited to a similar reason. That they occurred in the oldest American colleges and universities during the last century but rarely occur in them now is due to the fact that these institutions are no longer Evangelical. Evangelical revivals are still occurring in the kind of higher educational institutions in which they occurred in times past.

Theologically considered, evangelical awakenings are possible while three factors remain in operation: the Word of God, for while the text of the New Testament is read, it seems to produce certain effects upon readers; the Church of God, more specifically believers in the New Testament as the final authority in faith and practice who personally have experienced these effects; and the Spirit of God, that divine Dynamic without Whom the phenomenon of evangelical awakening is unexplainable, and Whose purposes at home and abroad are so strikingly advanced thereby.

For a century and a half, Christian liberal arts colleges have been founded and have been liquidated. More and more, their sponsors have been finding them difficult to maintain in the face of state competition. But many of them are as lively as ever. If the Christian liberal arts college were to become obsolete, history shows that the forces of evangelical revival would continue to operate in little different form in the voluntary associations of believing Christian students. Who knows what another great awakening in the population at large may not achieve? It is certainly needed.

CHAPTER I: THE EVANGELICAL HERITAGE

1   A standard dictionary definition of the word 'Evangelical' is 'pertaining to the Gospel,' more particularly 'emphasizing the teachings and authority of the Scriptures (especially of the New Testament) in opposition to the institutional authority of the Church itself.' Evangelical Christianity stresses the importance of a personal experience of Christian realities.

2   Islamic primary education was generally poor, providing the rudiments of reading, writing and arithmetic along with learning the Quran and catechism. The Jews adapted themselves to the educational institutions of their hosts, and showed unusual brilliance in the fields of medicine and the sciences.

3   see W. Boyd, THE HISTORY OF WESTERN EDUCATION, pp. 52ff; cf. PROVERBS 1: 8;   6: 23;   12: 1;   ECCLESIASTES 12: 1.

4   PSALM 110: 10.

5   The Lord Jesus used straightforward lecturing, 'questions and answers,' parables, and recitation—which reflected the Hebrew practice of the day.

6   cf. Luke 4: 18 & Isaiah 61: 1.

7   cf. Mark 16: 15 & Matthew 28: 19-20.

8   Matthew 26: 35-45.   9   John 14: 12 & 16: 7.

10 see J. Smart, THE TEACHING MINISTRY OF THE CHURCH, passim.

11 M. Joynt, THE LIFE OF St. GALL, p. 15; & H. Rashdall, THE UNIVERSITIES OF EUROPE IN THE MIDDLE AGES, passim.

12 S. Derenzi, STORIA DEL SCUOLA MEDICA DI SALERNO.

13 G. Cassani, DELL'ANTICO STUDIO DI BOLOGNA.

14 R. Delegne,   L'UNIVERSITE DE PARIS, 1224-1244, & A. O. Norton, MEDIEVAL UNIVERSITIES, passim.

15 K. S. Latourette, A HISTORY OF THE EXPANSION OF CHRISTIANITY, Volume II, p. 390.

16 W. Boyd, THE HISTORY OF WESTERN EDUCATION, p. 186.

17 Martin Luther, LETTER TO THE BURGOMASTERS AND COUNCILLORS OF ALL TOWNS IN GERMAN LANDS, URGING THE ESTABLISHMENT & MAINTENANCE OF CHRISTIAN SCHOOLS, 1524; cf. W. Boyd, THE HISTORY OF WESTERN EDUCATION, p. 188.

18 F. V. N. Painter, LUTHER ON EDUCATION (Philadelphia, 1889).

19 see J. W. Richard, PHILIP MELANCHTHON, THE PRECEPTOR OF GERMANY; W. Boyd, THE HISTORY OF WESTERN EDUCATION, p. 191ff.

20 Not only academic degeneration occurred, but an upsurge of immorality in universities provoked Luther's wrath. It ran rampant till Pietism arose.

21 see Ulrich Zwingli, THE CHRISTIAN EDUCATION OF BOYS, 1523.

22 for example, in LEGES ACADEMICAE GENEVENSIS (John Calvin, 1559)

23 W. Boyd, THE HISTORY OF WESTERN EDUCATION, p. 200.

24 John Knox, THE WORKS OF JOHN KNOX, Volume II, pp. 209ff.

25 see M. W. Keatinge, COMENIUS, (1932).

26 J. A. Comenius (translated by M. W. Keatinge), THE GREAT DIDACTIC, (Second Edition), p. 66.

27 cf. W. Boyd, THE HISTORY OF WESTERN EDUCATION, p. 247; and John Locke, SOME THOUGHTS CONCERNING EDUCATION (edited by E. Daniel, London, 1880).

28 W. Boyd, THE HISTORY OF WESTERN EDUCATION, pp. 269ff.

29 S. E. Morison, THE FOUNDING OF HARVARD COLLEGE, passim.

30 H. B. Adams, THE COLLEGE OF WILLIAM AND MARY, pp. 11-12.

31 E. Oviatt, THE BEGINNINGS OF YALE, 1701-1726, passim.

CHAPTER II: THE EVANGELICAL REVIVAL

1   W. Boyd, THE HISTORY OF WESTERN EDUCATION, p. 281.
2   Edward Gibbon, MEMOIRS OF MY LIFE AND WRITINGS, in WORKS, 1796, Volume I, pp. 32–39.
3   P. J. Spener, PIA DESIDERIA, 1675. (The bibliography is extraordinary —seven volumes folio, sixty three quarto, seven octavo and forty six duo, which is something of a record.)
4   see H. E. F. Guericke, A. H. FRANCKE, 1827 (London 1837); cf. W. Boyd, THE HISTORY OF WESTERN EDUCATION, p. 283.
5   see P. Monroe, A TEXT-BOOK IN THE HISTORY OF EDUCATION, p. 498.
6   W. O. B. Allen & E. McClure, TWO HUNDRED YEARS: THE HISTORY OF THE SOCIETY FOR PROMOTING CHRISTIAN KNOWLEDGE, 1698-1898, pp. 61ff.
7   C. Birchenough, A HISTORY OF ELEMENTARY EDUCATION IN ENGLAND AND WALES, Third Edition, pp. 3ff.
8   W. Wordsworth, ADDRESS TO THE SCHOLARS OF THE VILLAGE SCHOOL, 1798.
9   I. Parker, DISSENTING ACADEMIES IN ENGLAND, pp. 2–9.
10   see W. Boyd, THE HISTORY OF WESTERN EDUCATION, p. 281, & I. Parker, DISSENTING ACADEMIES IN ENGLAND, pp. 43, 101.
11   M. G. Jones, THE CHARITY SCHOOL MOVEMENT, pp. 29ff.
12   cf. W. Boyd, THE HISTORY OF WESTERN EDUCATION, p. 282; and M. G. Jones, THE CHARITY SCHOOL MOVEMENT, p. 61.
13   M. G. Jones, THE CHARITY SCHOOL MOVEMENT, p. 347.
14   F. Rudolph, editor, ESSAYS ON EDUCATION IN THE EARLY REPUBLIC, passim.
15   D. Jones, THE LIFE AND TIMES OF GRIFFITH JONES, p. 4.
16   A. W. Morton, THE CONTRIBUTION OF THE EVANGELICAL REVIVAL TO THE PHILOSOPHY AND PRACTICE OF EDUCATION, unpublished doctoral thesis, University of Oxford, 1949, an excellent study but limited in scope to Britain.
17   WELCH PIETY (accounts of the Circulating Schools in Wales, published annually from 1740), edition of 1749-50, Cardiff, p. 65 & p. 80.
18   The figures are found in the accounts of the Circulating Schools in Wales— see WELCH PIETY, 1760-61, passim.
19   D. Jones, THE LIFE AND TIMES OF GRIFFITH JONES, p. 162.
20   WELCH PIETY (accounts of the Circulating Schools in Wales, published annually from 1740), edition of 1748-49, Cardiff, p. 113.
21   see F. A. Cavenagh, THE LIFE AND WORK OF GRIFFITH JONES, pp. 61–62.
22   C. Mather, THE DIARY OF COTTON MATHER, Part II, p. 347.
23   cf. A. P. Marvin, THE LIFE AND TIMES OF COTTON MATHER, p. 158.
24   C. P. Shedd, TWO CENTURIES OF STUDENT CHRISTIAN MOVEMENTS, pp. 6ff.
25   Jonathan Edwards, THE LIFE OF DAVID BRAINERD, (1764), p. 19.
26   C. P. Shedd, TWO CENTURIES OF STUDENT CHRISTIAN MOVEMENTS, p. 20.
27   see William Law, THE OXFORD METHODISTS: BEING AN ACCOUNT OF SOME YOUNG GENTLEMEN IN THAT CITY, Third Edition, 1738. (The pamphlet was published anonymously, but attributed to Law).

28 cf. J. S. Simon, THE REVIVAL OF RELIGION IN ENGLAND IN THE EIGHTEENTH CENTURY, pp. 167ff.
29 L. Tyerman, THE OXFORD METHODISTS, p. 159.
30 George Whitefield, A FURTHER ACCOUNT OF GOD'S DEALINGS WITH THE REV. MR. GEORGE WHITEFIELD (1747, edition Wale, 1905), p. 67.
31 see William Cowper, HOPE POEMS, London, 1841, Volume I, p. 124; & Whitefield's FURTHER ACCOUNT, p. 82.
32 L. Tyerman, THE LIFE OF THE REV. GEORGE WHITEFIELD, 1876-77, Volume I, p. 494.
33 see THE AUTOBIOGRAPHY OF BENJAMIN FRANKLIN, (edited by O.S. Coad), New York, 1929.
34 see A CONTINUATION OF THE REV. MR. WHITEFIELD'S JOURNAL, edition of 1829, pp. 83ff.
35 L. Tyerman, THE LIFE OF THE REV. GEORGE WHITEFIELD, Volume I, pp. 325ff.
36 see A CONTINUATION OF THE REV. MR. WHITEFIELD'S JOURNAL.
37 T. J. Wertenbaker, PRINCETON: 1746-1896, passim.
38 E. P. Cheney, HISTORY OF THE UNIVERSITY OF PENNSYLVANIA, 1740-1940.
39 A. D. Belden, GEORGE WHITEFIELD, THE AWAKENER, pp. 237-238.
40 J. H. van Amringe, A HISTORY OF COLUMBIA UNIVERSITY, 1754-1904.
41 W. H. S. Demarest, A HISTORY OF RUTGERS COLLEGE, 1766-1924; L. B. Richardson, A HISTORY OF DARTMOUTH COLLEGE; W. C. Bronson, THE HISTORY OF BROWN UNIVERSITY.
42 THE TESTIMONY OF THE PRESIDENT, PROFESSORS, TUTORS AND HEBREW INSTRUCTOR OF HARVARD COLLEGE IN CAMBRIDGE AGAINST THE REV. MR. GEORGE WHITEFIELD AND HIS CONDUCT, Boston, 1744; J. Gillies, editor, MEMOIRS OF THE LIFE of the Rev. GEORGE WHITEFIELD, p. 241.
43 J. Boswell, THE LIFE OF SAMUEL JOHNSON, edition of J. W. Crocker, London, 1876, p. 734.
44 John Wesley, WORKS, edition of 1872, Volume II, p. 301.
45 A. W. Morton, THE CONTRIBUTION OF THE EVANGELICAL REVIVAL TO THE PHILOSOPHY AND PRACTICE OF EDUCATION, unpublished doctoral thesis, University of Oxford, 1949.
46 John Wesley, WORKS, Volume I, p. 45.
47 A. H. Body, JOHN WESLEY AND EDUCATION, p. 54.
48 L. Tyerman, THE LIFE OF THE REV. GEORGE WHITEFIELD, 1890 edition, Volume I, pp. 191-192.
49 John Wesley, A PLAIN ACCOUNT OF KINGSWOOD SCHOOL, 1871.
50 see John Wesley's tract, INSTRUCTIONS FOR CHILDREN, London, 1743.
51 M. G. Jones, THE CHARITY SCHOOL MOVEMENT, p. 139.
52 cf. John Wesley, A PLAIN ACCOUNT OF KINGSWOOD SCHOOL, and A. H. Body, JOHN WESLEY AND EDUCATION, passim.
53 see E. H. Wright, THE MEANING OF ROUSSEAU, Oxford, 1929.
54 Francis Asbury and Thomas Coke, founders of Cokesbury College, were appointed by Wesley as superintendents of the Methodist societies in the United States. (see A. Lowrey, THE LIFE AND WORK OF FRANCIS ASBURY, New York, 1894; and S. Drew, THE LIFE OF THE REV. THOMAS COKE, LL.D., London, 1817 (p. 124).
55 J. T. McNeill, THE CHRISTIAN HOPE FOR WORLD SOCIETY, p. 221; J. A. Green, LIFE AND WORK OF PESTALOZZI, London, 1913.

NOTES

CHAPTER III: DESPAIR AND RECOVERY

1 cf. W. W. Sweet, REVIVALISM IN AMERICA, p. 117 & C. L. Thompson, TIMES OF REFRESHING, p. 68.
2 B. R. Lacy, REVIVALS IN THE MIDST OF THE YEARS, p. 65.
3 G. A. Koch, REPUBLICAN RELIGION AND THE CULT OF REASON, passim; L. A. Weigle, AMERICAN IDEALISM, p. 139.
4 F. Rudolph, THE AMERICAN COLLEGE AND UNIVERSITY, pp. 38-39; A. B. Strickland, THE GREAT AMERICAN REVIVAL, p. 35.
5 Timothy Dwight, TRAVELS, Volume IV, pp. 376ff.
6 A. B. Strickland, THE GREAT AMERICAN REVIVAL, p. 40.
7 Lyman Beecher, AUTOBIOGRAPHY, Volume I, p. 43.
8 A. B. Strickland, THE GREAT AMERICAN REVIVAL, p. 33.
9 F. Rudolph, THE AMERICAN COLLEGE AND UNIVERSITY, pp. 38-39, & A. B. Strickland, THE GREAT AMERICAN REVIVAL, p. 33.
10 S. E. Morison, THE CENTURIES OF HARVARD, p. 185.
11 F. Rudolph, THE AMERICAN COLLEGE AND UNIVERSITY, p. 38.
12 T. J. Wertenbaker, PRINCETON, 1746-1896, p. 156.
13 see C. P. Shedd, TWO CENTURIES OF STUDENT CHRISTIAN MOVEMENTS, pp. 20 & 53.
14 T. J. Wertenbaker, PRINCETON, 1746-1896, pp. 134-137.
15 cf. S. E. Morison, THREE CENTURIES OF HARVARD, p. 162, & T. J. Wertenbaker, PRINCETON, 1746-1896, p. 127.
16 W. W. Sweet, THE STORY OF RELIGION IN AMERICA, p. 224.
17 Bishop Provoost. An Episcopal historian considered the period as one of suspended animation—C. C. Tiffany, A HISTORY OF THE PROTESTANT EPISCOPAL CHURCH IN THE UNITED STATES OF AMERICA, p. 388.
18 W. W. Sweet, THE STORY OF RELIGION IN AMERICA, p. 224.
19 G. M. Trevelyan, ENGLISH SOCIAL HISTORY, p. 355.
20 see J. Edwin Orr, THE LIGHT OF THE NATIONS, pp. 29-35.
21 see Sverre Norborg, HANS NIELSEN HAUGE, for the most recent biography (in Norwegian). For the other Scandinavian countries, references are found in J. Edwin Orr, THE LIGHT OF THE NATIONS, pp. 38-39.
22 S. B. Halliday, THE CHURCH IN AMERICA AND ITS BAPTISMS OF FIRE, p. 386.
23 C. C. Cleveland, THE GREAT REVIVAL IN THE WEST, pp. 62ff; & C. A. Johnson, FRONTIER CAMP MEETING, passim.
24 W. E. Farndale, THE SECRET OF MOW COP, pp. 15-19; cf. Young & Ashton, BRITISH SOCIAL WORK IN THE NINETEENTH CENTURY, p. 35.
25 W. Carus, THE LIFE OF CHARLES SIMEON, passim.
26 A. Haldane, THE LIVES OF ROBERT & JAMES ALEXANDER HALDANE.
27 Ami Bost, L'HISTOIRE DU REVEIL RELIGIEUX DES EGLISES PROTESTANTES DE LA SUISSE ET DE LA FRANCE.
28 P. Scharpff, GESCHICHTE DER EVANGELISATION, pp. 121ff.
29 E. Molland, CHURCH LIFE IN NORWAY, pp. 73ff.
30 F. W. Horn, GRUNDTVIGS LIV OG GJERNING, Copenhagen, 1883.
31 Gunnar Westin, DEN KRISTNA FRIFORSAMLINGEN I NORDEN, pp. 24ff.
32 cf. J. Edwin Orr, EVANGELICAL AWAKENINGS IN AFRICA, Chapter III; & J. Edwin Orr, EVANGELICAL AWAKENINGS IN INDIA, Chapter II.
33 K. S. Latourette, A HISTORY OF THE EXPANSION OF CHRISTIANITY, Volume VI, Introduction.
34 W. W. Sweet, THE STORY OF RELIGION IN AMERICA, p. 205.

CHAPTER IV: COLLEGIATE AWAKENINGS, 1800—

1 B. R. Lacy, REVIVALS IN THE MIDST OF THE YEARS, pp. 68ff.
2 C. L. Thompson, TIMES OF REFRESHING, p. 79.
3 C. P. Shedd, TWO CENTURIES OF STUDENT CHRISTIAN MOVEMENTS, pp. 37ff.
4 RECORD BOOK, Theological Society, 24 April 1808, Dartmouth College MS.
5 Reuben Guild, EARLY RELIGIOUS HISTORY OF BROWN UNIVERSITY, (MS).
6 CONSTITUTION of the Saturday Evening Religious Society, 1802 (MS), Harvard University.
7 Timothy Dwight, THE NATURE AND DANGER OF INFIDEL PHILOSOPHY, 1797; A DISCOURSE ON SOME EVENTS OF THE LAST CENTURY, 1801; (New Haven).
8 Timothy Dwight, BACCALAUREATE SERMON, Yale College, 1796.
9 PRINCETON REVIEW, 1859, XXXI, p. 39; cf. Letter of 21 June 1815 from the Praying Society of Brown University to Bowdoin College, (MS) Brown University.
10 Careful scrutiny of primary and secondary sources has revealed not one instance of fanaticism.
11 cf. C. A. Johnson, THE FRONTIER CAMP MEETING, passim.
12 F. G. Beardsley, A HISTORY OF AMERICAN REVIVALS, p. 89.
13 JOURNAL OF XLI ANNUAL CONVENTION OF THE PROTESTANT EPISCOPAL CHURCH IN THE DIOCESE OF OHIO, p. 28.
14 F. Rudolph, THE AMERICAN COLLEGE AND UNIVERSITY, pp. 79-80; the cynics called it a Day of Whist, in times of spiritual decline.
15 cf. PRINCETON REVIEW, 1859, XXXI, pp. 28ff; & A. B. Strickland, THE GREAT AMERICAN REVIVAL, pp. 133ff.
16 H. B. Wright, TWO CENTURIES OF CHRISTIAN ACTIVITY AT YALE, pp. 64-65.
17 C. Durfee, A HISTORY OF WILLIAMS COLLEGE, p. 117.
18 C. P. Shedd, TWO CENTURIES OF STUDENT CHRISTIAN MOVEMENTS, pp. 74-80.
19 PRINCETON REVIEW, 1859, XXXI, p. 42.
20 cf. C. P. Shedd, TWO CENTURIES OF STUDENT CHRISTIAN MOVE- MENTS, p. 77, & PRINCETON REVIEW, 1859, XXXI, p. 41.
21 PRINCETON REVIEW, 1859, XXXI, p. 39.
22 F. Rudolph, THE AMERICAN COLLEGE AND UNIVERSITY, pp. 80ff.
23 PRINCETON REVIEW, 1859, XXXI, p. 42.
24 J. C. Pollock, A CAMBRIDGE MOVEMENT, Chapter I.
25 W. Carus, THE LIFE OF CHARLES SIMEON, passim.
26 L. E. Binns, THE EVANGELICAL MOVEMENT IN THE ENGLISH CHURCH, pp. 37ff; & G. M. Trevelyan, ENGLISH SOCIAL HISTORY, passim.
27 G. Smith, HENRY MARTYN, passim.
28 S. P. Carey, WILLIAM CAREY, FELLOW OF THE LINNAEAN SOCIETY.
29 see University of London CALENDAR, 1970-71.
30 A. B. Wentz, FLIEDNER THE FAITHFUL, p. 13.
31 P. Scharpff, GESCHICHTE DER EVANGELISATION, pp. 121ff.
32 A. Haldane, THE LIVES OF ROBERT & JAMES ALEXANDER HALDANE, pp. 375ff.
33 Ami Bost, L'HISTOIRE DU REVEIL RELIGIEUX DES EGLISES PRO- TESTANTES DE LA SUISSE ET DE LA FRANCE, passim.

CHAPTER V: THE IMPACT ON EDUCATION

1 W. Boyd, THE HISTORY OF WESTERN EDUCATION, p. 281.
2 A. Gregory, ROBERT RAIKES: JOURNALIST AND PHILANTHROPIST, p. 145; cf. J. H. Harris, ROBERT RAIKES: THE MAN AND HIS WORK.
3 E. W. Rice, THE SUNDAY SCHOOL MOVEMENT, 1780-1917, passim.
4 F. Smith, LIFE & WORK OF SIR JAMES KAY SHUTTLEWORTH, p. 6.
5 W. Roberts, MEMOIR OF THE LIFE OF HANNAH MORE, passim.
6 J. M. D. Meiklejohn, AN OLD EDUCATIONAL REFORMER, 1881.
7 D. Salmon, editor, THE PRACTICAL PARTS OF LANCASTER'S IMPROVEMENTS AND BELL'S EXPERIMENT: Introduction.
8 cf. J. M. D. Meiklejohn and D. Salmon, cited above.
9 D. Salmon, editor, LANCASTER AND BELL, Introduction.
10 D. Salmon, JOSEPH LANCASTER, p. 7.
11 J. H. Harris, ROBERT RAIKES: THE MAN AND HIS WORK, p. 324.
12 M. Lyte, A HISTORY OF ETON COLLEGE, pp. 52ff.
13 D. Salmon, JOSEPH LANCASTER, p. 5.
14 D. Salmon, editor, LANCASTER AND BELL, p. viii.
15 W. Corston, THE LIFE OF JOSEPH LANCASTER, p. 16.
16 D. Salmon, JOSEPH LANCASTER, passim.
17 W. Corston, THE LIFE OF JOSEPH LANCASTER, p. 11.
18 H. C. Barnard, A HISTORY OF ENGLISH EDUCATION, pp. 56ff.
19 D. Salmon, editor, LANCASTER AND BELL, Introduction.
20 D. Salmon, JOSEPH LANCASTER, pp. 55ff.
21 D. Salmon, editor, LANCASTER AND BELL, Introduction.
22 H. C. Barnard, A HISTORY OF ENGLISH EDUCATION, pp. 56ff.
23 HANSARD, Volume IX, 1178, 11 August 1807.
24 W. Boyd, THE HISTORY OF WESTERN EDUCATION, pp. 369ff.
25 H. C. Barnard, A HISTORY OF ENGLISH EDUCATION, pp. 56ff.
26 W. Boyd, THE HISTORY OF WESTERN EDUCATION, pp. 307, 361.
27 H. C. Barnard, A HISTORY OF ENGLISH EDUCATION, pp. 56ff.
28 This landmark leglislation closely followed the Evangelical Awakening of the 1860s in England, which gave an impetus to mass education.
29 F. D. Washburn, FIFTY YEARS ON: GROTON SCHOOL.
30 see DICTIONARY OF AMERICAN BIOGRAPHY, Volume XII, pp. 240ff; Volume III, pp. 74ff; Volume I, pp. 621ff; & K. S. Latourette, A HISTORY OF THE EXPANSION OF CHRISTIANITY, Volume IV, p. 416 & note.
31 K. S. Latourette, A HISTORY OF THE EXPANSION OF CHRISTIANITY, Volume IV, p. 417.
32 L. G. Bacon, A HISTORY OF AMERICAN CHRISTIANITY, pp. 243-246.
33 G. Spring, MEMOIRS OF SAMUEL J. MILLS, 1820.
34 L. G. Bacon, A HISTORY OF AMERICAN CHRISTIANITY, pp. 256.
35 F. Rudolph, THE AMERICAN COLLEGE AND UNIVERSITY, p. 57.
36 There were often tests for faculty and trustees.
37 F. Rudolph, THE AMERICAN COLLEGE AND UNIVERSITY, p. 53.
38 W. Havighurst, THE MIAMI YEARS, 1809-1959, pp. 11ff.
39 Osborne & Gronert, WABASH COLLEGE, 1832-1932, pp. 45ff.
40 D. G. Tewkesbury, THE FOUNDING OF AMERICAN COLLEGES AND UNIVERSITIES BEFORE THE CIVIL WAR, passim.
41 K. S. Latourette, A HISTORY OF THE EXPANSION OF CHRISTIANITY, Volume IV, p. 221; D. G. Tewkesbury, op. cit., p. 69.
42 A. D. Waller, A SHORT HISTORY OF THE UNIVERSITY OF LONDON.

CHAPTER VI: EDUCATIONAL PIONEERING OVERSEAS

1 T. C. Richards, THE LIFE OF SAMUEL J. MILLS, pp. 30ff.
2 G. Spring, MEMOIRS OF SAMUEL J. MILLS, pp. 38ff.
3 W. Ellis, POLYNESIAN RESEARCHES, Volume I, pp. 248ff.
4 E. W. Dwight, MEMOIRS OF HENRY OBOOKIAH, New Haven, 1818.
5 H. Bingham, A RESIDENCE OF TWENTY-ONE YEARS IN THE SAND-WICH ISLANDS, pp. 57ff.
6 R. Lovett, THE HISTORY OF THE LONDON MISSIONARY SOCIETY, Volume I, pp. 122ff, 208ff.
7 R. Anderson, A HISTORY OF THE HAWAIIAN MISSION, pp. 48f; for refutation of James Michener, see CHRISTIAN LIFE, June 1967.
8 B. M. Brain, THE TRANSFORMATION OF HAWAII, pp. 113ff.
9 W. J. van der Merwe, THE DEVELOPMENT OF MISSIONARY ATTITUDES IN THE DUTCH REFORMED CHURCH IN SOUTH AFRICA, pp. 73ff.
10 J. du Plessis, A HISTORY OF CHRISTIAN MISSIONS IN SOUTH AFRICA, pp. 50ff, & R. Lovett, HISTORY OF THE L.M.S., Volume I, passim.
11 D. J. Kotze, editor, LETTERS OF THE AMERICAN MISSIONARIES, 1835-1838, p. 33.
12 W. Canton, HISTORY OF THE BRITISH AND FOREIGN BIBLE SOCIETY, Volume II, pp. 84ff, 92ff, & 347ff.
13 see J. Thomson, LETTERS ON THE MORAL AND RELIGIOUS STATE OF SOUTH AMERICA, passim.
14 K. G. Grubb, THE WEST COAST REPUBLICS OF SOUTH AMERICA, pp. 69, 77.
15 W. Canton, BRITISH & FOREIGN BIBLE SOCIETY, Volume II, pp. 347ff
16 see G. Smith, HENRY MARTYN, & S. P. Carey, WILLIAM CAREY.
17 J. C. Marshman, LIFE & TIMES OF CAREY, MARSHMAN & WARD.
18 see Charles Grant, OBSERVATIONS ON THE STATE OF SOCIETY AMONG THE ASIATIC SUBJECTS OF GREAT BRITAIN; K. Ingham, REFORMERS IN INDIA, pp. 58-59; J. Richter, A HISTORY OF MISSIONS IN INDIA, p. 192.
19 M. R. Paranjpe, A SOURCE BOOK OF MODERN INDIAN EDUCATION, 1797-1902, p. viii.
20 Nurullah & Naik, A HISTORY OF EDUCATION IN INDIA, p. 165.
21 K. Ingham, REFORMERS IN INDIA, p. 59.
22 MISSIONARY REGISTER, Madras, 1819, pp. 106, 107; 1828, pp. 81 & 88.
23 K. Ingham, REFORMERS IN INDIA, p. 73.
24 cf. J. R. Fleming, A HISTORY OF THE CHURCH IN SCOTLAND, p. 50.
25 W. Paton, THE LIFE OF ALEXANDER DUFF, p. 59.
26 see J. Edwin Orr, EVANGELICAL AWAKENINGS IN INDIA, pp. 23-24.
27 K. Ingham, REFORMERS IN INDIA, p. 96.
28 P. Hartog, SOME ASPECTS OF INDIAN EDUCATION, p. 6.
29 Nurullah & Naik, HISTORY OF EDUCATION IN INDIA, p. 162; H. Sharp, SELECTIONS FROM EDUCATIONAL RECORDS, Part I; M. A. Sherring, A HISTORY OF PROTESTANT MISSIONS IN INDIA, pp. 442-447.
30 M. A. Sherring, A HISTORY OF PROTESTANT MISSIONS IN INDIA, p. 75.
31 H. Sharp, SELECTIONS FROM EDUCATIONAL RECORDS, Part II, p. 44.
32 Evangelicals in the United States had switched from promotion of elementary education to the founding of colleges.
33 J. Richter, A HISTORY OF PROTESTANT MISSIONS IN INDIA, pp. 192ff.
34 Nurullah & Naik, A HISTORY OF EDUCATION IN INDIA, p. 170.

CHAPTER VII: THE MID-CENTURY DECLINE

1   H. D. Sheldon, THE HISTORY AND PEDAGOGY OF AMERICAN STUDENT SOCIETIES, 1901; see also BAIRD'S MANUAL: AMERICAN COLLEGE FRATERNITIES, 1940. These works were written before the decline of the fraternities and sororities in the turbulent 1960s.

2   F. Rudolph, THE AMERICAN COLLEGE AND UNIVERSITY, p. 146.

3   For two hundred and fifty years, from the formation of the Private Meeting at Harvard College till the series of college awakenings in 1970, confession of sin was a mark of the outbreak of spiritual revival on college campus. (A discussion of the subject is made available in the concluding chapters.)

4   F. Rudolph, THE AMERICAN COLLEGE AND UNIVERSITY, p. 147.

5   J. Edwin Orr, THE LIGHT OF THE NATIONS, Chapter XI, 'Dissension and Decline.' (This is Volume VIII in the Paternoster Series, edited by Prof. F. F. Bruce of the University of Manchester).

6   F. G. Beardsley, A HISTORY OF AMERICAN REVIVALS, pp. 213ff.

7   G. Spring, MEMOIRS OF SAMUEL J. MILLS, passim. There is also an extensive bibliography in T. C. Richards, SAMUEL J. MILLS, 1906.

8   J. H. Fairchild, A HISTORY OF OBERLIN, p. 22.

9   W. S. Tyler, A HISTORY OF AMHERST, pp. 246-250.

10   J. H. Fairchild, OBERLIN: THE COLONY AND THE COLLEGE, pp. 53-56, 64.

11   F. D. Nichol, THE MIDNIGHT CRY, is cited to disprove the charges of other excesses made against the Adventist enthusiasts. The Coming predicted for 1844 has been spiritualized—the Investigate Judgment doctrine.

12   The years between 1843 and 1846 have been described as years of real spiritual dearth in the colleges, as (for example) in F. Rudolph, MARK HOPKINS AND THE LOG: WILLIAMS COLLEGE, p. 118.

13   F. Rudolph, MARK HOPKINS AND THE LOG: WILLIAMS COLLEGE, p. 99.

14   W. S. Tyler, PRAYER FOR COLLEGES, p. 136.

15   Of the total of 745 students professing faith in these New England colleges—mid-fifties statistics—348 were preparing for the ministry.

16   Harvard College was still dominated by its Unitarian professors in the 1850 classes. See S. E. Morison, THREE CENTURIES OF HARVARD, p. 244.

17   F. Rudolph, MARK HOPKINS AND THE LOG: WILLIAMS COLLEGE, p. 126.

18   E. M. Coulter, COLLEGE LIFE IN THE OLD SOUTH, pp. 82-83.

19   C. H. Rammelkamp, ILLINOIS COLLEGE: A CENTENNIAL HISTORY, 1829-1929, p. 80; see F. Rudolph, THE AMERICAN COLLEGE AND UNIVERSITY, pp. 76-77.

20   F. G. Beardsley, A HISTORY OF AMERICAN REVIVALS, p. 216. Each account of the awakening to follow has stressed the general prosperity.

21   For a secular account of the economic conditions, see H. V. Faulkner, in AMERICAN ECONOMIC HISTORY, p. 217.

22   F. G. Beardsley, A HISTORY OF AMERICAN REVIVALS, p. 217. Other manufacturing cities were severely hit.

23   This contemporary opinion was cited in THE NOON PRAYER MEETING, by T. W. Chambers (p. 284).

24   J. Edwin Orr, THE LIGHT OF THE NATIONS, Chapter XII, described as the 'American Hour of Prayer.' It is surely strange that for one hundred and twenty years, no standard work on the 1858 Awakening appeared.

CHAPTER VIII: THE 1858-59 AWAKENING

1 H. S. Smith, R. T. Handy & L. A. Loetscher, AMERICAN CHRISTIANITY, Volume II, p. 64.
2 cf. W. G. McLoughlin, MODERN REVIVALISM, p. 163, & J. Edwin Orr, THE LIGHT OF THE NATIONS, p. 103.
3 NEW YORK DAILY TRIBUNE, 24 February 1858.
4 NEW YORK HERALD, 22 March 1858.
5 J. Shaw, TWELVE YEARS IN AMERICA, pp. 182-184.
6 CHRISTIAN ADVOCATE AND JOURNAL, New York, 3 June 1858.
7 THE UNITED STATES CENSUS, 1910, Volume I, p. 127, gives the figures 23,191,876 for 1850 and 31,443,321 for 1860.
8 cf. W. A. Candler, GREAT REVIVALS AND THE GREAT REPUBLIC, pp. 215-216, & J. Edwin Orr, THE LIGHT OF THE NATIONS, p. 165.
9 C. P. McIlvaine, BISHOP McILVAINE on the REVIVAL OF RELIGION, 1858.
10 see Address of the Rev. Morgan Dix, condemning the Revival as occurring among those, who (by their own choice) were without Episcopal order and government, THE EVANGELIST, New York, 8 April 1858.
11 see W. A. Candler, GREAT REVIVALS AND THE GREAT REPUBLIC, pp. 222-223.
12 W. W. Sweet, REVIVALISM IN AMERICA, p. 160.
13 C. P. Shedd, TWO CENTURIES OF STUDENT CHRISTIAN MOVEMENTS.
14 see Chapters V, VI & VII, and index of C. P. Shedd's work.
15 F. Rudolph, THE AMERICAN COLLEGE AND UNIVERSITY, p. 502.
16 THE EVANGELIST, New York, 19 November 1857.
17 OBERLIN EVANGELIST, 28 April 1858.
18 D. G. Tewkesbury, THE FOUNDING OF AMERICAN COLLEGES AND UNIVERSITIES BEFORE THE CIVIL WAR, p. 69.
19 F. Rudolph, THE AMERICAN COLLEGE AND UNIVERSITY, p. 83.
20 NATIONAL INTELLIGENCER, Washington, D.C., 20 March 1858.
21 see CONGREGATIONAL QUARTERLY, January 1859, and CHRISTIAN ADVOCATE AND JOURNAL, New York, 15 July 1858.
22 J. Shaw, TWELVE YEARS IN AMERICA, pp. 182-184.
23 CHRISTIAN ADVOCATE AND JOURNAL, 13 May 1858, & W. C. Conant, NARRATIVE OF REMARKABLE CONVERSIONS, pp. 379-380; OBERLIN EVANGELIST, 5 May 1858, & EVANGELICAL REPOSITORY, June 1858.
24 THE EVANGELIST, New York, 22 April 1858.
25 W. C. Conant, NARRATIVE OF REMARKABLE CONVERSIONS, pp. 379-380; THE EVANGELIST, New York, 11 March & 8 July 1858.
26 NEW YORK TRIBUNE, 15 March; OBERLIN EVANGELIST, 31 March 1858; W. C. Conant, NARRATIVE OF REMARKABLE CONVERSIONS, p. 429.
27 THE EVANGELIST, New York, 25 March 1858.
28 W. C. Conant, NARRATIVE OF REMARKABLE CONVERSIONS, p. 429.
29 THE EVANGELIST, New York, 15, 22 & 29 April; OBERLIN EVANGELIST, 28 April & 12 May 1858.
30 EVANGELICAL REPOSITORY, June 1858, pp. 31ff; CONGREGATIONAL YEAR BOOK, 1859, pp. 147ff.
31 THE EVANGELIST, New York, 29 April 1858.
32 S. E. Morison, THREE CENTURIES OF HARVARD, 1636-1936, pp. 244-5.
33 THE EVANGELIST, New York, 11 March; CHRISTIAN REGISTER, 3 April; MONTHLY RELIGIOUS MAGAZINE, 1858, pp. 333-356.

34   THE EVANGELIST, New York, 15 & 22 April 1858; see F. D. Huntington, PERMANENT REALITIES OF RELIGION AND THE PRESENT RELIGIOUS INTEREST, Boston, 1858.
35   A. S. Huntington, MEMOIRS & LETTERS OF F. D. HUNTINGTON, 1906.
36   CONGREGATIONAL QUARTERLY, January 1858.
37   PRESBYTERIAN MAGAZINE, June 1858.
38   OBERLIN EVANGELIST, 28 April 1858; EVANGELICAL REPOSITORY, June 1858, pp. 31ff; CHRISTIAN ADVOCATE AND JOURNAL, New York, 13 May 1858; THE EVANGELIST, New York, 22 April 1858.
39   THE EVANGELIST, New York, 10 June 1858; CONGREGATIONAL YEAR BOOK, 1859, pp. 147ff; cf. Reynolds, Fisher & Wright, TWO CENTURIES OF RELIGIOUS ACTIVITY AT YALE, passim.
40   W. C. Conant, NARRATIVE OF REMARKABLE CONVERSIONS, pp. 369ff.
41   NATIONAL INTELLIGENCER, Washington, D.C., 23 March 1858; see also W. C. Conant, NARRATIVE OF REMARKABLE CONVERSIONS, p. 372.
42   OBERLIN EVANGELIST, 28 April 1858.
43   THE EVANGELIST, New York, 25 February 1858.
44   cf. C. E. Allison, A HISTORICAL SKETCH OF HAMILTON COLLEGE, passim, & THE EVANGELIST, New York, 22 July 1858.
45   W. C. Conant, NARRATIVE OF REMARKABLE CONVERSIONS, p. 368.
46   cf. W. H. S. Demarest, A HISTORY OF RUTGERS COLLEGE, 1766-1924, & W. C. Conant's NARRATIVE, pp. 432-433.
47   THE EVANGELIST, New York, 22 April 1858.
48   C. P. Shedd, TWO CENTURIES OF STUDENT CHRISTIAN MOVEMENTS, pp. 127-128.
49   W. F. P. Noble, A CENTURY OF GOSPEL WORK, p. 420; EVANGELICAL CHRISTENDOM, London, 1858, pp. 177-178.
50   CHRISTIAN ADVOCATE AND JOURNAL, 6 May 1858; W. F. P. Noble, A CENTURY OF GOSPEL WORK, p. 421.
51   EVANGELICAL CHRISTENDOM, 1858, pp. 177-178.
52   W. F. P. Noble, A CENTURY OF GOSPEL WORK, p. 422.
53   R. E. Francis, 'The Religious Revival of 1858 in Philadelphia,' in LXX, PENNSYLVANIA MAGAZINE OF HISTORY AND BIOGRAPHY, January 1946, p. 72; see 5th Annual Report, Y.M.C.A. Philadelphia, 1860, p. 28.
54   EVANGELICAL REPOSITORY, June 1858, pp. 31ff.
55   A. Godbold, THE CHURCH COLLEGE IN THE OLD SOUTH, p. 117.
56   THE EVANGELIST, 22 April 1858; A. Godbold, THE CHURCH COLLEGE IN THE OLD SOUTH, pp. 113, 142.
57   OBERLIN EVANGELIST, 12 May 1858.
58   T. L. Smith, REVIVALISM AND SOCIAL REFORM, p. 153.
59   C. G. Finney, MEMOIRS, 1908 edition, p. 444.
60   F. G. Beardsley, A HISTORY OF AMERICAN REVIVALS, pp. 227-228.
61   W. A. Candler, GREAT REVIVALS AND THE GREAT REPUBLIC, p. 216.
62   PRESBYTERIAN MAGAZINE, June 1858.
63   R. P. Brooks, THE UNIVERSITY OF GEORGIA, p. 43.
64   OBERLIN EVANGELIST, 28 April 1858; cf. A. P. Tankersley, COLLEGE LIFE AT OLD OGLESTHORPE, p. 147.
65   see H. M. Bullock, A HISTORY OF EMORY UNIVERSITY, p. 98; E. M. Coulter, COLLEGE LIFE IN THE OLD SOUTH, pp. 162-165.
66   THE EVANGELIST, New York, 17 June 1858.
67   A. Godbold, THE CHURCH COLLEGE IN THE OLD SOUTH, p. 142; & K. P. Battle, HISTORY of the UNIVERSITY of NORTH CAROLINA, p. 691.

68 THE EVANGELIST, New York, 17 June 1858.
69 see C. P. Shedd, TWO CENTURIES OF STUDENT CHRISTIAN MOVE-MENTS, pp. 98ff.
70 C. H. Hopkins, HISTORY OF THE Y.M.C.A. IN NORTH AMERICA, p. 38.
71 Y.M.C.A. JOURNAL, V: pp. 202-205 (January 1860).
72 W. C. Conant, NARRATIVE OF REMARKABLE CONVERSIONS, pp. 374 & 434.
73 T. W. Chambers, THE NOON PRAYER MEETING, pp. 196-197.
74 THE EVANGELIST, New York, 20 May 1858.
75 C. P. Shedd, TWO CENTURIES OF STUDENT CHRISTIAN MOVEMENTS, pp. 95ff.
76 J. Shaw, TWELVE YEARS IN AMERICA, pp. 182-184; PRESBYTERIAN MAGAZINE, June 1858.
77 THE EVANGELIST, New York, 3 June 1858.
78 G. W. Chessman, DENISON: THE STORY OF AN OHIO COLLEGE, p. 139.
79 THE EVANGELIST, New York, 15 July 1858. Besides Miami in Ohio, there were awakenings at Wabash College in Indiana, and Illinois College.
80 CHICAGO DAILY PRESS, 25 March 1858, and following issues.
81 THE EVANGELIST, New York, 4 March 1858.
82 H. I. Hester, A HISTORY OF WILLIAM JEWELL COLLEGE, p. 33.
83 THE EVANGELIST, New York, 24 June 1858, and prior issues.
84 W. W. Ferrier, ORIGIN AND DEVELOPMENT OF THE UNIVERSITY OF CALIFORNIA, p. 273.
85 THE EVANGELIST, New York, 8 July 1858.
86 F. Rudolph, THE AMERICAN COLLEGE AND UNIVERSITY, p. 312—the woman's college 'most closely resembling a good man's college.' See THE EVANGELIST, 1 July 1858.
87 The encouraging progress of the raising of funds for the projected University of Chicago is cited in THE EVANGELIST, 12 August 1858.
88 C. P. McIlvaine, BISHOP McILVAINE ON THE REVIVAL OF RELIGION, New York, 1858.
89 A. Godbold, THE CHURCH COLLEGE OF THE OLD SOUTH, p. 137.
90 J. T. Carson, GOD'S RIVER IN SPATE, Belfast, 1958; J. Edwin Orr, THE SECOND EVANGELICAL AWAKENING IN BRITAIN, Chapter II.
91 Eifion Evans, WHEN HE IS COME, Bala, 1959; J. Edwin Orr, THE SECOND EVANGELICAL AWAKENING IN BRITAIN, Chapters III & IV.
92 J. Edwin Orr, THE LIGHT OF THE NATIONS, Chapter XVIII.
93 J. Edwin Orr, THE SECOND EVANGELICAL AWAKENING IN BRITAIN, pp. 209ff.
94 THE NONCONFORMIST, London, 30 November 1859; THE RECORD, London, 5 December 1859 & 2 January 1860; THE FREEMAN, London, 7 December 1859.
95 C. E. Wood, MEMOIR AND LETTERS OF CANON HAY AITKEN, pp. 76ff.
96 THE REVIVAL, 3 March 1863; see J. B. Lancelot, FRANCIS JAMES CHAVASSE, pp. 26-27; A. C. Downer, A CENTURY OF EVANGELICAL RELIGION IN OXFORD, passim; G. I. F. Thomson, THE OXFORD PASTORATE, Foreword; J. B. Harford & F. C. Macdonald, HANDLEY CARR GLYN MOULE, p. 14.
97 J. C. Pollock, A CAMBRIDGE MOVEMENT, passim.
98 The Inter-Varsity movement entered the United States from Canada in 1940.
99 THE FREEMAN, 28 September 1859; J. W. Bready, DR. BARNARDO: PHYSICIAN, PIONEER, PROPHET, passim.

CHAPTER IX: POST-1860 OVERSEAS IMPACT

1   cf. C. P. Shedd, TWO CENTURIES OF STUDENT CHRISTIAN MOVE-MENTS, passim; K. S. Latourette, A HISTORY OF THE EXPANSION OF CHRISTIANITY, Volume IV, p. 81, 101, etc.

2   J. Hudson Taylor went to China, John Clough to India, George Grenfell to the Congo, and Ashbel Green Simonton to Brazil. The list is inexhaustible —as a cursory glance through biographies would confirm. James Thoburn became the missionary bishop of Southern Asia; James Chalmers was the martyred missionary to the South Seas.

3   M. W. Retief, HERLEWINGS IN ONS GESKIEDENIS, Chapters IV & V, & W. Taylor, CHRISTIAN ADVENTURES IN SOUTH AFRICA, passim; see also J. Edwin Orr, EVANGELICAL AWAKENINGS IN AFRICA.

4   J. Whiteside, HISTORY OF THE WESLEYAN METHODIST CHURCH IN SOUTH AFRICA, passim.

5   United Nations figures of percentages of population in school in Africa and South African statistics based on race indicate that South Africa—and its enclave, Lesotho—enjoy the highest school attendance among all blacks in Africa, and exceed the proportion reported from North African states, despite their centuries of civilization. Southern African progress must be attributed to the work of the missions rather than government action.

6   J. S. Dennis, CHRISTIAN MISSIONS AND SOCIAL PROGRESS, Volume II, p. 69.

7   J. H. Speke, WHAT LED TO THE DISCOVERY OF THE SOURCE OF THE NILE, p. 366.

8   E. Stock, HISTORY OF THE CHURCH MISSIONARY SOCIETY, Volume III, pp. 410-412; cf. S. C. Neill, A HISTORY OF CHRISTIAN MISSIONS, p. 385.

9   S. C. Neill, A HISTORY OF CHRISTIAN MISSIONS, p. 306.

10   J. Richter, A HISTORY OF MISSIONS IN INDIA, pp. 346ff.

11   K. Ingham, REFORMERS IN INDIA; Lal Behari Day, RECOLLECTIONS OF ALEXANDER DUFF, AND THE MISSION COLLEGE WHICH HE FOUNDED AT CALCUTTA, passim. See also G. Smith, THE LIFE OF ALEXANDER DUFF; W. Paton, ALEXANDER DUFF, PIONEER OF MISSIONARY EDUCATION.

12   Mrs. W. I. Chamberlain, FIFTY YEARS IN FOREIGN FIELDS, the work of the Reformed Church in America, in China, Japan, India, Arabia, etc, pp. 24-25.

13   M. A. Sherring, THE INDIAN CHURCH DURING THE GREAT REBELLION, p. 218.

14   J. Richter, A HISTORY OF MISSIONS IN INDIA, pp. 347ff.

15   Mrs. R. Hoskins, CLARA A. SWAIN, M.D., FIRST MEDICAL MISSIONARY TO THE WOMEN OF THE ORIENT, passim.

16   C. Reynolds, PUNJAB PIONEER: DR. EDITH BROWN; W. Wanless, AN AMERICAN DOCTOR AT WORK IN INDIA; M. P. Jeffrey, DR. IDA: INDIA, passim. (The writer was acquainted with only the last-named, Dr. Ida Scudder, having stayed as a guest in her home in Vellore)

17   Christian Medical Association, TALES FROM THE INNS OF HEALING, p. 144.

18   C. B. Firth, AN INTRODUCTION TO INDIAN CHURCH HISTORY, p. 203.

19   see Sam Higginbotham, THE GOSPEL AND THE PLOW; G. R. Hess, SAM HIGGINBOTHAM OF ALLAHABAD, 1967.

20 W. S. Hunt, THE ANGLICAN CHURCH IN TRAVANCORE AND COCHIN, pp. 154ff.
21 A. D. Lindsay, CHRISTIAN HIGHER EDUCATION IN INDIA, p. 298.
22 Nurullah & Naik, A HISTORY OF EDUCATION IN INDIA, pp. 881ff.
23 K. S. Latourette, A HISTORY OF CHRISTIAN MISSIONS IN CHINA, pp. 441-451.
24 J. J. Morgan, THE '59 REVIVAL IN WALES, pp. 85-86; K. S. Latourette, A HISTORY OF THE EXPANSION OF CHRISTIANITY, Volume VI, p. 318; see also E. W. Price-Evans, TIMOTHY RICHARD.
25 C. H. Peake, NATIONALISM AND EDUCATION IN MODERN CHINA, pp. 43, 44; cf. W. E. Soothill, TIMOTHY RICHARD OF CHINA.
26 see Baron Dairoku Kikuchi, JAPANESE EDUCATION. (a national view); W. E. Griffis, HEPBURN OF JAPAN, passim.
27 W. E. Griffis, A MAKER OF THE NEW ORIENT, SAMUEL ROBBINS BROWN, pp. 137ff.
28 W. E. Griffis, VERBECK OF JAPAN, passim.
29 Keenleyside & Thomas, A HISTORY OF JAPANESE EDUCATION, p. 258.
30 A. S. Hardy, LIFE AND LETTERS OF JOSEPH HARDY NEESIMA, pp. 188ff. J. D. Davis, A SKETCH OF THE LIFE OF REV. JOSEPH HARDY NEESIMA, Second Edition, 1894.
31 Otis Cary, A HISTORY OF CHRISTIANITY IN JAPAN, Volume II, p. 209.
32 MINUTES of the Hawaiian Evangelistic Association, 1858-1862; J. Rauws et al, THE NETHERLANDS INDIES, pp. 53-54; W. Ellis, THE MARTYR CHURCH OF MADAGASCAR, pp. 373ff; WESLEYAN CHRONICLE, 1860 statistics, December 1860, p. 269 (Melbourne).
33 J. J. Considine, NEW HORIZONS IN LATIN AMERICA, p. 241; P. R. Rivera, INSTITUCIONES PROTESTANTES EN MEXICO, pp. 152-153; these provide a valuable Roman Catholic view, reflecting the toleration, and even sympathy, prevailing in the later twentieth century.
34 Braga & Grubb, THE REPUBLIC OF BRAZIL, pp. 50ff; S. R. Gammon, THE EVANGELICAL INVASION OF BRAZIL, pp. 111ff.
35 F. de Azevedo, BRAZILIAN CULTURE, p. 419.
36 W. R. Wheeler, MODERN MISSIONS IN CHILE AND BRAZIL, Chapter IX. (The Presbyterians maintained their educational traditions).
37 Braga & Grubb, THE REPUBLIC OF BRAZIL, pp. 33, 61, 76, etc.
38 W. R. Wheeler, MODERN MISSIONS IN CHILE AND BRAZIL, Chapter IX.
39 quoted in W. E. Browning, THE RIVER PLATE REPUBLICS, p. 72.
40 Lauro Bretones, REDEMOINHOS DO SUL: UM ANO DE REAVIVA-MENTO NO BRASIL COM O DR. J. EDWIN ORR, passim.
41 cf. Martinez & Lewandowski, THE ARGENTINE IN THE TWENTIETH CENTURY, p. 120.
42 see J. G. Guerra, SARMIENTO, SU VIDA Y SUS OBRAS, passim.
43 W. E. Browning, THE RIVER PLATE REPUBLICS, pp. 67-68.
44 A. H. Luiggi, SIXTY-FIVE VALIANTS, pp. 17, 35ff.
45 J. B. Zubiaur, SINOPSIS DE LA EDUCACION EN LA REPUBLICA ARGENTINA, pp. 31-44.
46 Browning, Ritchie & Grubb, THE WEST COAST REPUBLICS OF SOUTH AMERICA, pp. 29ff.
47 Penzotti came north from the Argentine; see Browning, Ritchie & Grubb, THE WEST COAST REPUBLICS OF SOUTH AMERICA, pp. 79, 80.
48 M. Rankin, TWENTY YEARS AMONG THE MEXICANS, pp. 88ff.
49 Camargo & Grubb, RELIGION IN THE REPUBLIC OF MEXICO, p. 44.

CHAPTER X: THE MULTIPLYING FELLOWSHIPS

1   E. D. Eddy, COLLEGES FOR OUR LAND AND TIME, passim.
2   see J. W. Jones, CHRIST IN THE CAMP, OR RELIGION IN LEE'S ARMY; W. W. Bennett, THE GREAT REVIVAL IN THE SOUTHERN ARMIES, passim.
3   W. W. Sweet, THE STORY OF RELIGION IN AMERICA, pp. 317ff.
4   L. Moss, ANNALS OF THE UNITED STATES CHRISTIAN COMMISSION.
5   R. C. Morse, 'Mr. Moody and the Y.M.C.A.,' in ASSOCIATION MEN, February 1900, pp. 81-96.
6   W. W. Bennett, THE GREAT REVIVAL IN THE SOUTHERN ARMIES.
7   J. W. Jones, CHRIST IN THE CAMP, p. 122.
8   CATALOGUE OF THE UNIVERSITY OF ROCHESTER, 1864.
9   C. P. Shedd, TWO CENTURIES OF STUDENT CHRISTIAN MOVEMENTS, p. 105.
10 Y.M.C.A. QUARTERLY, May 1868, p. 94.
11 C. P. Shedd, STUDENT CHRISTIAN MOVEMENTS, pp. 110-111.
12 J. B. Lancelot, FRANCIS JAMES CHAVASSE, pp. 26-27.
13 J. C. Pollock, A CAMBRIDGE MOVEMENT, p. 25.
14 Harford & Macdonald, HANDLEY CARR GLYN MOULE, p. 14.
15 J. C. Pollock, A CAMBRIDGE MOVEMENT, pp. 41ff.
16 W. R. Moody, THE LIFE OF DWIGHT L. MOODY, pp. 182ff, 197ff.
17 see issues of THE CHRISTIAN, London, for September, October and December, 1874; January, February & onward, 1875.
18 W. R. Moody, THE LIFE OF DWIGHT L. MOODY, pp. 223ff.
19 L. D. Wishard, 'The Beginning of the Students' Era in Christian History,' pp. 1-24 (MS), in Y.M.C.A. Historical Library.
20 see J. McCosh, THE ULSTER REVIVAL AND ITS PHYSIOLOGICAL ACCIDENTS, London, 1859 (Evangelical Alliance Address, Belfast, 1859)
21 C. P. Shedd, STUDENT CHRISTIAN MOVEMENTS, p. 127.
22 see issues of January 1876, PHILADELPHIA INQUIRER.
23 THE WATCHMAN, Y.M.C.A., Chicago, 1 November 1879.
24 L. D. Wishard, 'The Beginning of the Students' Era in Christian History,' pp. 52-53, (MS) Y.M.C.A. Historical Library; cf. H. Notter, THE ORIGINS OF THE FOREIGN POLICY OF WOODROW WILSON, pp. 7-10.
25 C. P. Shedd, STUDENT CHRISTIAN MOVEMENTS, p. 138.
26 L. D. Wishard, 'The Beginning of the Students' Era in Christian History,' p. 62 (MS).
27 C. P. Shedd, STUDENT CHRISTIAN MOVEMENTS, p. 139.
28 L. D. Wishard, 'The Beginning of the Students' Era in Christian History,' p. 73 (MS).
29 THE WATCHMAN, Y.M.C.A., Chicago, 1 January 1877.
30 L. D. Wishard, 'The Beginning of the Students' Era in Christian History,' p. 73, (MS).
31 PROCEEDINGS OF THE 22nd ANNUAL CONVENTION OF THE YOUNG MEN'S CHRISTIAN ASSOCIATIONS, Louisville, Kentucky, 6-10 June, 1877, p. 77.
32 C. P. Shedd, STUDENT CHRISTIAN MOVEMENTS, p. 155.
33 THE COLLEGE BULLETIN, New York, November 1878, pp. 1-2.
34 C. P. Shedd, STUDENT CHRISTIAN MOVEMENTS, p. 159.
35 THE CHRISTIAN, London, 19 February 1885.
36 G. A. Smith, THE LIFE OF HENRY DRUMMOND, passim.

CHAPTER XI: THE STUDENT VOLUNTEERS

1 N. P. Grubb, C. T. STUDD: CRICKETER AND PIONEER.
2 J. C. Pollock, A CAMBRIDGE MOVEMENT, p. 57.
3 W. R. Moody, THE LIFE OF DWIGHT L. MOODY, pp. 350ff.
4 J. C. Pollock, A CAMBRIDGE MOVEMENT, pp. 59-60.
5 J. C. Pollock, MOODY: A BIOGRAPHICAL PORTRAIT, pp. 228ff.
6 J. C. Pollock, A CAMBRIDGE MOVEMENT, p. 58.
7 CAMBRIDGE REVIEW, issues of November 1882.
8 W. R. Moody, THE LIFE OF DWIGHT L. MOODY, pp. 350-357.
9 J. C. Pollock, A CAMBRIDGE MOVEMENT, p. 70.
10 see THE CHRISTIAN, London, 23 November 1882.
11 THE CHRISTIAN, London, 18 February 1885.
12 Wilfred Grenfell, A LABRADOR DOCTOR (Autobiography).
13 J. C. Pollock, THE CAMBRIDGE SEVEN, passim.
14 THE COLLEGE BULLETIN, New York, March 1885.
15 J. C. Pollock, A CAMBRIDGE MOVEMENT, p. 83.
16 Phyllis Thompson, D. E. HOSTE: A PRINCE WITH GOD, passim.
17 Marshall Broomhall, W. W. CASSELS: FIRST BISHOP IN WEST CHINA.
18 N. P. Grubb, C. T. STUDD: CRICKETER AND PIONEER.
19 L. D. Wishard, 'The Students' Era in Christian History,' p. 138.
20 see Basil Mathews, JOHN R. MOTT, WORLD CITIZEN; John R. Mott, THE WORLD'S STUDENT CHRISTIAN FEDERATION.
21 THE COLLEGE BULLETIN, New York, April 1880.
22 L. D. Wishard, 'The Students' Era in Christian History,' pp. 129-130.
23 C. P. Shedd, STUDENT CHRISTIAN MOVEMENTS, pp. 248ff.
24 see REPORT OF THE FIRST INTERNATIONAL CONVENTION OF THE STUDENT VOLUNTEER MOVEMENT, Cleveland, Ohio, pp. 161-163.
25 C. P. Shedd, STUDENT CHRISTIAN MOVEMENTS, pp. 259-262.
26 cf. SPRINGFIELD REPUBLICAN, 2 August 1886; & John R. Mott, THE HISTORY OF THE STUDENT VOLUNTEER MOVEMENT, p. 12.
27 C. P. Shedd, STUDENT CHRISTIAN MOVEMENTS, p. 267.
28 THE INTERCOLLEGIAN, May 1887.
29 W. R. Moody, THE LIFE OF DWIGHT L. MOODY, p. 358.
30 C. P. Shedd, STUDENT CHRISTIAN MOVEMENTS, p. 275.
31 see J. H. Oldham, THE STUDENT CHRISTIAN MOVEMENT OF GREAT BRITAIN AND IRELAND, p. 13.
32 G. A. Smith, THE LIFE OF HENRY DRUMMOND, pp. 370ff.
33 C. P. Shedd, STUDENT CHRISTIAN MOVEMENTS, p. 280.
34 G. A. Smith, THE LIFE OF HENRY DRUMMOND, p. 378.
35 C. K. Ober, LUTHER D. WISHARD, pp. 122ff.
36 L. D. Wishard, 'The Students' Era in Christian History,' pp. 178-212.
37 THE INTERCOLLEGIAN, December 1889.
38 THE SPRINGFIELD UNION, 7 July 1892 (Report of O. O. Williams, of the University of London); cf. J. H. Oldham, THE STUDENT CHRISTIAN MOVEMENT OF GREAT BRITAIN AND IRELAND, pp. 14-15.
39 G. A. Smith, THE LIFE OF HENRY DRUMMOND, pp. 386ff.
40 Basil Mathews, JOHN R. MOTT: WORLD CITIZEN, pp. 112-114.
41 J. H. Oldham, STUDENT CHRISTIAN MOVEMENT (Britain), pp. 21ff.
42 C. P. Shedd, STUDENT CHRISTIAN MOVEMENTS, Chapter XXIII.
43 K. S. Latourette, A HISTORY OF THE EXPANSION OF CHRISTIANITY, Volume IV, pp. 97-98.

CHAPTER XII: SPORADIC REVIVALS OVERSEAS

1   cf. P. G. Mode, THE FRONTIER SPIRIT IN AMERICAN CHRISTIANITY, & W. W. Sweet, REVIVALISM IN AMERICA, which propounded the idea that Revival was a frontier phenomenon—considered untenable.
2   R. H. W. Shepherd, LOVEDALE, SOUTH AFRICA. THE STORY OF A CENTURY, 1841-1941.
3   K. S. Latourette, A HISTORY OF THE EXPANSION OF CHRISTIANITY, Volume V, p. 353.
4   South African Native Races Committee, ed., THE NATIVES OF SOUTH AFRICA, p. 188.
5   R. Laws, REMINISCENCES OF LIVINGSTONIA, pp. 5, 6.
6   J. Wells, THE LIFE OF JAMES STEWART, p. 171.
7   MISSIONARY REVIEW OF THE WORLD, 1899, pp. 98ff.
8   Student Christian Association of South Africa, REPORT OF THE (1904) WORCESTER CONFERENCE, p. 45.
9   Sesotho-speaking students were able to reach the Barotse people of Zambia, Xhosa- and Zulu-speaking, the many related Nguni tribes to the north.
10 J. S. Dennis, CHRISTIAN MISSIONS AND SOCIAL PROGRESS, Volume II, p. 101.
11 ZAMBESI INDUSTRIAL MISSION MONTHLY, November 1903.
12 see Harford Battersby, PILKINGTON OF UGANDA, Chapter XII; cf. Statistics of the Uganda Mission 1892 & 1907, in PROCEEDINGS OF THE CHURCH MISSIONARY SOCIETY, appropriate dates. Prof. J. du Plessis in THE EVANGELIZATION OF PAGAN AFRICA cites much larger figures for the whole C.M.S. fields in East Africa.
13 J. S. Dennis, CHRISTIAN MISSIONS AND SOCIAL PROGRESS, Volume II, pp. 68-69.
14 Sir Harry Hamilton Johnston's remarkable career, as an explorer and administrator is told in his autobiography, THE STORY OF MY LIFE.
15 SCRIBNER'S MAGAZINE, New York, August 1910.
16 W. L. S. Churchill, MY AFRICAN JOURNEY, passim.
17 J. S. Dennis, CHRISTIAN MISSIONS AND SOCIAL PROGRESS, Volume II, p. 101.
18 BAPTIST MISSIONARY MAGAZINE, Boston, 1897, p. 70; J. du Plessis, THE EVANGELIZATION OF PAGAN AFRICA, pp. 211ff.
19 J. S. Dennis, CHRISTIAN MISSIONS AND SOCIAL PROGRESS, Volume II, p. 102.
20 Mali, Niger, Ethiopia and Somalia have the fewest children in school in all of Africa, and were the latest entered by evangelical missionary forces.
21 C. W. Iglehart, PROTESTANT CHRISTIANITY IN JAPAN, p. 42.
22 Otis Cary, A HISTORY OF CHRISTIANITY IN JAPAN, Volume II, p. 167.
23 C. W. Iglehart, PROTESTANT CHRISTIANITY IN JAPAN, p. 73.
24 See Otis Cary, Volume II, Chapter VI; Iglehart, Chapter III; and sequel.
25 T. Richard, FORTY-FIVE YEARS IN CHINA, p. 297.
26 Beach & St. John, WORLD STATISTICS OF CHRISTIAN MISSIONS, p. 78. K. S. Latourette, A HISTORY OF THE EXPANSION OF CHRISTIANITY, Volume VI, pp. 353-354.
27 CHINA MISSION YEAR BOOK, 1913, pp. 293-297.
28 THE CHRISTIAN MOVEMENT IN THE JAPANESE EMPIRE, annual, 1915, pp. 476-477, 491.
29 Reminiscences of Dr. W. N. Blair, veteran Korean missionary.

CHAPTER XIII: THE AWAKENINGS OF THE 1900s

1   J. Edwin Orr, THE FLAMING TONGUE, p. 216.
2   Eifion Evans, THE WELSH REVIVAL OF 1904, is the most recent (1969) account of the movement in Wales.
3   see D. M. Phillips, EVAN ROBERTS, THE GREAT WELSH REVIVALIST, 1906; there are at least forty published books and booklets for reference.
4   D. M. Phillips, EVAN ROBERTS, p. 194.
5   G. T. B. Davis, WHEN THE FIRE FELL, p. 79.
6   J. V. Morgan, THE WELSH RELIGIOUS REVIVAL, pp. 248-249.
7   The Rev. Myrddyn Lewis (of Birmingham) assured the writer that in his Welsh home town in the Rhondda Valley the Court was opened at 10 a.m. one Monday morning, and closed at 10.05 a.m.
8   J. Penn-Lewis, THE AWAKENING IN WALES, p. 23.
9   R. B. Jones, RENT HEAVENS, passim.
10 Gipsy Smith, in THE CHRISTIAN, London, 5 January 1905.
11 THE CHRISTIAN, 13 April 1905.
12 see 'The Religious Revival,' CARNARVON AND DENBIGH HERALD, 16 December 1904.
13 WESLEYAN METHODIST MAGAZINE, London, 1905, p. 65.
14 THE CHRISTIAN, London, 2 March 1905.
15 THE ADVANCE, Chicago, 9 February 1905.
16 YR HERALD CYMRAEG, Aberystwyth, 24 January 1905.
17 for Lloyd-George's comments, YR HERALD CYMRAEG, 24 & 31 January 1905.
18 THE RECORD, London, 16 June 1905.
19 METHODIST RECORDER, London, 9 February 1905.
20 METHODIST TIMES, London, 16 March 1905.
21 J. Edwin Orr, THE FLAMING TONGUE, pp. 49-50.
22 ASSOCIATION MEN, Chicago, XXX, 7: April 1905.
23 Editorial, THE OXFORD STUDENT MOVEMENT, March 1905; see also A. W. Davies, in THE BRITISH STUDENT MOVEMENT, 1905, cited in ADDRESSES AND PAPERS OF JOHN R. MOTT, Volume II, THE WORLD'S STUDENT CHRISTIAN FEDERATION, p. 352.
24 THE RECORD, London, cited in the above, p. 354.
25 J. C. Pollock, A CAMBRIDGE MOVEMENT, & G. T. B. Davis, TORREY AND ALEXANDER, passim.
26 Report of Kenneth McPherson, in Basil Mathews, JOHN R. MOTT, p. 157.
27 'The Irish and Scottish Awakenings,' in J. Edwin Orr, THE FLAMING TONGUE, Chap. IV; cf. MISSIONARY RECORD, Edinburgh, 1905, p. 213.
28 SCOTTISH BAPTIST MAGAZINE, Glasgow, 1905, pp. 66, 67, 75 & 86.
29 MISSIONARY REVIEW OF THE WORLD, 1905, pp. 523ff.
30 J. Edwin Orr, THE FLAMING TONGUE, pp. 33-36.
31 MISSIONARY REVIEW OF THE WORLD, 1906, p. 151.
32 J. Edwin Orr, THE FLAMING TONGUE, pp. 59-63.
33 Student Volunteer Movement, STUDENTS AND THE MODERN MISSIONARY CRUSADE, p. 70.
34 'Greetings from the Students of Germany,' STUDENTS AND THE MODERN MISSIONARY CRUSADE, p. 71.
35 J. Edwin Orr, THE FLAMING TONGUE, Chap. XIV; INTERCOLLEGIAN, December 1905, p. 75.
36 J. Edwin Orr, THE FLAMING TONGUE, Chapter XV.

37 J. Edwin Orr, THE FLAMING TONGUE, p. 61.
    (There is no other published account of the 1905 Awakenings)
38 THE EXAMINER, New York, 26 January & 16 February 1905.
39 MICHIGAN CHRISTIAN ADVOCATE, Adrian, 9 December 1905.
40 BAPTIST HOME MISSION MONTHLY, 1905, p. 92 & passim.
41 CHRISTIAN ADVOCATE, New York, 25 January 1906; 17 January 1907.
42 INTERCOLLEGIAN, Chicago, XXVII, January 1905, p. 73.
43 INTERCOLLEGIAN, Chicago, XXVII, April 1905, p. 167.
44 ASSOCIATION MEN, Chicago, XXX: 7, March 1905, p. 263.
45 ASSOCIATION MEN, Chicago, XXX: 5, February 1905, p. 199.
46 Editorial, THE WATCHMAN, Boston, 4 May 1905.
47 J. Edwin Orr, THE FLAMING TONGUE, p. 85.
48 INTERCOLLEGIAN, Chicago, XXVIII, May 1906, p. 199.
49 INTERCOLLEGIAN, Chicago, XXVIII, April 1906, p. 176.
50 Letter to J. R. Mott, quoted in G. Stewart, LIFE OF HENRY B. WRIGHT,
    p. 45. (Robert E. Speer was a Student Volunteer layman, a key leader in
    Presbyterian missions)
51 G. Stewart, LIFE OF HENRY B. WRIGHT, p. 47.
52 CHRISTIAN ADVOCATE, New York, 9 February 1905.
53 MICHIGAN CHRISTIAN ADVOCATE, Adrian, 11 February 1905.
54 CHRISTIAN ADVOCATE, New York, 26 January 1905, quoting EVENING
    POST & SCHENECTADY GAZETTE, January issues.
55 INTERCOLLEGIAN, XL, May 1908, p. 188.
56 THE CHRISTIAN, London, 9 March 1905.
57 INTERCOLLEGIAN, XXVII, April 1905, p. 163.
58 CHRISTIAN ADVOCATE, New York, 4 January 1906.
59 YEAR BOOK, Y.M.C.A. of North America, 1905-06, pp. 220-221, 234-235,
    giving tables of statistics.
60 CHRISTIAN ADVOCATE, New York, 6 April 1905.
61 Editorial, CHRISTIAN ADVOCATE, 9 March 1905.
62 INTERCOLLEGIAN, XXVII, January & February 1905.
63 CHRISTIAN HERALD, London, 12 January 1905.
64 J. Edwin Orr, THE FLAMING TONGUE, pp. 86-87.
65 INTERCOLLEGIAN, XXVII, May 1905, p. 188.
66 INTERCOLLEGIAN, XXVIII, February 1906, p. 130.
67 INTERCOLLEGIAN, XXVII, April 1905, p. 167.
68 BAPTIST ARGUS, Louisville, 6 April 1905.
69 INTERCOLLEGIAN, XXVII, March 1905, p. 144.
70 JOURNAL & MESSENGER, Cincinnati, 2 February 1905.
71 YEAR BOOK, Y.M.C.A. of North America, 1905-06, pp. 212-213.
72 PENTECOSTAL HERALD, Louisville, 19 April 1905 & INTERCOLLEGIAN,
    XXVII, April 1905, p. 167.
73 CHRISTIAN OBSERVER, Louisville, 1 March 1905.
74 BAPTIST ARGUS, Louisville, 25 May 1905.
75 BAPTIST ARGUS, Louisville, 13 April & 5 May 1905; the missionary in-
    terest in Baylor University is cited in INTERCOLLEGIAN, XXVII, p. 167
    (April 1905).
76 YEAR BOOK, Y.M.C.A. of North America, 1905-06, pp. 210-211.
77 THE WATCHMAN, Boston, 23 March 1905.
78 INTERCOLLEGIAN, XXVII, June 1905, p. 213.
79 The Bible Institute of Los Angeles was founded in the downtown area, 1908,
    Lyman Stewart, T. C. Horton and other able men taking the initiative.

80 The Los Angeles Baptist City Mission Society was founded 1906, at a time when local churches were thriving, PACIFIC BAPTIST, 22 March 1905.
81 THE PACIFIC BAPTIST, 8 February & 26 April 1905.
82 INTERCOLLEGIAN, XXVIII, April 1906, p. 178.
83 INTERCOLLEGIAN, XXVIII, June 1906, p. 228.
84 THE PACIFIC BAPTIST, 19 April 1905.
85 Statistics from THE PACIFIC BAPTIST, 1 March 1905.
86 Letter of L. W. Riley, THE PACIFIC BAPTIST, 1 March 1905.
87 TELEPHONE-REGISTER, McMinnville, 11 & 12 February 1905.
88 C. W. Ruth's ministry is mentioned in several issues of the TELEPHONE-REGISTER, 13 January, 11 March, etc.
89 see TELEPHONE-REGISTER, 3 June 1905.
90 H. Wyse Jones's ministry is mentioned in the TELEPHONE-REGISTER, 15 April 1905; PACIFIC BAPTIST, 11 January & 1 February 1905, etc, it being said that Salem had not experienced such revival for many years.
91 see PACIFIC BAPTIST, 29 March 1905 (Pullman awakening); 24 May 1905 (Renton revival); etc.
92 Seattle Ministers' Conference, quoted in PACIFIC BAPTIST, 31 May 1905.
93 C. Hoyt Watson, MS History of Seattle Pacific College, Chapter IV, 'The Golden Era,' p. 20 (quotations courtesy of Seattle Pacific College).
94 CHRISTIAN ADVOCATE, New York, 2 February; CHRISTIAN HERALD, Philadelphia, 15 February; THE EXAMINER, Boston, 6 April 1905.
95 SERVICE, Baptist Young People's Union, Chicago, 1905, p. 43; EVENING POST, Burlington, quoted in CHRISTIAN ADVOCATE, 2 February 1905.
96 cf. INTERCOLLEGIAN, XXVII, January 1905; April 1905; December 1905; YEAR BOOK, Y.M.C.A. of North America, 1905-06, pp. 214-215.
97 INTERCOLLEGIAN, XXVIII, June 1906, p. 228.
98 CENTRAL BAPTIST, St. Louis, 13 & 27 April 1905; also CHRISTIAN ENDEAVOR WORLD, Boston, 30 March 1905.
99 INTERCOLLEGIAN, XXVII, June 1905, p. 216; cf. YEAR BOOK, 1905, Y.M.C.A. of North America, pp. 212-213.
100 INTERCOLLEGIAN, XXVII, May 1905, p. 189.
101 INTERCOLLEGIAN, XXVII, February 1905, p. 135.
102 BAPTIST HOME MISSION MONTHLY, 1905, p. 112.
103 YEAR BOOK, Y.M.C.A. of North America, 1906-07, pp. 222-223.
104 CHRISTIAN HERALD, Philadelphia, 15 February 1905; PENTECOSTAL HERALD, 1 & 22 February 1905.
105 PENTECOSTAL HERALD, Louisville, 22 February 1905.
106 J. Edwin Orr, THE FLAMING TONGUE, pp. 89-90.
107 SERVICE, Baptist Young People's Union, Chicago, 1904-05, p. 561; and 1905-06, p. 50.
108 BAPTIST HOME MISSION MONTHLY, 1905, p. 254.
109 YEAR BOOK, Y.M.C.A. of North America, 1905-06, pp. 240-241.
110 INTERCOLLEGIAN, XXVIII, March 1906, p. 149.
111 BAPTIST HOME MISSION MONTHLY, 1905, pp. 86, 359.
112 THE WATCHMAN, Boston, 20 April 1905; SERVICE, Chicago, 1905-06, p. 257; YEAR BOOK, Y.M.C.A. of North America, 1905-06, pp. 210-211.
113 YEAR BOOK, Y.M.C.A. of North America, 1905-06, pp. 210-211; and 1906-07, pp. 210-211.
114 BAPTIST ARGUS, Louisville, 23 March 1905; YEAR BOOK, Y.M.C.A. of North America, 1905-06, pp. 210-211.
115 F. Rudolph, THE AMERICAN COLLEGE AND UNIVERSITY, pp. 84, 502.

CHAPTER XIV: THE 1905 AFTERMATH

1   CHRISTIAN ADVOCATE, New York, 8, 22 & 29 June 1905; see WORLD'S WORK, 1905, pp. 6639ff.
2   CHRISTIAN ADVOCATE, New York, 4 January 1906.
3   WESTERN CHRISTIAN ADVOCATE, 31 January 1906.
4   Conversation with Dr. Edwin T. Dahlberg and subsequent correspondence.
5   INTERCOLLEGIAN, XXVII, May 1905, p. 189; XXVIII, March 1905, p. 151.
6   Report in INTERCOLLEGIAN, XXVII, April 1905, p. 164.
7   INTERCOLLEGIAN, XXVIII, March 1906, p. 150; May 1906, p. 199.
8   XXVIII, March 1906, p. 150.   9   XXVIII, May 1906, p. 198.
10 INTERCOLLEGIAN, XXVII, February 1905, pp. 109ff.
11 YEAR BOOK, Y.M.C.A. of North America, 1902-03, p. 220.
12 Table VII, in YEAR BOOK, 1904-05.
13 YEAR BOOK, Y.M.C.A. of North America, 1905-06, p. 239.
14 Table VII, in YEAR BOOK, 1907-08.
15 INTERCOLLEGIAN, XXVIII, May 1906, p. 199.
16 W. N. Stearns, RELIGIOUS EDUCATION, II: February 1908, pp. 202-203.
17 ANNUAL OF THE NORTHERN BAPTIST CONVENTION, 1910, p. 165.
18 W. N. Stearns, RELIGIOUS EDUCATION, I: February 1907, pp. 209-210.
19 C. P. Shedd, THE CHURCH FOLLOWS ITS STUDENTS, p. 19.
20 see also S. A. Smith, THE AMERICAN COLLEGE CHAPLAINCY.
21 M. H. Towner, RELIGION IN HIGHER EDUCATION, p. 252; & MINUTES, GENERAL ASSEMBLY, PRESBYTERIAN CHURCH, U.S.A., 1906, p. 56.
22 C. P. Shedd, THE CHURCH FOLLOWS ITS STUDENTS, p. 16.
23 see also S. A. Smith, THE AMERICAN COLLEGE CHAPLAINCY.
24 C. P. Shedd, THE CHURCH FOLLOWS ITS STUDENTS, p. 22.
25 B. Mathews, JOHN R. MOTT, WORLD CITIZEN, pp. 104ff.
26 INTERCOLLEGIAN, XXVII, January 1905, pp. 83-84; cf. YEAR BOOK, Y.M.C.A. of North America, 1905-06, pp. 210-211; 1906-07, pp. 208-209.
27 INTERCOLLEGIAN, XXVII, January 1905, p. 84; cf. YEAR BOOK.
28 YEAR BOOK, Y.M.C.A. of North America, 1905-06, pp. 218-219; and INTERCOLLEGIAN, XXVII, January 1905, p. 85.
29 INTERCOLLEGIAN, XXVIII, April 1906, p. 176; cf. YEAR BOOK.
30 INTERCOLLEGIAN, XXVIII, April 1906, p. 179; cf. YEAR BOOK.
31 INTERCOLLEGIAN, XXIX, April 1907, p. 157.
32 John R. Mott, THE WORLD'S STUDENT CHRISTIAN FEDERATION, p. 93.
33 C. H. Fahs, article: 'Student Missionary Volunteer Band Ideals,' in the INTERCOLLEGIAN, XXVII, November 1904, p. 39.
34 INTERCOLLEGIAN, XXVII, January 1905, p. 97; June 1905, p. 213; & YEAR BOOK, Y.M.C.A. of North America, 1905-06, pp. 234-235.
35 YEAR BOOK, 1905-06, p. 234.   36   YEAR BOOK, 1905-06, p. 238.
37 MISSIONARY REVIEW OF THE WORLD, 1906, p. 370.
38 MISSIONARY REVIEW OF THE WORLD, 1906, p. 367.
39 MISSIONARY REVIEW OF THE WORLD, 1905, p. 545; 1906, p. 163.
40 INTERCOLLEGIAN, XXVIII, March 1906, p. 116; also XXIX, April 1905, p. 167; and XXX, March 1908, p. 144.
41 Conversation with Dr. E. Stanley Jones at Asbury College, 1969.
42 K. S. Latourette, BEYOND THE RANGES, passim.
43 Mrs. Howard Taylor, BORDEN OF YALE, passim.
44 G. Stewart, LIFE OF HENRY B. WRIGHT, pp. 46-47.
45 W. T. Ellis, MEN AND MISSIONS, pp. 71-80.

CHAPTER XV: COLLEGIATE AWAKENINGS OVERSEAS

1   MISSIONARY REVIEW OF THE WORLD, 1905, pp. 523ff.
2   W. Canton, HISTORY OF THE BRITISH & FOREIGN BIBLE SOCIETY, Volume III, pp. 294-295; and passim.
3   Issues of DE KERKBODE, Capetown, 1901-1902, indexed (in Dutch); for a summary, see J. Edwin Orr, EVANGELICAL AWAKENINGS IN AFRICA, Chapter XVII.
4   A. F. Louw, MY EERSTE NEENTIG JAAR, passim.
5   CHRISTIAN STUDENT, Capetown, September 1901. The Student Christian Movement had begun in South Africa in 1896.
6   G. B. Gerdener, RECENT DEVELOPMENTS IN THE SOUTH AFRICAN MISSION FIELD, pp. 15-16.
7   MISSIONARY REVIEW OF THE WORLD, 1904, p. 79; see CHRISTIAN EXPRESS, Lovedale, issues of 1903.
8   MISSIONARY REVIEW OF THE WORLD, 1906, pp. 645ff.
9   D. MacGillivray, A CENTURY OF PROTESTANT MISSIONS IN CHINA, pp. 277-278; Student Volunteer Movement, STUDENTS AND THE MODERN MISSIONARY CRUSADE, p. 193.
10 MISSIONARY REVIEW OF THE WORLD, 1900, p. 652.
11 INTERCOLLEGIAN, XXVIII, February 1906, p. 116; Student Volunteer Movement, STUDENTS AND THE MODERN MISSIONARY CRUSADE.
12 MISSIONARY REVIEW OF THE WORLD, 1906, p. 643.
13 MISSIONARY REVIEW OF THE WORLD, 1907, p. 642; & 1908, p. 451. (It is of interest that Chiang Kai-shek was a student in Japan at that time, though he did not become a Christian until much later.)
14 R. Goforth, GOFORTH OF CHINA, passim. The writer enjoyed cordial fellowship with Dr. Goforth in Toronto, years later.
15 WORLD MISSIONARY CONFERENCE, Edinburgh, 1910, Volume I, pp. 36ff —giving a report by the Rev. Jonathan Goforth.
16 Student Volunteer Movement, STUDENTS AND THE MODERN MISSIONARY CRUSADE, p. 193.
17 W. N. Blair, GOLD IN KOREA, Chapter XVII, 'The Korean Pentecost'— which chapter heading was Dr. Blair's original title.
18 REPORT, Board of Missions, Methodist Episcopal Church, South, 1909.
19 Reminiscences of Dr. W. N. Blair, retired missionary, Duarte, California, now deceased.
20 B. Mathews, JOHN R. MOTT, WORLD CITIZEN, p. 183.
21 MISSIONARY REVIEW OF THE WORLD, 1910, p. 598.
22 K. S. Latourette, A HISTORY OF THE EXPANSION OF CHRISTIANITY, Volume VI, pp. 441ff.
23 J. Edwin Orr, EVANGELICAL AWAKENINGS IN INDIA, Chapter VIII.
24 M. M. Thomas & R. W. Taylor, editors, TRIBAL AWAKENING, pp. 23ff.
25 TRIBAL AWAKENING, pp. 226ff.
26 J. Edwin Orr, EVANGELICAL AWAKENINGS IN INDIA, Chapter IX.
27 J. A. Baker, CONTENDING THE GRADE, p. 105.
28 J. Edwin Orr, EVANGELICAL AWAKENINGS IN INDIA, Chapter X.
29 A. J. Thottungal, 'The History and Growth of the Mar Thoma Church,'— unpublished thesis, School of World Mission, Pasadena—p. 100.
30 J. Edwin Orr, EVANGELICAL AWAKENINGS IN INDIA, Chapter XII.
31 H. S. Dyer, PANDITA RAMABAI, passim.
32 Nicol MacNicol, PANDITA RAMABAI, p. 118.

CHAPTER XVI: VOLUNTEER OBJECTIVES OVERSEAS

1   Institute of International Education, New York, 1961: 'Survey of the African Student,' p. 7.
2   P. F. Bohannon, AFRICA AND AFRICANS, p. 235.
3   STATISTICAL YEAR BOOK OF THE UNITED NATIONS; see also the UNITED NATIONS MONTHLY BULLETIN OF STATISTICS. The first group of countries, almost all in southern Africa, range from approximately 15% in Lesotho and South Africa to approximately 10% in Malawi.
4   C. Manshardt, CHRISTIANITY IN A CHANGING INDIA, p. 147.
5   A. F. C. Bourdillon, VOLUNTARY SOCIAL SERVICES, p. 45, quoting Mrs. Thomas Barnardo, the wife of the founder of the world's largest private orphanage system.
6   R. G. Wilder, MISSION SCHOOLS IN INDIA, pp. 36-37.
7   Nurullah & Naik, A HISTORY OF EDUCATION IN INDIA, p. 60.
8   G. Smith, THE LIFE OF ALEXANDER DUFF, passim.
9   W. Paton, ALEXANDER DUFF, PIONEER OF MISSIONARY EDUCATION, p. 57.
10 G. B. Kanungo, THE LANGUAGE CONTROVERSY IN INDIAN EDUCATION, (p. 7) cites the missionaries as the initiators of a policy which afterwards in fact provided Indian nationalism with a lingua franca.
11 P.J. Braisted, INDIAN NATIONALISM & THE CHRISTIAN COLLEGES, pp. 86-91.
12 Sir Sarvapalli Radhakrishnan became President of the Republic of India. Dr. M. M. Thomas has published a well-documented work on the influence of Christianity upon Hindu thinkers—THE ACKNOWLEDGED CHRIST OF THE INDIAN RENAISSANCE, Bangalore, 1970.
13 A. D. Lindsay, CHRISTIAN HIGHER EDUCATION IN INDIA, pp. 64ff. cf. DIRECTORY OF CHRISTIAN MISSIONS IN INDIA, 1928-1929.
14 DIRECTORY OF CHRISTIAN MISSIONS IN INDIA, 1928-1929.
15 A. D. Lindsay, CHRISTIAN HIGHER EDUCATION IN INDIA, pp. 12ff.
16 The writer's ministry in India has taken him to a score of these colleges, most of them affiliated with the Senate of Serampore College, founded by William Carey in 1818, of which he is a graduate.
17 A. D. Lindsay, CHRISTIAN HIGHER EDUCATION IN INDIA, p. 373.
18 p. 374. This appeared to be true of arts and science colleges, rather than of theological institutions.
19 The writer stayed on the campus of a Christian college where shortly before the Hindu students had rioted and besieged the Principal in his office for forty-eight hours, all because a Hindu student had sought baptism in the nearest city, without the connivance of the college authorities.
20 see CHRISTIAN HANDBOOK OF INDIA, 1962.
21 The Lutheran work at Chota Nagpur was founded by the Gossner Mission.
22 D. A. McGavran, CHURCH GROWTH IN JAMAICA, pp. 113-114.
23 see M. W. Randall, PROFILE FOR VICTORY, NEW PROPOSALS FOR MISSIONS IN ZAMBIA, Chapter VI.
24 The writer heard none other than Mr. Krishna Menon complain of this sad handicap to India's progress.
25 see Meyer, Fortes & Evans-Pritchard, AFRICAN POLITICAL SYSTEMS, for contrasting pre-colonial and post-educational values.
26 R. Gray, THE TWO NATIONS, p. 138.
27 R. L. Buell, THE NATIVE PROBLEM IN AFRICA, Volume II, p. 80.

CHAPTER XVII: DECLINE OF A GREAT MOVEMENT

1   Student Volunteer Movement, STUDENTS AND WORLD ADVANCE, New York, 1920.
2   W. H. Beahm, 'Factors in the Development of the Student Volunteer Movement for Foreign Missions,' unpublished Ph.D. dissertation, University of Chicago, 1941, p. 13.
3   see, for example, Paul Kanamori's optimistic report on Japan.
4   MISSIONARY REVIEW OF THE WORLD, 1932, p. 67.
5   'Student Volunteers at Indianapolis,' in MISSIONARY REVIEW OF THE WORLD, 1936, p. 68.
6   W. A. Omulogoli, 'The Student Volunteer Movement: Its History and Contribution,' unpublished M.A. thesis, Wheaton College, 1967, passim.
7   W. H. Beahm, 'Factors in the Development of the Student Volunteer Movement for Foreign Missions,' p. 16.
8   The writer observed both interest and results in the Philippines.
9   R. D. Winter, TWENTY-FIVE UNBELIEVABLE YEARS, passim.
10 Religious News Service report, 1 April 1969.
11 see NEWS NOTES, Department of Higher Education, National Council of Churches of Christ in U.S.A., New York, March 1969, number 3.
12 YEAR BOOK, 1921, Y.M.C.A. of North America, pp. 390ff.
13 W. H. Beahm, 'Factors in the Development of the Student Volunteer Movement for Foreign Missions,' pp. 14-15.
14 This is obvious from a reading of C. Howard Hopkins, HISTORY OF THE Y.M.C.A. IN NORTH AMERICA, pp. 642-645.
15 C. Howard Hopkins, HISTORY OF THE Y.M.C.A. IN NORTH AMERICA, pp. 362ff.
16 see 'The Y.M.C.A. and the Religious Climate,' op. cit., pp. 375ff.
17 author's analysis.
18 The League of Evangelical Students owed much to Prof. J. Gresham Machen, (D. Johnson, A BRIEF HISTORY OF THE INTERNATIONAL FELLOW SHIP OF EVANGELICAL STUDENTS, p. 161.
19 For a summary, see A. J. Appasamy, WRITE THE VISION, pp. 72ff.
20 see 1936 YEAR BOOK, Y.M.C.A. of Canada & Y.M.C.A. of the U.S.A., pp. 82-83.
21 'What Religious Activities Should Y.M.C.A's. Emphasize?' pp. 44-45.
22 INTERCOLLEGIAN, Volume 53, October 1935—May 1936.
23 see J. Edwin Orr, THIS IS THE VICTORY, p. 19; cf. A. J. Appasamy, WRITE THE VISION, p. 75.
24 N. P. Grubb, MODERN VIKING: THE STORY OF ABRAHAM VEREIDE, PIONEER IN CHRISTIAN LEADERSHIP, passim.
25 J. Edwin Orr, THIS IS THE VICTORY, p. 23. The remarks on atheism at the University of Washington were made by the Hon. Arthur Langley.
26 J. Edwin Orr, THIS IS THE VICTORY, pp. 23-24.
27 CHRISTIAN EDUCATION, XXI, October 1937, pp. 43-46.
28 'A National Survey of the Religious Preferences of Students in American Colleges and Universities,' CHRISTIAN EDUCATION, XXI, pp. 49ff, 1936.
29 C. Howard Hopkins, HISTORY OF THE Y.M.C.A. IN NORTH AMERICA, p. 645.   30 1936 YEAR BOOK, Y.M.C.A., p. 73.
31 T. Driberg, THE MYSTERY OF MORAL REARMAMENT, New York, 1965; see also Peter Howard, REMAKING THE WORLD, London, 1948, etc.
32 A. J. Russell, FOR SINNERS ONLY, London, 1932.

CHAPTER XVIII: A SLOW EVANGELICAL RECOVERY

1   see W. W. Willard, FIRE ON THE PRAIRIE, Wheaton College, 1950.
2   Data extracted from DOCTORAL RECIPIENTS FROM UNITED STATES UNIVERSITIES, 1958-66, National Academy of Sciences, Washington, 1967; U. S. Office of Education, EDUCATION DIRECTORY, Part III, 1966-67.
3   Information received from C. Adrian Heaton, 1941; cf. WHEATON RECORD, Volume 76, 7 February 1957, p. 1; Volume 49, 8 January 1936, p. 1.
4   A. J. Appasamy, WRITE THE VISION, p. 147; cf. W. W. Willard, p. 188.
5   WHEATON RECORD, Volume 50, 29th January 1936, p. 4.
6   Peter Stam, Jr., 'How the Revival Came to Wheaton College,' SUNDAY SCHOOL TIMES, 7 March 1936, pp. 158-159.
7   cf. David M. Howard, STUDENT POWER IN WORLD EVANGELISM, p. 98.
8   SUNDAY SCHOOL TIMES, 7 March 1936, pp. 158-159.
9   A. J. Appasamy, WRITE THE VISION, p. 147.
10   Extract of Alumni Records, Wheaton College.
11   David M. Howard, STUDENT POWER IN WORLD EVANGELISM, p. 98.
12   Marguerite McQuilkin, ALWAYS IN TRIUMPH (R. C. McQuilkin), 1956.
13   David M. Howard, STUDENT POWER IN WORLD EVANGELISM, p. 101.
14   Chapel Records, February 1936, courtesy of Columbia Bible College.
15   MONTHLY NEWS LETTER, Columbia Bible College, 20 February 1936.
16   cf. A. J. Appasamy, WRITE THE VISION, pp. 147-148.
17   A. J. Appasamy, WRITE THE VISION, p. 78.
18   cf. WHEATON RECORD, Volume 50, 29 January 1936, p. 4; & report of Prof. W. H. Wrighton (Georgia), in THE CHRISTIAN, 21 May 1936.
19   MONTHLY NEWS LETTER, Columbia Bible College, 24 March 1936.
20   J. Edwin Orr, THIS IS THE VICTORY, pp. 110ff; Pres. R. Wayne Gardner, 11 March 1936; J. Cameron, EASTERN NAZARENE COLLEGE, pp. 201ff.
21   D. Johnson, A BRIEF HISTORY OF THE INTERNATIONAL FELLOWSHIP OF EVANGELICAL STUDENTS, p. 40.
22   Tissington Tatlow, THE STORY OF THE S. C. M., pp. 381ff.
23   N. P. Grubb, ONCE CAUGHT, NO ESCAPE, p. 55.
24   D. Johnson, A BRIEF HISTORY OF THE I. F. E. S., p. 44.
25   Of these, Joe Blinco and Tom Rees are deceased.
26   Personal knowledge of Bryan Green, the best-known Church evangelist.
27   F. D. Coggan, editor, CHRIST AND THE COLLEGES, pp. 216ff.
28   Personal knowledge, and access to Howard Guinness's diaries and letters.
29   D. Johnson, I. F. E. S., pp. 121ff; and Guinness's diaries and letters.
30   Personal knowledge of C. Stacey Woods (likewise for thirty five years).
31   D. Johnson, A BRIEF HISTORY OF THE I.F.E.S., pp. 119ff.
32   Private Prayer Letters, courtesy of Dr. Howard W. Guinness.
33   F. D. Coggan, editor, CHRIST AND THE COLLEGES, passim.
34   Several Moderators of the Presbyterian Church; cf. Coggan, pp. 127ff.
35   D. Johnson, A BRIEF HISTORY OF THE I.F.E.S, p. 13ff.
36   cf. D. Johnson, A BRIEF HISTORY OF THE I.F.E.S., pp. 160ff.
37   WHEATON RECORD, Volume 56, 5-16 February 1943.
38   Graham had been a student at Trinity College in Florida, when the writer first met him; he then transferred to Wheaton College.
39   Extract of Alumni Records, Wheaton College, 1943.
40   See Mel Larson, YOUNG MAN ON FIRE, THE STORY OF TORREY JOHNSON AND YOUTH FOR CHRIST, Chapter VII.
41   see J. Edwin Orr, I SAW NO TEARS, Chapter III.

CHAPTER XIX: MID-CENTURY RESURGENCE

1   A. J. Appasamy, WRITE THE VISION, p. 117.
2   After its first century, St. Catherine's Society became an Oxford college.
3   G. I. F. Thomson, THE OXFORD PASTORATE, passim.
4   Guinness accomplished excellent work in Oxford in the post-war years, then served well for twenty years under Archbishop Howard Mowll of Sydney.
5   THE LIFE OF FAITH, London, 16 February 1949.
6   The Ministers' Prayer Fellowship is still active and effective after 20 years.
7   THE LIFE OF FAITH, 25 May 1949.
8   Christ for Greater Los Angeles Committee was fully interdenominational.
9   THE LIFE OF FAITH, 25 May 1949.
10   The Korean War interrupted the church-building projects in California.
11   'Signs of Revival,' Rev. J. O. Gisselquist, United Spiritual Advance, in the inter-synodical Lutheran magazine, EVANGELIZE, February 1949.
12   F. W. Hoffman, REVIVAL TIMES IN AMERICA, pp. 163-164.
13   Mimeographed report of United Spiritual Advance, Minneapolis, 8 June 1949.
14   Report of President Henry C. Wingblade to United Spiritual Advance, cited.
15   THE STANDARD, Chicago, 6 & 13 May 1949.
16   Report of President Henry C. Wingblade to United Spiritual Advance, cited.
17   A. J. Appasamy, WRITE THE VISION, p. 151.
18   Mimeographed report of United Spiritual Advance, Minneapolis, 8 June 1949.
19   J. Edwin Orr, GOOD NEWS IN BAD TIMES, pp. 59-60.
20   Report of Dr. T. W. Wilson, Minneapolis, to THE LIFE OF FAITH.
21   Mimeographed report of United Spiritual Advance, Minneapolis, 8 June 1949.
22   E. M. Baldwin & D. V. Benson, HENRIETTA MEARS, Chapter VI.
23   J. Edwin Orr, GOOD NEWS IN BAD TIMES, p. 61; cf. E. M. Baldwin & D. V. Benson, HENRIETTA MEARS, p. 232.
24   J. Edwin Orr, GOOD NEWS IN BAD TIMES, p. 62.
25   A. J. Appasamy, WRITE THE VISION, p. 151.
26   E. M. Baldwin & D. V. Benson, HENRIETTA MEARS, p. 252; cf. J. Edwin Orr, FULL SURRENDER, p. 127 & Introduction by Billy Graham; with J. C. Pollock, BILLY GRAHAM, pp. 52-53; also Stanley High, BILLY GRAHAM, on the turning-point in Graham's ministry, at Forest Home.
27   C. T. Cook, THE BILLY GRAHAM STORY, p. 18.
28   Billy Graham, REVIVAL IN OUR TIME, passim.
29   Reports of President C. W. Koller, Professor J. R. Mantey, and the Student Council of Northern Baptist Theological Seminary, October 1949.
30   W. R. Bright, AWAKENING BULLETIN, Los Angeles, April 1950.
31   THE NORTHERN, Chicago, October 1950, p. 3; cf. Report of Alastair C. Walker, student body president, AWAKENING BULLETIN, October 1950.
32   J. Edwin Orr, GOOD NEWS IN BAD TIMES, p. 64.
33   No complete list of colleges affected by the movement has been discovered.
34   W. W. Willard, FIRE ON THE PRAIRIE: THE STORY OF WHEATON COLLEGE, Wheaton, Illinois, 1950.
35   Report of Chaplain W. Wyeth Willard, AWAKENING BULLETIN, April 1950, cited in J. Edwin Orr, GOOD NEWS IN BAD TIMES, pp. 76-77.
36   AWAKENING BULLETIN, editor W. R. Bright, April 1950.
37   J. Edwin Orr, GOOD NEWS IN BAD TIMES, p. 75.
38   THE WHEATON RECORD, 9 February 1950, p. 1.
39   J. Edwin Orr, GOOD NEWS IN BAD TIMES, p. 77.
40   V. R. Edman to J. Edwin Orr, sometime in 1950.

41 Report of Chaplain W. W. Willard, AWAKENING BULLETIN, April 1950.
42 H. C. James & P. Rader, HALLS AFLAME, Wilmore, Kentucky, 1966.
43 J. Edwin Orr, GOOD NEWS IN BAD TIMES, p. 80; cf. HALLS AFLAME, p. 8; F. W. Hoffman, REVIVAL TIMES IN AMERICA, p. 166.
44 PENTECOSTAL HERALD, Louisville, 15 March 1950, p. 4.
45 J. Edwin Orr, GOOD NEWS IN BAD TIMES, p. 80.
46 H. C. James & P. Rader, HALLS AFLAME, p. 18.
47 SEATTLE PACIFIC BULLETIN, Seattle, March 1950.
48 J. Edwin Orr, GOOD NEWS IN BAD TIMES, pp. 67-68.
49 J. M. Carroll, A HISTORY OF TEXAS BAPTISTS, Dallas, 1923, p. 237; cf. E. F. Williams, 'A History of Baylor University,' unpublished M.A. thesis, July 1941, p. 147 & passim.
50 M. L. Brown, 'Survey and Evaluation of the Youth Revival Movement in the South and Southwest since 1945,' unpublished M.A. thesis, Baylor University, May 1949, p. 6 & passim. (Personal knowledge of youth leaders cited)
51 C. E. Bryant, 'News in Texas,' BAPTIST STANDARD, 1 February 1951, p. 5.
52 WHEATON RECORD, 17 February 1950, p. 4, noted that newspapers in Miami, Louisville, Knoxville, Seattle, Omaha, New York, Newark, Chicago, Des Moines, Detroit, Cleveland & Los Angeles gave front-page space.
53 LIFE, 22 February 1950, pp. 40-41, headlined two pages of pictures and descriptions, 'College Revival Becomes Marathon,' popularizing an unfortunate, and wholly inaccurate, journalistic judgment.
54 TIME, 20 February 1950.
55 President Edman was quoted as saying: 'These kids are tired out. The testimonies have mostly to do with private matters. After all, the principal confessions are to Almighty God—not to a public audience.' (TIME).
56 J. Edwin Orr, GOOD NEWS IN BAD TIMES, pp. 77-78.
57 Editorial, BISBEE GAZETTE, quoted in J. Edwin Orr, GOOD NEWS IN BAD TIMES, p. 79.
58 AWAKENING BULLETIN, April 1950, q. Walter Kiernan.
59 COMMUNITY NEWS, Lexington, Kentucky, 3 March 1950, Editor's report: 'Impressions of Asbury Revival.'
60 F. W. Hoffman, REVIVAL TIMES IN AMERICA, pp. 166-167; J. Edwin Orr, GOOD NEWS IN BAD TIMES, pp. 84-85.
61 On Houghton College, see J. Edwin Orr, GOOD NEWS IN BAD TIMES, pp. 84-85; F. W. Hoffman, REVIVAL TIMES IN AMERICA, p. 166.
62 There was another unusual awakening at Asbury College in 1958, described in H. C. James & P. Rader, HALLS AFLAME, pp. 53ff.
63 Lauro Bretones, REDEMOINHOS DO SUL, Um Ano de Reavivamento no Brasil com o Dr. J. Edwin Orr, Teresopolis, 1953.
64 American Bible Society, ANNUAL REPORT, New York, 1953.
65 INTERNATIONAL REVIEW OF MISSIONS, January 1954, p. 54.
66 American Bible Society, ANNUAL REPORT, New York, 1953. The British and Foreign Bible Society, ANNUAL REPORT, 1955, stated that 'Brazil is being shaken by the winds of the Spirit as never before,' describing 1952 as 'a year of triumph.'
67 A. J. Appasamy, WRITE THE VISION, p. 188.
68 Lauro Bretones, REDEMOINHOS DO SUL, p. 80.
69 A. J. Appasamy, WRITE THE VISION, p. 154.
70 Lauro Bretones, REDEMOINHOS DO SUL, Chapter X, 'Escolas de Profetas.'
71 A. J. Appasamy, WRITE THE VISION, p. 145.
72 H. Reinhardt, 'When the Spirit Came,' CALL TO PRAYER, April 1966.

CHAPTER XX: THE EVANGELISM OF THE 'FIFTIES

1   J. Edwin Orr, GOOD NEWS IN BAD TIMES, p. 84.
2   Editorial, HIS Magazine, January 1956, p. 2, citing Stanley Rowland, in NEW YORK TIMES, 22 & 24 October 1955.
3   J. Edwin Orr, GOOD NEWS IN BAD TIMES, p. 66.
4   AWAKENING BULLETIN, W. R. Bright, editor, April 1950.
5   J. Edwin Orr, GOOD.NEWS IN BAD TIMES, p. 70.
6   Mimeographed report of Robert C. Cummings, president of the Religious Council of the University of Washinton, and three college presidents.
7   see UNIVERSITY OF WASHINGTON DAILY, 12-17 February 1950.
8   Mimeographed report of Robert C. Cummings.
9   J. Edwin Orr, GOOD NEWS IN BAD TIMES, p. 71.
10 Mimeographed report of Robert C. Cummings.
11 Editorial, HIS Magazine, October 1949.
12 see HIS Magazine, issues of October 1950 to May 1951.
13 'News of the Campus,' HIS Magazine, December 1950, p. 34.
14 see 'A Year of Evangelism,' issues of October 1950 to May 1951.
15 The Rev. Leith Samuel since became a regular Keswick Convention speaker.
16 J. Edwin Orr, GOOD NEWS IN BAD TIMES, p. 72.
17 A. J. Appasamy, WRITE THE VISION, p. 142.
18 Telegram, Rev. R. F. McMurray, president, Varsity Christian Fellowship,
19 E. M. Baldwin & D. V. Benson, HENRIETTA MEARS, p. 246.
20 W. R. Bright, COME HELP CHANGE THE WORLD, p. 24.
21 This advisory board gave advice on request, individually.
22 W. R. Bright, COME HELP CHANGE THE WORLD, p. 30.
23 J. Edwin Orr, INSIDE STORY OF THE HOLLYWOOD CHRISTIAN GROUP.
24 The researchist himself was the evangelist in these I.V.-C.C. campaigns.
25. W. R. Bright, COME HELP CHANGE THE WORLD, p. 33.
26 E. M. Baldwin & D. V. Benson, HENRIETTA MEARS, pp. 268-269.
27 W. R. Bright, COME HELP CHANGE THE WORLD, p. 131ff; see also LOS ANGELES EXAMINER, 27 December 1954 (full-page spread).
28 Information following from Campus Crusade headquarters, San Bernardino.
29 International Christian Leadership, Washington, D.C.
30 CHRISTIANITY TODAY, 23 April 1971, p. 38.
31 Dawson Trotman's Journals, 1931-41; NAVIGATORS' LOG; letters.
32 Christian Athletes' Fellowship, Kansas City, Missouri.
33 International Students, Washington, D.C.
34 Extracts, Billy Graham Association records, Minneapolis and Atlanta.
35 Editorial, HIS Magazine, January 1956, pp. 1-4.
36 M. E. Marty, THE NEW SHAPE OF AMERICAN RELIGION, pp. 14-15.
37 Editorial, HIS Magazine, January 1956, pp. 1-4.
38 Stanley Rowland, NEW YORK TIMES, 22 & 24 October 1955.
39 Reinhold Niebuhr, 'Is There a Revival of Religion?' in NEW YORK TIMES MAGAZINE, 19 November 1950, pp. 13, 60 & 62.
40 see M. E. Marty, THE NEW SHAPE OF AMERICAN RELIGION, pp. 6ff.
41 J. Edwin Orr, GOOD NEWS IN BAD TIMES, described the manifestations of the awakening among Evangelicals, and condemned the national immorality.
42 see W. L. Miller, 'Hollywood and Religion,' in RELIGION AND LIFE, XXII, Spring 1953, pp. 273-279.
43 The most effective counter-attack on drug addiction came from the charismatic wing of the Evangelical constituency, for example.

CHAPTER XXI: THE UNBELIEVABLE YEARS

1   J. Edwin Orr, I SAW NO TEARS, p. 111.
2   Letter of 11 August 1945, to Carol Orr, at Oribi, on Pondoland's borders.
3   N. A. Horner, ed., PROTESTANT CROSSCURRENTS IN MISSIONS, p. 39.
4   R. D. Winter, THE TWENTY-FIVE UNBELIEVABLE YEARS, p. 39.
5   N. Goodall, ed., MISSIONS UNDER THE CROSS, p. 40.
6   cf. N. A. Burr, A CRITICAL BIBLIOGRAPHY OF RELIGION IN AMERICA, 'Recent Revival,'   pp. 1162ff.
7   cf. D. M. Stowe, 'Changing Patterns of Missionary Service in Today's World,' OCCASIONAL BULLETIN, XX, January 1969, Missionary Research Library.
8   see A. J. Appasamy, WRITE THE VISION, passim.
9   VIDA PRESBITERIANA, Sao Paulo, 25 October 1952.
10   W. Stanley Rycroft, Board of Foreign Missions of the Presbyterian Church in the U.S.A., 52-1403, 17-18 November 1952.
11   Young Nak Presbyterian Church, Seoul, Dr. Kyung Chik Han, pastor.
12   An espousal of the notion that social action is evangelism led to the neglect of evangelism, to the dismay of those who believed in both.
13   An Anglican friend is now writing a history of the East African Revival.
14   David Barrett, 'The Expansion of Christianity in Africa in the Twentieth Century,' CHURCH GROWTH BULLETIN, V, May 1969; TIME, 12 January 1970, p. 35.
15   R. D. Winter, THE TWENTY-FIVE UNBELIEVABLE YEARS, p. 56.
16   see, for example, WHEATON ALUMNI, March 1971, pp. 1-2.
17   on Dr. Paul Carlson, see C. P. Anderson, THERE WAS A MAN, p. 31.
18   D. M. Howard, STUDENT POWER IN WORLD EVANGELISM, pp. 104-105.
19   W. M. Beahm, 'Factors in the Development of the Student Volunteer Movement for Foreign Missions,' pp. 276-278, notes that the Student Consultation in Toronto in 1940 was limited, but that it had 'the backing of the entire Student Christian movement of U.S.A.—including Church groups, Y.M.C.A., Y.W.C.A., S.V.M. & regional movements—as well as of the S.C.M. of Canada.'
20   D. M. Howard, STUDENT POWER IN WORLD EVANGELISM, p. 103.
21   R. D. Winter, THE TWENTY-FIVE UNBELIEVABLE YEARS, p. 56.
22   K. S. Latourette, MISSIONS TOMORROW, pp. 127-131.
23   D. M. Howard, STUDENT POWER IN WORLD EVANGELISM, p. 106.
24   Both the Evangelical Foreign Missions Association and the Interdenominational Foreign Missions Association established Personnel and Student Affairs Commissions—see D. M. Howard, p. 108.
25   P. F. Barkman, E. R. Dayton & E. L. Gruman, CHRISTIAN COLLEGIANS AND FOREIGN MISSIONS, 1969, p. xii.
26   'The Delegates to Urbana,' CHRISTIAN COLLEGIANS AND FOREIGN MISSIONS, pp. 4-7.
27   'The Delegates to Urbana,' pp. 8-9; 12-15; 24-27; 30-31; 38-39.
28   W. R. Bright, COME HELP CHANGE THE WORLD, Chapter XVIII.
29   International Students, Colorado Springs. Colorado.
30   R. Gehman, LET MY HEART BE BROKEN, 1960.
31   Overseas Crusades, Palo Alto, California.
32   Wycliffe Bible Translators, Santa Ana, California.
33   Missionary Aviation Fellowship, Fullerton, California.
34   Far East Broadcasting Company, Whittier, California.
35   Moody Institute of Science, Whittier, California.
36   Gospel Recordings, Los Angeles, California.

CHAPTER XXII: EPILOGUE: 1970

1 But not President V. R. Edman, WHEATON RECORD, 9 February 1950.
2 WHEATON RECORD, 10 January & 29 May 1957, & passim.
3 Most striking was a letter received by the writer in 1964 from a Wheaton graduate, now a college president, urgently requesting prayer.
4 Personal knowledge.
5 WHEATON RECORD, 11 February 1965.
6 CHRISTIANITY TODAY, 12 March 1965; cf. BULLETIN, Wheaton College, March 1965, p. 5.
7 News Release, Evangel College, Springfield, Missouri, 18 November 1969 & 15 August 1970.
8 Neo-Pentecostalism, or the 'charismatic movement,' owes its development more to the ministry of Dr. David DuPlessis than any other human factor. A South African, he served as Secretary of the Pentecostal World Alliance, but became a free-lance 'missionary' to the other denominations.
9 K. & D. Ranaghan, CATHOLIC PENTECOSTALS, Chapters I & II.
10 Information received from David DuPlessis personally.
11 K. & D. Ranaghan, CATHOLIC PENTECOSTALS, pp. 51ff.
12 The American Association of Evangelical Students voted in 1971 to expand its membership, and form chapters on secular university campuses—see CHRISTIANITY TODAY, 23 April 1971, p. 38.
13 LEXINGTON LEADER, 18 February 1970.
14 CHRISTIANITY TODAY, 13 March 1970.
15 Mimeographed Report, Prof. H. A. Hanke, February 1970.
16 CHRISTIANITY TODAY, 13 March 1970.
17 see ASBURY COLLEGIAN, 25 February 1970.
18 WHEATON RECORD, 13 & 20 February 1970.
19 News Release, Greenville College, Greenville, Illinois, February 1970; & CHRISTIANITY TODAY, 13 March 1970.
20 ANDERSON HERALD, 24 February 1970; ANDERSON COLLEGE NEWS, March 1970; VITAL CHRISTIANITY, Anderson, Indiana, 5 & 19 April 1970; & correspondence with the campus minister, James Earl Massey.
21 CHRISTIANITY TODAY, 13 March 1970.
22 INDIANAPOLIS STAR, 23 February 1970; & CHRISTIANITY TODAY, 13 March 1970.
23 Letter of President Haggard, Azusa Pacific College, 10 March 1970.
24 SEATTLE TIMES, 25 March 1970.
25 THE ORACLE, Tulsa, Oklahoma, 6 March 1970.
26 SAN ANTONIO EXPRESS, 6 April 1970.
27 THE SEMINARY TOWER, Kansas City, Summer 1970.
28 CHRISTIANITY TODAY, 13 March 1970.
29 Reports of Dr. Roy L. Fish & Dr. L. Jack Gray, Southwestern Baptist Theological Seminary, Fort Worth, Texas, April 1970.
30 Associated Press reporter at Asbury College, quoted in R. E. Coleman, ed., ONE DIVINE MOMENT, p. 90.
31 Special Reports, Asbury College, February-April 1970; cf. R. E. Coleman, ed., ONE DIVINE MOMENT, Chapter VI.
32 Special Reports, Asbury College, February-April 1970; and private letter to the author.
33 'Does Nation Face Spiritual Awakening?' INDIANAPOLIS STAR, article, 23 February 1970.

CHAPTER XXIII: PATTERN OF COLLEGE REVIVALS

1 F. Rudolph, THE AMERICAN COLLEGE AND UNIVERSITY, p. 80.
2 UNITED EVANGELICAL ACTION, 15 March 1951.
3 J. Edwin Orr, GOOD NEWS IN BAD TIMES, p. 84.
4 Letters from various college presidents, addressed to Alastair C. Walker, Chicago, dated variously in April 1951.
5 Report of United Spiritual Advance, Minneapolis, 8 June 1949.
6 E. M. Baldwin & D. V. Benson, HENRIETTA MEARS, p. 232.
7 J. Edwin Orr, FULL SURRENDER, introduction by Billy Graham.
8 Reported to the writer by faculty members, Wheaton College, 1950.
9 F. Rudolph, THE AMERICAN COLLEGE AND UNIVERSITY, p. 80.
10 F. Rudolph, MARK HOPKINS AND THE LOG: WILLIAMS COLLEGE, 1836-1872, p. 100.
11 G. W. Chessman, DENISON: THE STORY OF AN OHIO COLLEGE, p. 81.
12 Recollections of Professor Myron Goldsmith, George Fox College.
13 This incident was reported to the writer years ago by the minister of the Tremont Temple in Boston.
14 Editorial, HIS Magazine, May 1950.
15 J. Edwin Orr, FULL SURRENDER, pp. 27ff.
16 Special Reports, Asbury College, February-April 1970.
17 CALIFORNIA SEMINARY NEWS, Los Angeles, November-December 1949, and J. Edwin Orr, GOOD NEWS IN BAD TIMES, pp. 65-66.
18 Letters in reply to inquiries made by the writer to college presidents, 1971.
19 F. Rudolph, THE AMERICAN COLLEGE AND UNIVERSITY, pp. 77-78.
20 His Excellency Sri Sri Prakasa, Governor of Madras State (now Tamilnadu) and later Governor of Bombay State (now Maharashtra).
21 K. S. Latourette, MISSIONS TOMORROW, pp. 127ff.
22 Professor Latourette often stated this conviction in public and private, as well as in the passage cited above.

CHAPTER XXIV: THEOLOGY OF COLLEGE REVIVALS

1 J. W. Ewing, GOODLY FELLOWSHIP, p. 17.
2 John the Baptist, Matthew 3: 2, "Repent ye, for the kingdom of heaven is at hand." Matthew 4: 17, 'From that time Jesus began to preach and to say, "Repent: for the kingdom of heaven is at hand." ' The twelve disciples, Mark 6: 12, 'And they went out, and preached that men should repent.' Acts 2: 38, 'Then Peter said unto them, "Repent . . ." ' Acts 26: 19-20, 'Whereupon, O king Agrippa, I was not disobedient unto the heavenly vision: but shewed first unto them of Damascus, and at Jerusalem, and throughout all the coasts of Judaea, and then to the Gentiles, that they should repent and turn to God, and do works meet for repentance.'
3 John 3: 3, 'Jesus answered and said unto him, "Except a man be born again, he cannot see the kingdom of God." '
4 I John 1: 9, 'If we confess our sins, he is faithful and just to forgive us our sins, and to cleanse us from all unrighteousness.'
5 Matthew 5: 23-24; Matthew 18: 15-17.
6 Leviticus 5: 5, '. . . he shall confess that he hath sinned in that thing.'
7 James 5: 16, 'Confess your faults one to another, and pray one for another, that ye may be healed. The effectual fervent prayer of a righteous man availeth much.'

BIBLIOGRAPHY

Periodicals: Daily, Weekly, Monthly, Quarterly & Annually

THE ADVANCE, Chicago, Illinois, 1905.
ANDERSON COLLEGE NEWS, Anderson, Indiana.
ANDERSON HERALD, Anderson, Indiana.
ANNUAL OF THE NORTHERN BAPTIST CONVENTION, Philadelphia, 1910.
ANNUAL REPORT, American Bible Society, New York, 1953.
ANNUAL REPORT, British & Foreign Bible Society, London, 1955.
ASBURY COLLEGIAN, Wilmore, Kentucky.
ASSOCIATION MEN, Y.M.C.A., Chicago, Illinois, 1900.
AWAKENING BULLETIN, W.R. Bright, editor, Los Angeles, 1950.
BAIRD'S MANUAL: American College Fraternities, Menasha, Wisconson, 1940.
BAPTIST ARGUS, Louisville, Kentucky, 1905.
BAPTIST HOME MISSION MONTHLY, Philadelphia, 1905.
BAPTIST MISSIONARY MAGAZINE, Boston, 1895-1905.
BAPTIST STANDARD, Dallas, Texas.
BISBEE GAZETTE, Bisbee, Arizona.
BRITISH STUDENT MOVEMENT, S.C.M., London, 1905.
CALENDAR OF THE UNIVERSITY OF LONDON, 1970-71.
CALIFORNIA SEMINARY NEWS, Los Angeles, 1949.
CALL TO PRAYER, Chicago, Illinois.
CAMBRIDGE REVIEW, Cambridge, England, issues of November 1882.
CARNARVON & DENBIGH HERALD, Denbigh, Wales, 1904.
CATALOGUE OF THE UNIVERSITY OF ROCHESTER, 1864.
THE CENTRAL BAPTIST, St. Louis, 1905.
CHINA MISSION YEAR BOOK, Shanghai, 1913.
CHICAGO DAILY PRESS, 1858.
THE CHRISTIAN, London, 1874ff.
CHRISTIAN ADVOCATE AND JOURNAL, New York, 1858ff & 1905ff.
CHRISTIAN EDUCATION, Chicago, 1937.
CHRISTIAN ENDEAVOR WORLD, Boston, 1905.
CHRISTIAN EXPRESS, Lovedale, South Africa, 1903.
CHRISTIAN HANDBOOK OF INDIA, Delhi, 1962.
THE CHRISTIAN HERALD, Philadelphia.
CHRISTIAN LIFE, Chicago, Illinois.
THE CHRISTIAN MOVEMENT in the Japanese Empire, Tokyo, 1915 (annual).
CHRISTIAN OBSERVER, Louisville, 1905.
CHRISTIAN REGISTER, Boston, 1858.
CHRISTIAN STUDENT, Capetown, 1900ff.
CHRISTIANITY TODAY, Washington, D.C.
CHURCH GROWTH BULLETIN, Palo Alto, California.
CHURCH HISTORY, Chicago.
THE CHURCHMAN, New York, 1858.
THE COLLEGE BULLETIN, New York, 1878.
COMMUNITY NEWS, Lexington, Kentucky.
CONGREGATIONAL QUARTERLY, Boston, 1858ff.
CONGREGATIONAL YEAR BOOK, Boston, 1859.
DE KERKBODE, Capetown, 1901-1902.
DIRECTORY OF CHRISTIAN MISSIONS IN INDIA, Nagpur, 1928-1929.

DOCTORAL RECIPIENTS FROM UNITED STATES UNIVERSITIES, 1958-66, National Academy of Sciences, Washington, D.C., 1967.
ENCYCLOPEDIA BRITANNICA, Chicago, 1970.
EVANGELICAL CHRISTENDOM, London, 1858 & 1905 (Quarterly).
EVANGELICAL REPOSITORY, New York, 1858.
THE EVANGELIST, New York, 1858.
EVANGELIZE, Minneapolis (Lutheran Evangelistic Movement).
EVENING POST, Burlington, Iowa, 1905.
EVENING POST, Schenectady, New York, 1905.
THE EXAMINER, New York, 1858 & 1905.
THE FREEMAN, London, 1859.
HANSARD, London, Volume IX, 1178, 11 August 1807.
HIS Magazine, Chicago, 1950ff.
INDIANAPOLIS STAR, Indianapolis.
THE INTERCOLLEGIAN, 1887ff.
INTERNATIONAL REVIEW OF MISSIONS, New York.
JOURNAL OF XLI ANNUAL CONVENTION OF THE PROTESTANT EPISCOPAL CHURCH IN THE DIOCESE OF OHIO, Cleveland, 1858.
THE JOURNAL AND MESSENGER, Cincinnati, 1905.
LEXINGTON LEADER, Lexington, Kentucky.
LIFE Magazine, New York.
LOS ANGELES EXAMINER.
METHODIST RECORDER, London, 1905.
METHODIST TIMES, London, 1905.
MICHIGAN CHRISTIAN ADVOCATE, Adrian, 1905.
MINUTES OF THE GENERAL ASSEMBLY OF THE PRESBYTERIAN CHURCH IN THE UNITED STATES OF AMERICA, Philadelphia, 1906.
MINUTES of the Hawaiian Evangelistic Association, Honolulu, 1858-1862.
THE MISSIONARY REGISTER, Madras, 1819.
MISSIONARY RECORD of the United Presbyterian Church, Edinburgh, 1905.
MISSIONARY REVIEW OF THE WORLD, New York, 1899ff.
MONTHLY NEWS LETTER, Columbia Bible College, South Carolina, 1936.
MONTHLY RELIGIOUS MAGAZINE, Boston, 1858.
NATIONAL INTELLIGENCER, Washington, D.C., 1858.
NAVIGATORS' LOG, Colorado Springs, Colorado.
NEW YORK DAILY TRIBUNE, 1858.
NEW YORK HERALD, 1858.
NEW YORK TIMES, 1955.
NEWS NOTES, Department of Higher Education, National Council of Churches of Christ in the U.S.A., New York, 1969.
THE NONCONFORMIST, London, 1859.
THE NORTHERN, Northern Baptist Theological Seminary, Chicago, 1949.
OBERLIN EVANGELIST, Oberlin, Ohio, 1858.
OCCASIONAL BULLETIN, Missionary Research Library, New York.
THE ORACLE, Oral Roberts University, Tulsa, Oklahoma.
THE OXFORD STUDENT MOVEMENT, Oxford, 1905.
THE PACIFIC BAPTIST, Portland, Oregon, 1905.
PENNSYLVANIA MAGAZINE OF HISTORY & BIOGRAPHY, Philadelphia, 1946.
THE PENTECOSTAL HERALD, Louisville, 1905.
THE PHILADELPHIA INQUIRER, 1876.
THE PRESBYTERIAN MAGAZINE, Philadelphia, 1858.
THE PRINCETON REVIEW, Princeton, 1859.

PROCEEDINGS OF THE CHURCH MISSIONARY SOCIETY, London.
PROCEEDINGS OF THE 22nd ANNUAL CONVENTION OF THE YOUNG MEN'S
    CHRISTIAN ASSOCIATIONS, Louisville, 1877.
THE RECORD, London, 1859 & 1905.
RELIGION IN LIFE, New York.
RELIGIOUS EDUCATION, Chicago, 1908.
REPORT, Board of Missions, Methodist Episcopal Church, Nashville, 1909.
REPORT OF THE FIRST INTERNATIONAL CONVENTION OF THE STUDENT
    VOLUNTEER MOVEMENT, Cleveland, Ohio, 1877.
THE REVIVAL, London, 1859ff (later known as THE CHRISTIAN).
SAN ANTONIO EXPRESS, San Antonio, Texas.
SCHENECTADY GAZETTE, Schenectady, New York, 1905.
SCRIBNER'S MAGAZINE, New York, 1910.
SCOTTISH BAPTIST MAGAZINE, Glasgow, 1905.
SEATTLE PACIFIC BULLETIN, Seattle, 1950.
SEATTLE TIMES, Seattle, Washington.
THE SEMINARY TOWER, Nazarene Theological Seminary, Kansas City.
SERVICE, organ of the Baptist Young People's Union, Chicago, 1905-1906.
SPRINGFIELD REPUBLICAN, Springfield, Massachusetts, 1886.
SPRINGFIELD UNION, Springfield, Massachusetts, 1892.
THE STANDARD, Chicago, 1949ff.
SUNDAY SCHOOL TIMES, Philadelphia, 1936.
TELEPHONE-REGISTER, McMinnville, Oregon, 1905.
TIME, the Weekly News Magazine, Chicago, 1950.
UNITED EVANGELICAL ACTION, Cincinnati.
UNITED STATES CENSUS, 1910.
U. S. Office of Education, EDUCATION DIRECTORY, Part III, 1966-67.
UNIVERSITY OF WASHINGTON DAILY, Seattle, 1950.
VIDA PRESBITERIANA, Sao Paulo, Brazil, 1952.
VITAL CHRISTIANITY, Anderson, Indiana.
THE WATCHMAN, Boston, 1905.
THE WATCHMAN, Y.M.C.A., Chicago, 1879.
WELCH PIETY (accounts of the Circulating Schools in Wales, published annu-
    ally from 1740), Cardiff, Wales, 1740-1750.
WESLEYAN CHRONICLE, Melbourne, 1860.
WESLEYAN METHODIST MAGAZINE, London, 1905.
WESTERN CHRISTIAN ADVOCATE, Cincinnati, 1905-1906.
WHEATON ALUMNI, Wheaton, Illinois.
WHEATON RECORD, Wheaton, Illinois.
THE WORLD'S WORK, Chicago, 1905.
YEAR BOOK OF THE AMERICAN CHURCHES, New York, 1923.
YEAR BOOK, the Young Men's Christian Associations of North America, 1906,
    1921 & 1936.
YR HERALD CYMRAEG, Aberystwyth, 1905.
Y.M.C.A. JOURNAL, New York, 1860.
Y.M.C.A. QUARTERLY, New York, 1868.
ZAMBESI INDUSTRIAL MISSION MONTHLY, London, 1903.

H. B. Adams, THE COLLEGE OF WILLIAM AND MARY, Washington, 1887.

W. O. B. Allen & E. McClure, TWO HUNDRED YEARS: THE HISTORY OF THE SOCIETY FOR PROMOTING CHRISTIAN KNOWLEDGE, 1698-1898, London, 1898.

C. E. Allison, A HISTORICAL SKETCH OF HAMILTON COLLEGE, Clinton, New York, 1889.

R. Anderson, A HISTORY OF THE HAWAIIAN MISSION, Boston, 1870.

A. J. Appasamy, WRITE THE VISION, London, 1964.

L. G. Bacon, THE HISTORY OF AMERICAN CHRISTIANITY, New York, 1897.

J. A. Baker, CONTENDING THE GRADE, Asheville, N.C., 1947.

E. M. Baldwin & D. V. Benson, HENRIETTA MEARS AND HOW SHE DID IT, Glendale, California, 1966.

P. F. Barkman, E. R. Dayton & E. L. Gruman, CHRISTIAN COLLEGIANS AND FOREIGN MISSIONS, Monrovia, California, 1969.

H. C. Barnard, A HISTORY OF ENGLISH EDUCATION, London, 1947.

K. P. Battle, HISTORY OF THE UNIVERSITY OF NORTH CAROLINA, Raleigh, 1907-1912, 2 Volumes.

H. P. Beach & B. St. John, WORLD STATISTICS OF CHRISTIAN MISSIONS, New York, 1916.

W. H. Beahm, 'Factors in the Development of the Student Volunteer Movement for Foreign Missions,' unpublished Ph.D. dissertation, University of Chicago, 1941.

F. G. Beardsley, A HISTORY OF AMERICAN REVIVALS, New York, 1904.

Lyman Beecher, AUTOBIOGRAPHY, CORRESPONDENCE, etc., New York, 1864-1865.

A. D. Belden, GEORGE WHITEFIELD, THE AWAKENER, New York, 1930.

W. W. Bennett, NARRATIVE OF THE GREAT REVIVAL WHICH PREVAILED IN THE SOUTHERN ARMIES DURING THE LATE CIVIL WAR, Philadelphia, 1877.

H. Bingham, A RESIDENCE OF TWENTY-ONE YEARS IN THE SANDWICH ISLANDS, Hartford, 1948.

L. E. Binns, THE EVANGELICAL MOVEMENT IN THE ENGLISH CHURCH, London, 1928.

C. Birchenough, A HISTORY OF ELEMENTARY EDUCATION IN ENGLAND AND WALES, Third Edition, London, 1938.

W. N. Blair, GOLD IN KOREA, Topeka, 1948.

A. H. Body, JOHN WESLEY AND EDUCATION, London, 1936.

P. F. Bohannon, AFRICA AND AFRICANS, Garden City, 1964.

Ami Bost, L'HISTOIRE DU REVEIL RELIGIEUX DES EGLISES PROTES-TANTES DE LA SUISSE ET DE LA FRANCE, Paris.

J. Boswell, THE LIFE OF SAMUEL JOHNSON, edition of J. W. Crocker, London, 1876.

A. F. C. Bourdillon, VOLUNTARY SOCIAL SERVICES, London, 1945.

W. Boyd, THE HISTORY OF WESTERN EDUCATION, Eighth Edition, New York, 1966—revised by Edmund J. King, University of London.

E. Braga & K. G. Grubb, THE REPUBLIC OF BRAZIL, London, 1932.

B. M. Brain, THE TRANSFORMATION OF HAWAII, New York, 1896.

P. J. Braisted, INDIAN NATIONALISM AND THE CHRISTIAN COLLEGES, New York, 1935.

Lauro Bretones, REDEMOINHOS DO SUL: UM ANO DE REAVIVAMENTO NO BRASIL COM O DR. J. EDWIN ORR, Teresopolis, 1953.

W. R. Bright, COME HELP CHANGE THE WORLD, Old Tappan, N.J., 1970.

W. C. Bronson, THE HISTORY OF BROWN UNIVERSITY, 1764-1914, Brown University, Providence, 1914.

R. P. Brooks, THE UNIVERSITY OF GEORGIA UNDER SIXTEEN ADMINI-STRATIONS, 1785-1955, Athens, Georgia, 1956.

Marshall Broomhall, W. W. CASSELS: FIRST BISHOP IN WEST CHINA, London, 1926.

M. L. Brown, 'Survey and Evaluation of the Youth Revival Movement in the South and Southwest,' unpublished M. A. thesis, Baylor University.

W. E. Browning, J. Ritchie & K. G. Grubb, THE WEST COAST REPUBLICS OF SOUTH AMERICA, Chile, Peru and Bolivia, London, 1930.

W. E. Browning, THE RIVER PLATE REPUBLICS, London, 1928.

R. L. Buell, THE NATIVE PROBLEM IN AFRICA, London, 1928, 2 Vols.

H. M. Bullock, A HISTORY OF EMORY UNIVERSITY, Nashville, 1936.

N. A. Burr, A CRITICAL BIBLIOGRAPHY OF RELIGION IN AMERICA, Princeton, 1961, 2 Volumes.

John Calvin, LEGES ACADEMICAE GENEVENSIS, Geneva, 1559.

G. B. Camargo & K. G. Grubb, RELIGION IN THE REPUBLIC OF MEXICO, London, 1935.

J. Cameron, EASTERN NAZARENE COLLEGE, Boston, 1965.

W. A. Candler, GREAT REVIVALS AND THE GREAT REPUBLIC, Nashville, 1904.

W. Canton, A HISTORY OF THE BRITISH AND FOREIGN BIBLE SOCIETY, London, 1904-1910, 5 Volumes.

S. P. Carey, WILLIAM CAREY, FELLOW OF THE LINNAEAN SOCIETY, London, 1934.

J. M. Carroll, A HISTORY OF TEXAS BAPTISTS, Dallas, 1923.

J. T. Carson, GOD'S RIVER IN SPATE, Belfast, 1958.

W. Carus, MEMOIRS OF THE LIFE OF THE Rev. CHARLES SIMEON, New York, 1847.

Otis Cary, A HISTORY OF CHRISTIANITY IN JAPAN, New York, 1909, 2 Vols.

G. Cassani, DELL'ANTICO STUDIO DI BOLOGNA, Bologna, 1888.

F. A. Cavenagh, THE LIFE AND WORK OF GRIFFITH JONES, Cardiff, 1930.

Mrs W. I. Chamberlain, FIFTY YEARS IN FOREIGN FIELDS, New York, 1925.

T. W. Chambers, THE NOON PRAYER MEETING, New York, 1858.

G. W. Chessman, DENISON: THE STORY OF AN OHIO COLLEGE, Granville, Ohio, 1957.

E. P. Cheyney, HISTORY OF THE UNIVERSITY OF PENNSYLVANIA, 1740-1940, Philadelphia, 1940.

Christian Medical Association of India, TALES FROM THE INNS OF HEALING, Nagpur, 1942.

W. L. S. Churchill, MY AFRICAN JOURNEY, London, 1908.

C. C. Cleveland, THE GREAT REVIVAL IN THE WEST, Chicago, 1916.

F. D. Coggan, editor, CHRIST AND THE COLLEGES, London, 1934.

Thomas Coke, A SERMON UPON EDUCATION, Sherbourne, 1774.

R. E. Coleman, editor, ONE DIVINE MOMENT, Wilmore, Kentucky, 1970.

J. A. Comenius, THE GREAT DIDACTIC, translated by M. W. Keatinge, 1910 (Second Edition), London.

W. C. Conant, NARRATIVE OF REMARKABLE CONVERSIONS, New York, 1858.

J. J. Considine, NEW HORIZONS IN LATIN AMERICA, New York, 1958.

C. T. Cook, THE BILLY GRAHAM STORY, London, 1954.

W. Corston, THE LIFE OF JOSEPH LANCASTER, London, 1861.

E. M. Coulter, COLLEGE LIFE IN THE OLD SOUTH, Athens, Georgia, 1951.

William Cowper, HOPE POEMS, London, 1841.

G. T. B. Davis, WHEN THE FIRE FELL, Philadelphia, 1945.

G. T. B. Davis, TORREY AND ALEXANDER, New York, 1905.

J. D. Davis, A SKETCH OF LIFE OF THE Rev. JOSEPH HARDY NEESIMA, Second Edition, Chicago, 1894.

Lal Behari Day, RECOLLECTIONS OF ALEXANDER DUFF, and the MISSION COLLEGE WHICH HE FOUNDED AT CALCUTTA, London, 1879.

F. de Azevedo, BRAZILIAN CULTURE, New York, 1950.

R. Delegne, L'UNIVERSITE DE PARIS, 1224-1244, Paris, 1902.

W. H. S. Demarest, A HISTORY OF RUTGERS COLLEGE, 1766-1924, New Brunswick, 1924.

J. S. Dennis, CHRISTIAN MISSIONS AND SOCIAL PROGRESS, New York, 1897-1906, 3 Volumes.

S. Derenzi, STORIA DEL SCUOLA MEDICA DI SALERNO, Naples, 1857.

DICTIONARY OF AMERICAN BIOGRAPHY, New York, 1928-37, 21 Volumes.

A. C. Downer, A CENTURY OF EVANGELICAL RELIGION IN OXFORD, London, 1938.

S. Drew, THE LIFE OF THE REV. THOMAS COKE, LL.D., London, 1817.

J. du Plessis, A HISTORY OF CHRISTIAN MISSIONS IN SOUTH AFRICA, London, 1911.

J. du Plessis, THE EVANGELIZATION OF PAGAN AFRICA, Capetown, 1930.

C. Durfee, A HISTORY OF WILLIAMS COLLEGE, Boston, 1860.

E. W. Dwight, MEMOIRS OF HENRY OBOOKIAH, New Haven, 1818.

Timothy Dwight, A DISCOURSE ON SOME EVENTS OF THE LAST CENTURY, New Haven, 1801.

Timothy Dwight, THE NATURE AND DANGER OF INFIDEL PHILOSOPHY, New Haven, 1798.

Timothy Dwight, TRAVELS, New Haven, 1821-1822.

H. S. Dyer, PANDITA RAMABAI, London, undated.

E. D. Eaton, HISTORICAL SKETCHES OF BELOIT COLLEGE, Beloit, 1928.

E. D. Eddy, COLLEGES FOR OUR LAND AND TIME, The Land-Grant Idea in American Education, New York, 1957.

Jonathan Edwards, THE LIFE OF DAVID BRAINERD, Edinburgh, 1765.

W. Ellis, THE MARTYR CHURCH IN MADAGASCAR, London, 1870.

W. Ellis, POLYNESIAN RESEARCHES, London, 1831, 2 Volumes.

W. T. Ellis, MEN AND MISSIONS, Philadelphia, 1909.

Eifion Evans, WHEN HE IS COME, Bala, Wales, 1959.

Eifion Evans, THE WELSH REVIVAL OF 1904, London, 1969.

J. W. Ewing, GOODLY FELLOWSHIP, the Life and Work of the Evangelical Alliance, 1846-1946, London, 1946.

J. H. Fairchild, OBERLIN: THE COLONY AND THE COLLEGE, Oberlin, 1883.

W. E. Farndale, THE SECRET OF MOW COP, London, 1950.

H. V. Faulkner, AMERICAN ECONOMIC HISTORY, New York, 1938.

W. W. Ferrier, ORIGIN AND DEVELOPMENT OF THE UNIVERSITY OF CALIFORNIA, Berkeley, 1930.

C. G. Finney, MEMOIRS OF CHARLES G. FINNEY, New York, 1876 & 1908.

C. B. Firth, INTRODUCTION TO INDIAN CHURCH HISTORY, Madras, 1961.

J. R. Fleming, A HISTORY OF THE CHURCH IN SCOTLAND, Edinburgh, 1927-1933. - ·

Benjamin Franklin, THE AUTOBIOGRAPHY OF BENJAMIN FRANKLIN, New York, 1929, edited by O. S. Coad.

S. R. Gammon, THE EVANGELICAL INVASION OF BRAZIL, Richmond, Va., 1910.

R. Gehman, LET MY HEART BE BROKEN, New York, 1960.

G. B. Gerdener, RECENT DEVELOPMENTS IN THE SOUTH AFRICAN MISSION FIELD, London, 1958.

Edward Gibbon, MEMOIRS OF MY LIFE AND WRITINGS, in WORKS, London, 1796.

J. Gillies, editor, MEMOIRS OF THE LIFE OF REV. GEORGE WHITEFIELD, London, 1774.

A. Godbold, THE CHURCH COLLEGE IN THE OLD SOUTH, Durham, 1944.

R. Goforth, GOFORTH OF CHINA, London, undated.

Norman Goodall, editor, MISSIONS UNDER THE CROSS, London, 1953.

Billy Graham, REVIVAL IN OUR TIME, Wheaton, Illinois, 1950.

R. Gray, THE TWO NATIONS, London, 1960.

J. A. Green, THE LIFE AND WORK OF PESTALOZZI, London, 1913.

A. Gregory, ROBERT RAIKES: JOURNALIST AND PHILANTHROPIST, London, 1877.

Wilfred Grenfell, A LABRADOR DOCTOR (Autobiography), New York, 1919.

W. E. Griffis, HEPBURN OF JAPAN, Philadelphia, 1913.

W. E. Griffis, A MAKER OF THE NEW ORIENT, Samuel Robbins Brown, Chicago, 1902.

W. E. Griffis, VERBECK OF JAPAN, Chicago, 1900.

N. P. Grubb, C. T. STUDD: CRICKETER AND PIONEER, London, 1933.

N. P. Grubb, ONCE CAUGHT, NO ESCAPE, (Autobiography), London, 1969.

N. P. Grubb, MODERN VIKING: THE STORY OF ABRAHAM VEREIDE, Grand Rapids, 1961.

K. G. Grubb, THE WEST COAST REPUBLICS OF SOUTH AMERICA, London, 1930.

H. E. F. Guericke, AUGUST HERMAN FRANCKE, London, 1837.

A. Haldane, THE LIVES OF ROBERT AND JAMES ALEXANDER HALDANE, New York, 1854.

S. B. Halliday & D. S. Gregory, THE CHURCH IN AMERICA AND ITS BAPTISMS OF FIRE, New York, 1896.

A. S. Hardy, THE LIFE AND LETTERS OF JOSEPH HARDY NEESIMA, Boston, 1892.

C. F. Harford-Battersby, PILKINGTON OF UGANDA, London, undated.

J. B. Harford & F. C. Macdonald, HANDLEY CARR GLYN MOULE, Bishop of Durham, London, 1922.

J. H. Harris, ROBERT RAIKES: THE MAN AND HIS WORK, London, 1899.

K. Hartfelder, PHILIPP MELANCHTHON ALS PRAECEPTOR GERMANIAE, Berlin, 1889.

Philip Hartog, SOME ASPECTS OF INDIAN EDUCATION, London, 1939.

W. Havighurst, THE MIAMI YEARS, 1809-1959, New York, 1958.

G. R. Hess, SAM HIGGINBOTHAM OF ALLAHABAD, New York, 1967.

H. I. Hester, A HISTORY OF WILLIAM JEWELL COLLEGE, Liberty, 1967.

Sam Higginbotham, THE GOSPEL AND THE PLOW, New York, 1921.

Stanley High, BILLY GRAHAM, New York, 1956.

F. W. Hoffman, REVIVAL TIMES IN AMERICA, Boston, 1956.

C. Howard Hopkins, HISTORY OF THE Y.M.C.A. IN NORTH AMERICA, New York, 1951.

271

F. W. Horn, GRUNDTVIGS LIV OG GJERNING, Copenhagen, 1883.

N. A. Horner, editor, PROTESTANT CROSSCURRENTS IN MISSIONS, New York, 1968.

Mrs R. Hoskins, CLARA A. SWAIN, M.D., FIRST MEDICAL MISSIONARY TO THE WOMEN OF THE ORIENT, Boston, 1912.

David M. Howard, STUDENT POWER IN WORLD EVANGELISM, Downer's Grove, Illinois, 1970.

W. S. Hunt, THE ANGLICAN CHURCH IN TRAVANCORE AND COCHIN, Kottayam, Kerala, 1933.

A. S. Huntington, MEMOIRS AND LETTERS OF F. D. HUNTINGTON, Boston, 1906.

F. D. Huntington, PERMANENT REALITIES OF RELIGION AND THE PRESENT RELIGIOUS INTEREST, Boston, 1858.

C. W. Iglehart, A CENTURY OF PROTESTANT CHRISTIANITY IN JAPAN, Tokyo, 1959.

Kenneth Ingham, REFORMERS IN INDIA, 1783-1833, London, 1956.

Institute of International Education, A SURVEY OF THE AFRICAN STUDENT, New York, 1961.

H. C. James & Paul Rader, HALLS AFLAME, Wilmore, Kentucky, 1966.

M. P. Jeffrey, DR. IDA: INDIA, THE LIFE STORY OF IDA S. SCUDDER, New York, 1938.

C. A. Johnson, THE FRONTIER CAMP MEETING, Dallas, 1955.

Sir H. H. Johnston, THE STORY OF MY LIFE, London, 1923.

D. Jones, THE LIFE AND TIMES OF GRIFFITH JONES, London, 1902.

J. W. Jones, CHRIST IN THE CAMP, OR RELIGION IN LEE'S ARMY, Richmond, 1887.

M. G. Jones, THE CHARITY SCHOOL MOVEMENT, Cambridge, 1938.

R. B. Jones, RENT HEAVENS, THE REVIVAL OF 1904, London, 1930.

M. Joynt, THE LIFE OF St. GALL, London, 1927.

G. B. Kanungo, THE LANGUAGE CONTROVERSY IN INDIAN EDUCATION, Chicago, 1962.

M. W. Keatinge, COMENIUS, London, 1932.

Keenleyside & Thomas, A HISTORY OF JAPANESE EDUCATION, Tokyo, 1937.

Baron Dairoku Kikuchi, JAPANESE EDUCATION, London, 1909.

John Knox, THE WORKS OF JOHN KNOX, edited by David Laing, Edinburgh, 1846-1864, 6 Volumes.

G. A. Koch, REPUBLICAN RELIGION: THE AMERICAN REVOLUTION AND THE CULT OF REASON, New York, 1933.

D. J. Kotze, editor, LETTERS OF THE AMERICAN MISSIONARIES, 1835-1838, Capetown, 1950.

B. R. Lacy, REVIVALS IN THE MIDST OF THE YEARS, Richmond, 1943.

J. B. Lancelot, FRANCIS JAMES CHAVASSE, Bishop of Liverpool, London, 1929.

Mel Larson, YOUNG MAN ON FIRE: THE STORY OF TORREY JOHNSON AND YOUTH FOR CHRIST, Chicago, 1945.

K. S. Latourette, BEYOND THE RANGES, (Autobiography), New York, 1968.

K. S. Latourette, A HISTORY OF CHRISTIAN MISSIONS IN CHINA, London, 1929.

K. S. Latourette, A HISTORY OF THE EXPANSION OF CHRISTIANITY, New York, 1938-1945.

K. S. Latourette, MISSIONS TOMORROW, New York, 1936.

S. S. Laurie, JOHN AMOS COMENIUS, London, 1887.

William Law, THE OXFORD METHODISTS: BEING AN ACCOUNT OF SOME YOUNG GENTLEMEN IN THAT CITY, Third Edition, London, 1738.

Robert Laws, REMINISCENCES OF LIVINGSTONIA, Edinburgh, 1934.

A. D. Lindsay, CHRISTIAN HIGHER EDUCATION IN INDIA, Oxford, 1931.

John Locke, SOME THOUGHTS CONCERNING EDUCATION (edited by E. Daniel), London, 1880.

A. F. Louw, MY EERSTE NEENTIG JAAR, Capetown, 1958.

Richard Lovett, THE HISTORY OF THE LONDON MISSIONARY SOCIETY, 1795-1895, London, 1899.

A. Lowrey, THE LIFE AND WORK OF FRANCIS ASBURY, New York, 1895.

A. H. Luiggi, SIXTY-FIVE VALIANTS, Gainesville, Florida, 1965.

Martin Luther, LETTER TO THE BURGOMASTERS AND COUNCILLORS OF ALL TOWNS IN GERMAN LANDS, URGING THE ESTABLISHMENT AND MAINTENANCE OF CHRISTIAN SCHOOLS, 1524.

M. Lyte, A HISTORY OF ETON COLLEGE, London, 1925.

J. McCosh, THE ULSTER REVIVAL AND ITS PHYSIOLOGICAL ACCIDENTS, London, 1859.

D. A. McGavran, CHURCH GROWTH IN JAMAICA, Lucknow, 1962.

D. MacGillivray, A CENTURY OF PROTESTANT MISSIONS IN CHINA, Shanghai, 1907.

C. P. McIlvaine, BISHOP McILVAINE ON THE REVIVAL OF RELIGION, New York, 1858.

W. G. McLoughlin, MODERN REVIVALISM, Charles Grandison Finney to Billy Graham, New York, 1959.

J. T. McNeill, THE CHRISTIAN HOPE FOR WORLD SOCIETY, Chicago, 1937.

Nicol MacNicol, PANDITA RAMABAI, Calcutta, 1926.

Marguerite McQuilkin, ALWAYS IN TRIUMPH. Westwood, N.J., 1956.

C. Manshardt, CHRISTIANITY IN A CHANGING INDIA, Calcutta, 1933.

J. C. Marshman, THE LIFE AND TIMES OF CAREY, MARSHMAN AND WARD, London, 1859.

M. E. Marty, THE NEW SHAPE OF AMERICAN RELIGION, New York, 1959.

A. P. Marvin, THE LIFE AND TIMES OF COTTON MATHER, Boston, 1892.

Cotton Mather, THE DIARY OF COTTON MATHER, Boston, 1911-1912.

Basil Mathews, JOHN R. MOTT, WORLD CITIZEN, New York, 1934.

J. M. D. Meiklejohn, AN OLD EDUCATIONAL REFORMER, Edinburgh, 1881.

Meyer, Fortes & Evans-Pritchard, AFRICAN POLITICAL SYSTEMS, London, 1950.

P. G. Mode, THE FRONTIER SPIRIT IN AMERICAN CHRISTIANITY, New York, 1923.

Einar Molland, CHURCH LIFE IN NORWAY, Minneapolis, 1957.

P. Monroe, A TEXT-BOOK IN THE HISTORY OF EDUCATION, New York, 1914.

W. R. Moody, THE LIFE OF DWIGHT L. MOODY, New York, 1900.

J. J. Morgan, THE '59 REVIVAL IN WALES, Mold, Wales, 1909.

J. V. Morgan, THE WELSH RELIGIOUS REVIVAL, London, 1909.

S. E. Morison, THE FOUNDING OF HARVARD COLLEGE, Cambridge, 1935.

S. E. Morison, THREE CENTURIES OF HARVARD, 1636-1936, Cambridge, 1936.

A. W. Morton, 'The Contribution of the Evangelical Revival to the Philosophy and Practice of Education,' unpublished D.Phil. dissertation, Oxford, 1949.

Lemuel Moss, ANNALS OF THE UNITED STATES CHRISTIAN COMMISSION, Philadelphia, 1868.

John R. Mott, ADDRESSES AND PAPERS of JOHN R. MOTT, New York, 1947.
John R. Mott, THE HISTORY OF THE STUDENT VOLUNTEER MOVEMENT, New York, 1947.
John R. Mott, THE WORLD'S STUDENT CHRISTIAN FEDERATION, 1947.
S. C. Neill, A HISTORY OF CHRISTIAN MISSIONS, London, 1965.
F. D. Nichol, THE MIDNIGHT CRY, Washington, 1944.
W. F. P. Noble, A CENTURY OF GOSPEL WORK, Philadelphia, 1876.
Sverre Norborg, HANS NIELSEN HAUGE, Oslo, 1967.
A. O. Norton, MEDIEVAL UNIVERSITIES, London, 1909.
H. Notter, THE ORIGINS OF THE FOREIGN POLICY OF WOODROW WILSON, Baltimore, 1937.
Syed Nurrulah & J. P. Naik, A HISTORY OF EDUCATION IN INDIA, Bombay, 1951.
C. K. Ober, LUTHER D. WISHARD, Philadelphia, 1900.
J. H. Oldham, THE STUDENT CHRISTIAN MOVEMENT OF GREAT BRITAIN AND IRELAND, London, 1920.
W. A. Omulogoli, 'The Student Volunteer Movement: Its History and Contribution,' unpublished M.A. thesis, Wheaton College, 1967.
J. Edwin Orr, EVANGELICAL AWAKENINGS IN AFRICA, Pretoria, 1969.
J. Edwin Orr, FULL SURRENDER, London, 1951.
J. Edwin Orr, GOOD NEWS IN BAD TIMES, Grand Rapids, 1953.
J. Edwin Orr, I SAW NO TEARS, London, 1946.
J. Edwin Orr, INSIDE STORY OF THE HOLLYWOOD CHRISTIAN GROUP, Grand Rapids, 1955.
J. Edwin Orr, THE LIGHT OF THE NATIONS, Grand Rapids, 1965.
J. Edwin Orr, THE SECOND EVANGELICAL AWAKENING IN BRITAIN, London, 1949.
J. Edwin Orr, EVANGELICAL AWAKENINGS IN INDIA, New Delhi, 1970.
J. Edwin Orr, THE FLAMING TONGUE, London, 1971.
J. Edwin Orr, THIS IS THE VICTORY, London, 1936.
E. Oviatt, THE BEGINNINGS OF YALE, 1701-1726, New Haven, 1916.
J. I. Osborne & T. G. Gronert, WABASH COLLEGE: THE FIRST HUNDRED YEARS, 1832-1932, Crawfordsville, Indiana, 1932.
F. V. N. Painter, LUTHER ON EDUCATION, Philadelphia, 1889.
M. R. Paranjpe, A SOURCE BOOK OF MODERN INDIAN EDUCATION, 1797-1901, Bombay, 1938.
I. Parker, DISSENTING ACADEMIES IN ENGLAND, Cambridge, 1914.
W. Paton, ALEXANDER DUFF, PIONEER OF MISSIONARY EDUCATION, London, 1923.
C. H. Peake, NATIONALISM AND EDUCATION IN MODERN CHINA, New York, 1932.
J. Penn-Lewis, THE AWAKENING IN WALES, London, 1905.
D. M. Phillips, EVAN ROBERTS, THE GREAT WELSH REVIVALIST, London, 1906.
H. M. Philpott, 'A History of the Student Y.M.C.A., 1900-1941,' unpublished Ph.D. dissertation, Yale University, 1947.
J. C. Pollock, BILLY GRAHAM, New York, 1966.
J. C. Pollock, A CAMBRIDGE MOVEMENT, London, 1950.
J. C. Pollock, THE CAMBRIDGE SEVEN, London, 1955.
J. C. Pollock, MOODY: A BIOGRAPHICAL PORTRAIT, New York, 1963.
C. H. Rammelkamp, ILLINOIS COLLEGE: A CENTENNIAL HISTORY, 1829-1929, New Haven, 1928.

K. & D. Ranaghan, CATHOLIC PENTECOSTALS, Toronto, 1969.

M. W. Randall, PROFILE FOR VICTORY, NEW PROPOSALS FOR MISSIONS IN ZAMBIA, South Pasadena, 1971.

M. Rankin, TWENTY-FIVE YEARS AMONG THE MEXICANS, Cincinnati, 1875.

H. Rashdall, THE UNIVERSITIES OF EUROPE IN THE MIDDLE AGES, Oxford, 1936.

J. Rauws et al, THE NETHERLANDS INDIES, London, 1935.

M. W. Retief, HERLEWINGS IN ONS GESKIEDENIS, Capetown, 1951.

C. Reynolds, PUNJAB PIONEER: DR. EDITH BROWN, New York, 1969.

E. W. Rice, THE SUNDAY SCHOOL MOVEMENT, 1780-1917, Philadelphia, 1917.

J. W. Richard, PHILIP MELANCHTHON, THE PRECEPTOR OF GERMANY, New York, 1898.

T. Richard, FORTY-FIVE YEARS IN CHINA, New York, 1916.

T. C. Richards, THE LIFE OF SAMUEL J. MILLS, Boston, 1906.

L. B. Richardson, A HISTORY OF DARTMOUTH COLLEGE, Hanover, N.H., 1932, 2 Volumes.

J. Richter, A HISTORY OF MISSIONS IN INDIA, London, 1909.

W. Roberts, MEMOIR OF THE LIFE AND CORRESPONDENCE OF HANNAH MORE, London, 1834.

F. Rudolph, THE AMERICAN COLLEGE AND UNIVERSITY, New York, 1962.

F. Rudolph, editor, ESSAYS ON EDUCATION IN THE EARLY REPUBLIC, New York,

F. Rudolph, MARK HOPKINS AND THE LOG: WILLIAMS COLLEGE, 1836-1872, New Haven, 1956.

D. Salmon, JOSEPH LANCASTER, London, 1904.

D. Salmon, editor, THE PRACTICAL PARTS OF LANCASTER'S IMPROVEMENTS AND BELL'S EXPERIMENT, Cambridge, 1932.

H. Sharp, SELECTIONS FROM EDUCATIONAL RECORDS, 1781-1839, London, 1920.

P. Scharpff, GESCHICHTE DER EVANGELISATION, Giessen, 1964.

J. Shaw, TWELVE YEARS IN AMERICA, London, 1867.

C. P. Shedd, TWO CENTURIES OF STUDENT CHRISTIAN MOVEMENTS: THEIR ORIGIN AND INTERCOLLEGIATE LIFE, New York, 1934.

C. P. Shedd, THE CHURCH FOLLOWS ITS STUDENTS, New York, 1938.

H. D. Sheldon, THE HISTORY AND PEDAGOGY OF AMERICAN STUDENT SOCIETIES, New York, 1901.

R. H. W. Shepherd, LOVEDALE, SOUTH AFRICA, the Story of a Century, 1841-1941, Lovedale, 1941.

M. A. Sherring, A HISTORY OF PROTESTANT MISSIONS IN INDIA, London, 1884.

M. A. Sherring, THE INDIAN CHURCH DURING THE GREAT REBELLION, London, 1859.

J. S. Simon, THE REVIVAL OF RELIGION IN ENGLAND IN THE EIGHTEENTH CENTURY, London, undated.

South African Native Races Committee, THE NATIVES OF SOUTH AFRICA, London, 1909.

F. Smith, THE LIFE AND WORK OF SIR JAMES KAY SHUTTLEWORTH, London, 1932.

G. Smith, THE LIFE OF ALEXANDER DUFF, London, 1899.

G. Smith, HENRY MARTYN, London, 1892.

G. A. Smith, THE LIFE OF HENRY DRUMMOND, New York, 1898.

H. S. Smith, R. T. Handy & L. A. Loetscher, AMERICAN CHRISTIANITY, An Historical Interpretation, New York, 1960.

S. A. Smith, THE AMERICAN COLLEGE CHAPLAINCY, New York, 1954.

T. L. Smith, REVIVALISM AND SOCIAL REFORM, Nashville, 1947.

W. E. Soothill, TIMOTHY RICHARD OF CHINA, London, 1923.

J. H. Speke, WHAT LED TO THE DISCOVERY OF THE SOURCE OF THE NILE, London, 1864.

P. J. Spener, PIA DESIDERIA, 1675.

G. Spring, MEMOIR OF THE REV. SAMUEL J. MILLS, New York, 1820.

G. Stewart, THE LIFE OF HENRY B. WRIGHT, New Haven, 1925.

E. Stock, THE HISTORY OF THE CHURCH MISSIONARY SOCIETY, London, 1899-1916, 4 Volumes.

A. B. Strickland, THE GREAT AMERICAN REVIVAL, Cincinnati, 1934.

Student Christian Association of South Africa, REPORT OF THE WORCESTER CONFERENCE, 1904, Capetown, 1904.

Student Volunteer Movement, STUDENTS AND THE MODERN MISSIONARY CRUSADE, New York, 1906.

Student Volunteer Movement, STUDENTS AND WORLD ADVANCE, New York, 1920.

W. W. Sweet, REVIVALISM IN AMERICA: Its Origin, Growth and Decline, New York, 1944.

W. W. Sweet, THE STORY OF RELIGION IN AMERICA, New York, 1950.

A. P. Tankersley, COLLEGE LIFE AT OLD OGLESTHORPE, Atlanta, 1951.

Tissington Tatlow, THE STORY OF THE STUDENT CHRISTIAN MOVEMENT OF GREAT BRITAIN AND IRELAND, London, 1933.

Mrs. Howard Taylor, BORDEN OF YALE, London, 1926.

W. Taylor, CHRISTIAN ADVENTURES IN SOUTH AFRICA, New York, 1877.

D. G. Tewkesbury, THE FOUNDING OF AMERICAN COLLEGES AND UNIVERSITIES BEFORE THE CIVIL WAR: with Particular Reference to the Religious Influences Bearing upon the College Movement, New York, 1932.

C. L. Thompson, TIMES OF REFRESHING: a History of American Revivals from 1740-1877, Chicago, 1877.

M. M. Thomas, THE ACKNOWLEDGED CHRIST OF THE INDIAN RENAISSANCE, Bangalore, 1970.

M. M. Thomas & R. W. Taylor, editors, TRIBAL AWAKENING, Bangalore, 1965.

Phyllis Thompson, D. E. HOSTE: A PRINCE WITH GOD, London, 1950.

G. I. F. Thomson, THE OXFORD PASTORATE, London, 1946.

J. Thomson, LETTERS ON THE MORAL AND RELIGIOUS STATE OF SOUTH AMERICA, London, 1830.

A. J. Thottungal, 'The History and Growth of the Mar Thoma Church,' unpublished M.A. thesis, School of World Mission, Pasadena, California.

C. C. Tiffany, A HISTORY OF THE PROTESTANT EPISCOPAL CHURCH IN THE UNITED STATES OF AMERICA, New York, 1895.

M. C. Towner, editor, RELIGION IN HIGHER EDUCATION, Chicago, 1931.

G. M. Trevelyan, ENGLISH SOCIAL HISTORY, London, 1944.

L. Tyerman, THE LIFE OF THE REV. GEORGE WHITEFIELD, London, 1876-1877, 2 Volumes.

L. Tyerman, THE OXFORD METHODISTS, London, 1873.

W. S. Tyler, A HISTORY OF AMHERST COLLEGE, Boston, 1896.

J. H. van Amringe, A HISTORY OF COLUMBIA UNIVERSITY, 1754-1904, New York, 1904.

W. J. van der Merwe, THE DEVELOPMENT OF MISSIONARY ATTITUDES IN THE DUTCH REFORMED CHURCH IN SOUTH AFRICA, Capetown, 1936.

A. D. Waller, A SHORT HISTORY OF THE UNIVERSITY OF LONDON, London, 1912.

W. Wanless, AN AMERICAN DOCTOR AT WORK IN INDIA, New York, 1932.

F. D. Washburn, FIFTY YEARS ON: GROTON SCHOOL, 1884-1934, New York, 1934.

C. Hoyt Watson, Ms History of Seattle Pacific College, unpublished, Seattle Pacific College.

L. A. Weigle, AMERICAN IDEALISM, New Haven, 1928.

J. Wells, THE LIFE OF JAMES STEWART, London, 1909.

A. B. Wentz, FLIEDNER THE FAITHFUL, Philadelphia, 1936.

T. J. Wertenbaker, PRINCETON: 1746-1896, Princeton, 1946.

John Wesley, INSTRUCTIONS FOR CHILDREN, London, 1743.

John Wesley, A PLAIN ACCOUNT OF KINGSWOOD SCHOOL, London, 1871.

John Wesley, WORKS, edition of 1872, London, 1872.

Gunnar Westin, DEN KRISTNA FRIFORSAMLINGEN I NORDEN, Stockholm, 1927.

W. R. Wheeler, MODERN MISSIONS IN CHILE AND BRAZIL, Philadelphia, 1926

J. Whiteside, HISTORY OF THE WESLEYAN METHODIST CHURCH IN SOUTH AFRICA, London, 1906.

George Whitefield, A CONTINUATION OF THE REV. MR. WHITEFIELD'S JOURNAL, edition of 1829, London, 1829.

George Whitefield, A FURTHER ACCOUNT OF GOD'S DEALINGS WITH THE REV. MR. GEORGE WHITEFIELD (1747, edition Wale, 1905).

W. W. Willard, FIRE ON THE PRAIRIE, Wheaton College, Illinois, 1950.

E. F. Williams, 'A History of Baylor University,' unpublished M. A. thesis, Baylor University, Waco, Texas.

R. D. Winter, THE TWENTY-FIVE UNBELIEVABLE YEARS, South Pasadena, 1970.

L. D. Wishard, 'The Beginning of the Students' Era in Christian History,' Ms. Y.M.C.A. Library, New York.

C. E. Wood, MEMOIR AND LETTERS OF CANON HAY AITKEN, London, 1928.

WORLD MISSIONARY CONFERENCE, Edinburgh, 1910.

W. Wordsworth, ADDRESS TO THE SCHOLARS OF THE VILLAGE SCHOOL, London, 1798.

E. H. Wright, THE MEANING OF ROUSSEAU, Oxford, 1929.

H. B. Wright, TWO CENTURIES OF CHRISTIAN ACTIVITY AT YALE, New Haven, 1925.

A. F. Young & E. T. Ashton, BRITISH SOCIAL WORK IN THE NINETEENTH CENTURY, London, 1956.

J. B. Zubiaur, SINOPSIS DE LA EDUCACION en La Republica Argentina, Buenos Aires, 1901.

Ulrich Zwingli, THE CHRISTIAN EDUCATION OF BOYS, Zurich, 1523.